MW00964131

The Substance of Things Hoped For

To Karl —

God bless you and

keep you

And make His face to

shine upon you!

Blessings,

Rod & Elaine

The Substance of Things Hoped For

Rod Taylor

Email: leader@chp.ca
Twitter: RodTaylor@CHPCanadaLeader
Facebook: RodTaylor.CHPCanadaLeader

The Substance of Things Hoped For

Copyright © 2018 by Rod Taylor. All rights reserved. No portion of this book may be reproduced in any form without written permission from the publisher, except for brief quotations in critical reviews.

ISBN 9781797718101

Dedication

To my father, Walt Taylor, who was, by his passionate commitment to the causes he believed in and to the ideal world he sought—a world in which people would treat each other better—a shining example to me and many others of the power of persistence even against the flow of misguided public opinion . . .

. . . and to my mother, Peggy Taylor, who was the embodiment of love for all her children and who took such sincere interest in others. Her patient sacrifices for the family and her encouraging and thoughtful words and deeds kept us all going.

Acknowledgments

No man is an island. Without the examples, the mentorship and friendship of others, few of us would choose high ideals over personal gain and comfort. I have been privileged to have many such examples, including some I have never met. Not yet.

This list cannot be comprehensive or it would become a book in itself. However, I want to acknowledge some of those people, by name or by generic groups, who have influenced my life in significant ways. Some of them have already passed on to glory. Others are still at their posts. There will be gaping holes in this list and I only intend it as a feeble attempt to recognize my small place in the ongoing discussion about the application of divine principles to the problems of mankind.

I acknowledge:
Almighty God, maker of heaven and earth. Without Him, we can do nothing but with Him, all things are possible.

Jesus Christ, the Saviour of mankind. He lived a sinless life, willingly took the punishment for our sins, was hated for his sinless perfection and rejected by the religious and political leaders of His day, was crucified, rose from the dead and offers forgiveness and eternal life to all who will believe and follow Him.

My dear wife, Elaine Taylor, who both inspires and encourages me. She has made great sacrifices for me and for our family throughout our 44 years of marriage. Never satisfied with mediocrity, she lifts for me a high standard in all our endeavours. She was in the faith before me and many of the things about which I write or even care, were topics she introduced to me.

Many of the authors or musicians or philosophers I like are ones which she has recommended. She even discovered the Christian Heritage Party in its infancy and brought it into our home.

She has put up with me in spite of all my shortcomings and she has raised our children with love and care. She has foregone many of her own personal goals and dreams to make our house a home, often with meagre resources. This book is possible because of her constant influence.

Our children and grandchildren, who have been such a source of pleasure and marvel over the years. While always wishing I had spent more intentional quality time with our children when they were young, I am grateful for the opportunities to interact with them as adults. It is now for them, their offspring and their peers that I advocate for family-friendly policies.

The prophets and martyrs going back to the beginning who made obedience to God a higher standard than the pleasing of men. From the Old Testament prophets who were stoned by jealous and angry mobs, to New Testament martyrs like Stephen, James and Paul . . . the Scottish Covenanters and other believers whose blood has been shed over the centuries, countless missionaries from the first century right up to the present time. These men and women have shown by their willingness to die for Christ that they saw their principles and their relationship with God to be of more value even than life itself . . . and in giving up their fleeting earthly lives have laid hold of the life that cannot die.

Modern martyrs like Martin Luther King, who was assassinated for his work to bring equality and justice to America. Modern prophetic witnesses like Linda Gibbons and Mary Wagner who have spent years in prison to rescue babies from abortion. Bill Whatcott and others like him who have also been in prison and faced unjust criminal charges for seeking to rescue young people from state-imposed gender confusion.

Lawyers like Charles Lugosi, John Carpay, Albertos Polizogopoulos, Andre Schutten (just to name a few) and many others who have represented—at great personal cost—people and principles being crushed by social and political forces which in recent years have been unleashed with exceeding fury against all that is holy and good.

All my teachers and pastors from my youth up who have guided me and helped me learn about history, literature and the wisdom of God.

Numberless authors, poets, musicians and artists who have given us a better and deeper understanding and appreciation for God's creative wisdom and care for all of us—not only for our physical needs but for our soul's love of beauty.

Politicians like Brad Trost, Maurice Vellacott, Rod Bruinooge, Stephen Woodworth, Rob Anders and many others too numerous to mention who have stood in the gap, fighting for life, family and moral values even when their own party has turned against them. Men like Bill Vander Zalm, 28th Premier of BC, who attempted to protect babies in BC from the scourge of taxpayer-funded abortion and bore the consequences of leftist outrage through backroom campaigns, media smears and orchestrated political maneuvers which ultimately took him out of office. I thank Bill for graciously agreeing to write the foreword for this book.

Writers and publishers like Ted Byfield, whose Report magazines highlighted current social and political ills and educated and mobilized a wave of political activism that took root and bore fruit in the Reform movement, even though its energy has since been diluted by pragmatism at many levels. The effort was worthwhile and the goals remain worthy goals.

Activist and advocacy groups like Campaign Life Coalition, Euthanasia Prevention Coalition, Association for Reformed Political Action, Canadian Taxpayers Federation, National Firearms Association and many others which are standing up for life, family and freedom. Of course, these are not just organizations but they represent the collective sacrificial work of their leaders and dedicated volunteers.

Ed Vanwoudenberg, founding leader of the Christian Heritage Party. Ron Gray, who led the party for 13 years and has given us all such a great example to follow. Jim Hnatiuk, party leader from 2008 to 2014 and who invited me to serve as his deputy. My local CHP electoral district association, our National Board, founding members, generous donors, gracious hosts and our many great candidates and volunteers.

Tasha Deschambault, my publisher at Beautiful Fields Publishing who guided me through the final steps in getting this book to print stage. I appreciate that help so much.

I'm grateful for all who have contributed to my life in any way.

TABLE of CONTENTS

Foreword

There are many books written about individual people, interesting and informative but basically all about one person. There are books written about history and historical events. We can learn from history, but the extent to which we would learn is mostly limited to that time or event. There are books written about political parties or people, but they are largely written to promote a political person, party or philosophy.

Rod Taylor, leader of the Christian Heritage Party, has not written this book to promote himself or to highlight an isolated historical event or some narrow philosophical viewpoint. This book is not just an attempt to persuade you to vote a particular way or to convert you to Christianity. One purpose of this book he has written is to illustrate the hypocrisy of the main-stream political parties in their efforts to please voters all across the political spectrum. In trying to please all, they often lose their way. Few people realize, for instance, that the federal political party that professes to be for all the people, the Canadian Liberal Party, now denies you the opportunity to be a candidate for the party if you're a pro-life Christian.

This book will show you that, once elected, your representative from the mainstream parties, in spite of his or her campaign promises, will often vote as he/she has been told to do by the Party Leader. For mainstream party advisors, it's no longer an issue of "right or wrong" it has now become an issue of "what will get us the votes?" Once elected, a candidate may discover that if you want to progress in party ranks, if you want to maintain the many benefits, that hefty pay package, and an extremely generous pension package, you do as you're told. Simply said, "this book is meant to be an eye opener".

Some will argue, understandably, "why should I read this book? what will it change?" "All the power and funding is with the big three established political parties, so why waste time?" Others will argue, and rightly so, that on the real value and moral issues, all three of the established political parties don't differ that much. Everyone should consider that legitimate, thoughtful policy positions based on thorough evaluation and consideration, come not from a party seeking to please a particular group for votes; nor does that bring us good government. They come from people whose decisions are based not on partisan trade-offs but on honestly held beliefs and principles.

We need a voice other than one based purely on campaign funding and votes, even if only to allow for debate from a totally value-based perspective. If all parties on the platform "throw in the towel" to get the votes, truth will cease to be a rudder and anchor for those in power.

One won't always agree with everything written in the following pages, but it is truly democratic, fair, honest and wise that people should at least listen to the opinions of somebody who became involved in the political process to further a spiritual objective, rather than one based on dollars and votes. A prime example of that, as this book so aptly illustrates is – our governments can make any amount of money available immediately for ending life, through abortion and euthanasia, but a terminally ill person may wait months for an operation or treatment, for lack of funds.

Some children are forced to go through life with an infirmity for lack of priority or funding, but an abortion can be provided immediately right up to the time of a healthy birth, and euthanasia is now being provided not for the benefit of the patient but to relieve inconvenienced relatives who have other plans to suit their lives.

This book reminded me of a vote held in parliament when the Conservatives were governing and the Liberals in the opposition. The vote asked parliament to resolve to ask the G8 (now G7) nations, to make available the resources needed to improve health outcomes for women and children in third world countries. The then-leader of the opposition, Michael Ignatieff, moved to amend the motion to include abortion and contraception – all about scoring political points and little or nothing about real care. That kind of cynical pragmatism continues to set the tone for the big parties grasping for or clinging to power. If they continue to accumulate debt with unaffordable campaign promises, the Progressives in both the Conservative and Liberal parties, will break us financially and economically. Another generation, 50 years from now, can probably fix that, but if they also break us spiritually, morally and ethically, that might be unfixable.

I'm beginning to think, and this book confirms much of it, that we could elect a bunch of robots, whose sole role would be to get the party re-elected, buy votes, no matter what you have to do or say, no matter how vile, dishonest, immoral, just get the votes.

You're not expected to like all you read in this book. If you liked everything you too might be a robot. In real life there are things you like and things you don't like, but hopefully when thinking about these you will not forget to use your conscience as a guide. Thank you Rod Taylor for giving us the opportunity to consider all we read here based on Christian principles that include empathy, sympathy, care, common sense and responsibility.

Bill Vander Zalm
28th Premier of British Columbia

September 2018

INTRODUCTION

The writer of Ecclesiastes tells us that there is "nothing new under the sun". That is certainly true of the chapters of this book, for it is little more than a compilation of articles I've published in the past. For the most part, they deal with situations, events and political or social developments within Canada that have taken place within the past 15 years, so the articles themselves—other than a few editorial adjustments or formatting changes—are not new.

Neither are the topics themselves unique to this book nor to the age in which we live. In my study of world history—including biblical history—many of the themes, the issues and the struggles of mankind are repeated over and over in different degrees and across many cultural and ethnic divides. Human nature has not changed. The grasping for power and prominence and the endless pursuit of wealth and rank, even the deep inner need for a sense of personal significance and value, have motivated men and women to words, deeds and social constructs that are both incredible and often boringly expected. The deepest mysteries of human behaviour seem to be those impulses that lead to tyranny and bloodshed. Within the semi-secure and comfortable confines of our vestigial Western civilization we may wonder at the slaughter of two-year olds in Herod's day, the Holocaust of Jews in Germany, the brutal treatment of black slaves in the United States, the starvation and beatings of millions under Stalin and on and on...

Unfortunately, these horrific examples of man's brutal treatment of his own kind are neither new to us nor have they been eliminated from the list of human behaviours today. Cain's murder of his brother Abel in the dawn of civilization was as ghastly as the beheadings of children by ISIS today. Those who look to the ancient past for a time of idyllic peace or who look to the future for the miraculous transformation of society through science or government structures will seek in vain for a pattern of cooperative and selfless human interaction…unless they look to the One who created all things, who came in human flesh and who died to bring reconciliation, forgiveness and new life.

In spite of the disappointments of the past and the failures of men and women and the nation-states in which they reside to address the issues of self and sin that have troubled all human history from the beginning to this present day, I offer this book and these thoughts in the hope that we—the citizens of Canada—might yet learn from the errors of the past, apply the wisdom of our loving God, adopt the attitude of our risen Saviour and experience that elusive sense of community for which we were designed.

The 11th chapter of the Book of Hebrews begins with these words: "Faith is the substance of things hoped for, the evidence of things not [yet] seen". If mankind had already discovered the keys to successful community living and the peaceful coexistence of neighbouring nation-states, we would each now be contentedly sitting "under our own vine and under our own fig tree". We would not be expending our energy dealing with human rights violations, breaches of the peace and selfish and tyrannical despots. If we already had the fulfilment of the dream, we would no longer need to be exercising our faith.

As Christians, we see something that the world does not see but we see it through the eyes of faith, we speak it into being with words of faith and we walk towards it with steps of faith.

The failures of former civilizations and former governments—to achieve broad success in human rights, to eliminate crime and corruption, to protect innocent human life or to ensure justice for their citizens—do not lift from our shoulders the responsibility for continuing to seek all those things today nor for endeavouring with every ounce of initiative and energy to create the kind of society where those outcomes are most likely. We must, however, recognize that such accomplishments are not possible without Divine intervention and that only by a national exercise of faith can they be achieved, even in part. "For without faith it is impossible to please Him".

With that brief introduction, I welcome you to my reflections in this random sampling of articles about current events (or events which were current at the time of their writing). Many of these articles will present the barest of details regarding an event, a bill being debated or a decision being made by the courts. The article may point out a flaw in logic or an inconsistency in approach or the need for a biblical perspective in assessing the challenges faced by our generation. Underlying every article and every issue is my confident belief that human reasoning alone is insufficient to deal with the problems created by flawed human character. I believe that "God is able to do exceedingly abundantly above all that we can ask or think", and that He has plans for us, "...plans for good and not for evil, plans to give us a future and a hope".

Like other good things in life, many of God's promises are conditional. He says, "If you will walk in my ways, you shall enjoy the good of the land and no evil shall befall you". By implication, if we do not walk in His ways, we have no justification for claiming the promises.

Canada, at this writing, is polluted with innocent blood. Over 100,000 babies are killed by abortion each year in our country. Our governments are trying to hide the statistics (as in B.C. and Ontario where abortion-related statistics, even the publicly-funded costs of abortions performed in private clinics have been excluded from published statistics). Organizations which should know better are ignoring peer-reviewed studies which show a link between abortion and breast cancer. Teachers' unions, which should have the interests of their members in mind, are ignoring the fact that the equivalent of 4,000 to 5,000 classrooms of children are being aborted in Canada each year. (For those who are not math teachers, that means 4,000 to 5,000 fewer teaching positions, more school closures, etc.)

On the business side, unlimited abortion in Canada means a loss of 100,000 potential employees, entrepreneurs, skilled technicians, doctors and researchers each year. For real estate people, that means fewer houses to be built and sold and for the government that means fewer taxpayers.

Immigration policy is affected as well. In a vain attempt to fill the workplace needs of this country, the government has been accepting hundreds of thousands of immigrants and refugees—with little regard for the skill sets, the financial strengths, the level of loyalty to Canadian values or the social commitment they bring. We now—in the second decade of this century—have become reluctantly aware of "home-grown terrorism" and "lone-wolf attacks" phenomena largely associated with Canada's changing cultural milieu. Unless there is a dramatic change in policy, these tragic attacks are likely to increase.

God cannot bless this nation while we tolerate the shedding of innocent human blood. We cannot separate morality from public policy. The impacts of harmful decisions, whether rendered by elected legislators or unelected judges, will touch every family and every community, simply by the natural logical progression of cause and effect. The failure of our family policies and the increasingly diverse demands on government resources have led to expansion of government bureaucracy, a shrinking of the taxpayer base and a mushrooming of the national debt . . . at this writing exceeding $671 billion dollars.

If we include the very real but less measurable costs of social dysfunction, broken homes, the increased incidence of violence and property crime, rising insurance costs, the ravages of unhinged mental illness and a culture hooked on drugs (both pharmaceutical and the street variety), the challenges increase dramatically . . . but there is yet another factor which we must consider:

We live on this planet as the invited guests of the One who made it all. Our Creator has designed all the weather and climate systems and the harmonious interaction of all our ecosystems. He has placed us the right distance from the sun, at the correct speed of rotation in our prescribed orbit and with an abundance of water, oxygen and minerals to permit us to live here and to enjoy our life together. We owe God everything. Without Him we can do nothing. He is our source of life and has just claims on our time and attitudes. We ought to live our lives as He directs. He is against the shedding of innocent human blood. When we flaunt our reckless disobedience to His revealed will, we must expect that a just and powerful God will hold us accountable for our actions.

It is time for a movement of national repentance for the sins of the past. It is time to dedicate this nation and ourselves to a renewed and conscious awareness of our Maker in an attitude of gratitude and submission, especially when it comes to respect for human life and honour for the institution of the family from which all human life flows. It is time for the churches of this nation to issue a call to their members for passionate and persistent prayer and a conscious effort to rid our land of the blight of abortion. It's time for politicians, bureaucrats, health care workers and judges to confront the evil of abortion, to call it by name and to courageously expel it from our coasts.

Although many of the topics discussed in the pages ahead invite sombre reflection, I do not yield any ground to the "prophets of doom". Our God does not call us to do anything for which He has not given us the requisite strength or ability. He promises that He will not allow us to be tested beyond our ability to bear it. Paul said "I can do all things through Him who strengthens me". And again, "With God ALL things are possible".

In the days ahead, let us serve our God and our nation by exercising our faith and allowing that faith to direct our actions. After all, **"Faith is the substance of things hoped for; the evidence of things not [yet] seen".**

Rod Taylor
November, 2018

Mercy and Justice

Without Mercy, Justice would be harsh,
But with her he is tender.
Without Justice, Mercy would be lost,
Having no defender.

So many in the courts today
And in the halls of power
Spend days pursuing Mercy
But give Justice not an hour.

They think by trading sword for shield
And banishing Truth's blade
They'll reap the fruit that virtues yield
Though virtue's image fade.

They think in Mercy only
They'll find a peaceful rest
Without Justice to provide them either
Measurement or test.

They hoist a flag uncoloured;
Pirates plunder fast their hold
But in shipwreck or surrender
Their hands will yet grow cold.

The shield of Mercy covers well;
Its edge is ever soft
And shelters many in its shade
When it is held aloft.

But it cannot turn the battle tide
Nor force the routed foe
The sword of Justice must be raised
While Mercy shields the blow.

So call forth now your banners!
Unfurl them one by one!
And call on deck your sleeping crew
And powder every gun!

The robbers of the open sea
Do seek our weak submission
But resolute and daring
We must meet them in collision.

Collusion is their frontispiece
And calumny their finis—
But we have taken sacred vows
And Justice lives within us!

Rod Taylor
March 2007

What are the "Things We Hope For"?

We hope for that which we do not yet see. If we already saw it, if we already had it in our hands, there would be no need for faith or hope, no great odds against which we must persevere. We hope for that which we have not yet attained. But this is not a groundless hope, not merely wishful thinking, but a confidence in the power and faithfulness of God.

What do I hope for? What is the goal, the earnest expectation, the desire which I hold dear . . . and not only I but countless others, both within and without the Christian Heritage Party?

The dream, the vision, the cherished end of our thoughts, our prayers, our labours and our commitments can be summed up in one phrase: the will of God. We want His will to be manifested in the earth, in Canada, in our communities and in our families. Most importantly, in ourselves. As we pray and work towards the responsible governance of cities, provinces and nations, we recognize that first we must accept and walk in "self-government" and take personal responsibility to govern our own thoughts and actions according to His will. "He who rules his own spirit is better than one who captures a city". Proverbs 16:32

Jesus taught His disciples to pray "Thy kingdom come, Thy will be done on earth as it is in heaven". All who ever prayed that prayer have been asking—consciously or not—for God to so move, in our lives and in the lives of those around us, that the great principles and themes of godly living, holy obedience and pure and fruitful relationships would be evident here and now, in this place we live, on this planet we call home.

If we truly want His kingdom on earth, we must live ourselves as citizens of that kingdom. We can't wait for others to establish His throne. We must first put the King on the throne of our own hearts, see the world through His eyes and demonstrate the kind of loyal citizenship that will allow others to see that which is now hidden from their sight.

Of course, this general and all-encompassing phrase, "the will of God" has many facets, many identifying characteristics, many practical outworkings in the interactions of family life, social constructs and even in political policies. Throughout history, mankind's strivings and efforts to establish certain elements in regard to the governance and control of events have been motivated alternately by self-interest or group-interest and sometimes by both. Most people have longed for justice—except those who have seen short-term personal advantage in injustice. The robber, the rapist, the power-hungry dictator have this in common: they want wealth, pleasure and power more than they want justice and the will of God. If they only knew that one day they would stand before a holy God and answer for their crimes, they would see that their momentary pleasures are nothing when weighed against the infinite and eternal joy of living in the kingdom of God.

What specific things do we hope for? What social patterns, policies and practices do we hope for on earth, in Canada, believing in faith that our God has already prepared them for us in the unseen realm?

Life: We love, value and respect every human life. We want to see that same respect for human life manifested in our laws and in public attitudes.

Marriage and Family: We want to see a restoration of respect for traditional marriage—the union of one man and one woman in a lifelong covenant—and the nurture of children within the bonds of sacrificial familial love. Laws cannot create or sustain love but are necessary for the defence of the institutions of family and marriage.

Justice: In any successful society, evil must be punished and good must be rewarded. In a corrupt and crumbling society such as ours, we see evildoers reaping benefits and good men and women hindered in their efforts. We desire to see laws enacted and judgments pronounced that promote godliness and deter wickedness.

Truth and Freedom: The Bible tells us "You shall know the truth and the truth shall make you free". In our days, we have seen the truth obscured and falsehoods promoted. We long to see this reversed: falsehoods exposed and the truth revealed.

Prosperity: Every human being desires for himself or herself and for his or her children an abundant supply of food, dry and comfortable shelter, adequate clothing and, of course, in our times, we want wheels (the ability to travel), cellphones and computers (the ability to communicate) and a variety of other luxuries which we in the Western world have come to expect.

Safety and Security: Most of us have never been exposed to "shot and shell" on the battlefield. We do not expect to be robbed at gunpoint, to have our houses broken into or to be threatened with violence. We hope that our data will not be hacked, that our emails and letters will reach their destination. We trust that our children will arrive safely at school and return home without incident. We deeply desire and expect privacy. As our society is unraveling and shared Christian values of civility, decency and respect for private property are eroding, many of these aspects of civilization are being threatened. In all these matters we long for God to take control, to keep us safe and to imbue us with a sense of His presence, His peace, His security.

King David, the Psalmist, expressed in a few lines the kind of society for which we all long:

> *I will sing a new song unto thee, O God: upon a psaltery and an instrument of ten strings will I sing praises unto thee.*
>
> *It is He that giveth salvation unto kings: who delivereth David his servant from the hurtful sword.*
>
> *Rid me, and deliver me from the hand of strange children, whose mouth speaketh vanity, and their right hand is a right hand of falsehood.*
>
> *That our sons may be as plants grown up in their youth; that our daughters may be as corner stones, polished after the similitude of a palace.*
>
> *That our garners may be full, affording all manner of store; that our sheep may bring forth thousands and ten thousands in our streets.*
>
> *That our oxen may be strong to labour; that there be no breaking in, nor going out; that there be no complaining in our streets.*
>
> *Happy is that people, that is in such a case: yea, happy is that people, whose God is the Lord.*　　*Psalm 144: 9-15*

God has answers, if we will only listen. We cannot achieve His goals by violating His precepts. We can't improve our lives by carelessly taking the lives of others. We can't enjoy prosperity by taking the wealth of others. We can't give ourselves more personal freedom by restricting the freedom of others. We can't expect others to tell the truth if we ourselves are lying. Justice must be blind, not biased. We can't borrow ourselves out of debt.

All of us want happiness but happiness without God is an illusion. As David said: "Happy is that people whose God is the Lord".

We hope for those things which we do not yet see. We trust in God to make us the kind of people who will be able to express His great love for our fellow-citizens and to—in some fragmented way—manifest His principles for living. We pray and long for "His kingdom to come and His will to be done on earth, as it is in Heaven".

Many of the articles in this book are meant to expose some of the social and political obstacles to the achievement of our hopes and dreams. To build a society where righteousness reigns requires both the (figurative) sword and the trowel. We must expose that which is evil and bring it into the light. We must uproot corrupt political structures which prevent good men and women from reaching their destiny.

While we are engaged in this aspect of social renewal, we must remember: without Him we can do nothing but with God ALL things are possible.

Life

I have set before you LIFE and death, blessing and cursing; therefore choose LIFE, that both thou and thy seed may live.   Deut. 30:19

Riding in the Dark

Every year we lose a riding in Canada. That is, we lose the population equivalent of one federal riding or electoral district. I refer, of course, to the more than 100,000 innocents killed each year by abortion.

My own riding, Skeena-Bulkley Valley, showed a population of 99,474 souls in 2004. Just think of it: the combined populations of Smithers, Telkwa, Terrace, the Hazeltons, Kitimat, Prince Rupert, Haida Gwaii, Moricetown, Dease Lake, Telegraph Creek, Atlin, Gitseguecla, Lower Post, Fort St. James, Houston, Burns Lake, New Aiyansh, Port Edward, Bella Bella, Bella Coola, Lachkaltsap, Iskut, Gitanyow, Quick and all the smaller communities add up to less than the number of babies we allow to be killed in Canada each year. The population of this great region of Northwestern BC is lower than the death toll extracted and destroyed by Canadian doctors otherwise considered to be professional healers and preservers of life.

What kind of impact would it have and how alarmed would the media be if the Skeena-Bulkley Valley District were suddenly hit by a massive plague, a fire, a flood, an earthquake or other calamity of such magnitude that every resident was destroyed? It would dwarf the 12,000 who perished in France's heat wave, it would make the thousands, who perished in Iraq seem like isolated losses. The fact is, we still have not grasped the dimensions of the self-mutilation taking place in Canada today. Because we do not see the faces every night on TV, we ignore the carnage and talk antiseptically of "choice".

Let's pause for a moment in our frantic flight from truth. Let's turn and face the reality of our "choice". We have the equivalent of a federal electoral district whose constituents have NO CHOICE and NO VOICE. We have allowed the courts to enfranchise convicted criminals with the right to vote, but these poor innocents—murdered in the dark, before they have seen the light of day—are denied even the recognition of their personhood. They receive no birth certificate and no death certificate. They have no vote today, nor will they have one tomorrow. When Parliament sits, there is no MP whose party has taken up their cause, no MP whose party will speak for them.

Therefore I refer to these 100,000 souls as constituents of a "Riding in the Dark". For them the sun never rises when Parliament sits. And next year another 100,000 will be sent to the Guillotine. We Christians marvel at the passivity of the French crowds who, in the days after the storming of the Bastille, watched and tolerated the cruel Guillotine. We shake our heads at the blindness of the crowds who watched as our Lord was crucified. We click our tongues at the German citizens who allowed Hitler to dominate and destroy his own people. But we have been too quick to judge those people, for whom resistance meant death. Here in Canada, we still have the right to vote. We still have the right to speak to our neighbour and the right to lobby for change. Are we doing all we can?

In Skeena-Bulkley Valley (and in every other electoral district in Canada), we have the right to elect a Member of Parliament who will take up the banner for these little ones. Since they have no vote themselves, let us vote for them. Since they have no voice themselves, let us be their voice for change. Let us adopt our little brothers and sisters and become their protectors. Let us give them hope. Let us become a light for them. Wherever you live, your riding could become the first federal district whose constituents would choose an MP representing a party that will stand up for these little ones. Let's give our MPs some extra responsibility:

besides representing voters in their districts of residence, let's encourage them to also represent the little people who live in the Riding in the Dark.

Riding in the Dark was one of the first articles I wrote as a CHP cabdidate. Back in 2004, it just suddenly dawned on me that the number of preborns killed by abortion was almost exactly the population of most federal ridings. I wanted to be their defender. I still do.

All Lives Matter; How an Ethnic Focus Undermines the Quest for Justice

Dallas again. In Dallas on November 22, 1963, the world sat stunned in the horrible aftermath of JFK's assassination and the subsequent shooting of Lee Harvey Oswald which played live on national TV. The motorcade, the sniper, the book depository, the Warren commission, the Zapruder footage, the endless questions about the Grassy Knoll and the Cuban connections . . . all these images and soundbites still mill about in our minds as we—those of us old enough to remember the Kennedy assassination—reflect on unthinkable acts by persons unknown until showcased for their brutal deeds.

This past week, Black Lives Matter mobilized in Dallas and across the country in response to two horrible acts by men wearing police uniforms in Minnesota and Baton Rouge. Even before those two killings, Black Lives Matter got airtime in Toronto for its unexpected appearance at the Gay Pride Parade, apparently delaying the march for two hours and extracting several promises from Pride organizers.

On July 7, 2016 Micah Johnson used the Black Lives Matter demonstration in Dallas as a convenient stage for shooting and killing five police officers and wounding seven others. Race concerns disappeared momentarily in collective grief; concerned citizens around the world shuddered to see race-blaming extended to the calculated murder of five officers sworn to uphold the peace. Our hearts go out to all those who have been affected by this terrible act of violence. We pray that peace and reconciliation may yet be established. Revenge killings can never restore the lives taken away; they only invite more bloodshed.

Individuals who happen to identify with a group either by shared race, language or occupation should not be treated differently, with less respect or under different rules than their fellow citizens. The "rule of law" which is foundational to Canada's Charter and the phrase "all men are created equal" which highlights America's Declaration of Independence both point to universal worth and the right to universal freedom and dignity. Donning a policeman's uniform should not make one a target of violence any more than being born with black or white or brown skin. Of course black lives matter; no responsible citizen could disagree. So do white lives, so do the lives of police officers, so do the lives of the preborn, the elderly and the disabled.

In Canada today and in the US, unjust laws and biased court interpretations have robbed the preborn of all races of the protection their lives deserve. The recent passage of C-14, which legalized the killing of the vulnerable by those who should be helping them to heal, has again sent the message to our young people that some lives matter more than others.

Author George Orwell was best known for his chilling novel *1984* but his other main commentary on human nature and the threat of dictatorship was *Animal Farm*. In both novels, he showed how the gradual twisting of language is capable of changing societal attitudes and leading a gullible public to accept hideous tyranny. In *1984*, he had the Ministry of Truth substituting false history and ultimately producing slogans like: "War is Peace". In *Animal Farm*, after the animals had thrown off the farmer's oppressive yoke, they first demonized humans and made high-sounding declarations like "All animals are created equal". Later, as some rose to positions of power and began living in luxury at the expense of others (becoming, in the process, more like their previous human oppressors), they subtly added the words ". . . but some are more equal than others".

This is the world we live in today. We have a Prime Minister who campaigned on the slogan "A citizen is a citizen is a citizen", meaning by that statement that even those who become citizens while planning to commit acts of terror will never be deprived of the rights of a citizen. In actual practice, neither he nor our courts nor our bureaucracy treat all citizens equally. Peaceful pro-life protesters like Linda Gibbons and Mary Wagner are hauled off to jail. Violent and aggressive protesters representing certain ethnic minorities are occasionally allowed to occupy streets, housing developments, or rail lines for hours or days before being forced to move. Where's the justice? Where's the "rule of law"?

All lives matter. More importantly, every individual life matters. Until our society recognizes the innate dignity of each human life and the value God has given to it, we will struggle with competing rights and interests. Instead of isolating ourselves in ethnic ghettoes, focused on revenge with unthinking gang-like loyalties, we need to step up as community leaders to bridge the gaps between races and income groups, between "us" and "them".

Because all lives matter, we need to hold policemen and politicians accountable for their actions and we need to wean troubled activists from the feel-good frenzy of adrenalin activism. Those who want to make the world a better place need to first of all show an example in their families and communities. Children need engaged parents who will protect and nurture them and teach them about the "supremacy of God and the rule of law". Our cities need engaged citizens who will step up to serve as mayors, councillors, MLAs, MPs, lawyers, judges—people who will not compromise on moral issues and who will not allow either ethnic bias or political correctness to cloud their vision. We need a collective hunger and thirst for righteousness in our land, for justice and for freedom.

The CHP values all human life and calls for a national return to biblical morality, a rededication to shared national values and a renewed commitment to "justice for all".

July 11, 2016

Aborting Canada's Health Initiatives

News reports circulating late last week indicated that a vote would be held on Tuesday, March 23 (today) that would put a "poison pill" in the government's proposal to seek resources through the G8 to improve health outcomes for women and children in other countries. Opposition MPs, led by the Hon. Michael Ignatieff are seeking to force the Prime Minister to include abortion and contraception in his offer of help to the world. Mr. Harper's public statements about the aid package, by contrast, were centered around clean water, medical training and other health-related initiatives.

The crass and blatantly partisan use of maternal health issues and tragic infant mortality rates to score political points in Canada is disgusting. Canada is a giving nation, a compassionate nation and a free nation. All of us expect to see Canada provide leadership in humanitarian initiatives. We all want to reduce suffering and untimely deaths. Our desire and our ability to assist millions of women and children around the world would be a breath of fresh air and a cup of cool water for those suffering in conditions of poverty, abuse and unpleasant social conditions.

This blatant attempt by the Leader of the Opposition to turn a humanitarian gesture into a platform for partisan wrangling is another signal that some people get into politics for the wrong reason.

To attempt to link compassionate aid to the stale and stagnant spectre of even more abortions, even more killings of innocent human beings is a ruse so despicable and morally bankrupt that it is hard to imagine. There is a promise of blessing to those who offer a cup of cold water for the thirsty but to those who promote death for the innocent and vulnerable there can be no moral confidence and no quietness of conscience. While logic cannot explain how killing children will reduce infant mortality neither can a blind subservience to dated policies justify the damage imposed on women by wholesale abortions in the face of growing evidence of the physical, emotional and psychological harm that such abortions cause.

Members of Parliament need to realize that their votes on matters of this nature will be recorded both in heaven and on earth. There is no medical or moral justification for promoting the untimely death of the innocent. Political posturing and partisan power plays on issues of life and death will bring shame to our nation and bring both lofty offices and titles of esteem into disrepute, not only in Canada but around the world. Canada has a great and noble role to fulfil in the development of the world community. If we will recognise it and act accordingly, we have a destiny to claim. It is to be a helper and healer, not a destroyer of life and dignity. As many prophetic voices have stated in recent years: "The leaves of the tree are for the healing of the nations". Canada's maple leaf should be a source of pride and inspiration. Let us hold it high and look for ways to promote and sustain life.

The Hon, Maurice Vellacott and the Hon. Brad Trost have produced a marvellous article which explains in helpful detail why the inclusion of abortion in efforts to help women in the developing nations is not only ethically flawed but medically harmful as well. They deserve our thanks for their tireless efforts in the House of Commons.

March 22, 2010

As this article explains, the issue of providing humanitarian aid to pregnant women and infants in the developing world was hijacked in debate by the Hon. Michael Ignatieff, then serving as

Leader of the Opposition. To their credit, the Conservatives resisted the pressure. Since then, our current PM, the Rt. Hon. Justin Trudeau has contaminated our foreign health care with "blood money" promoting abortion around the world including countries where it is still illegal.

The letter to the Saskatoon Star-Phoenix by the Hon. Brad Trost and Hon. Maurice Vellacott can be found here: http://freenorthamerica.ca/viewtopic.php?f=2&t=6611

A National Suicide Pact

Last week, the Liberal governments (both in Ottawa and Toronto) committed to sending emergency teams and yet more money to Attawapiskat to try to derail the plague of suicides among First Nations youth there and in other indigenous communities. On Thursday, the other shoe dropped. The federal government tabled its long-anticipated Bill C-14, designed to free up hospital beds by killing old people. Ironically—and almost simultaneously—governments are intervening to prevent some people from ending it all while "helping" others to end their lives. This schizophrenic approach is called Medical Assistance in Dying (MAID) and is paid for with healthcare dollars.

Of course, that's not the narrative they want you to believe. They want you to think C-14 is all about "choice" and "death with dignity". Underneath all the hubris and heart-wrenching tales of tragedy, "intolerable suffering" may be more about the frantic antics of federal and provincial budget teams trying to deal with the demographic imbalance of payers and users of health care than it is about patient comfort. Statistically, there simply aren't enough hospital facilities for our aging population nor enough working young people—thanks, in part to abortion—to pay for extended care for the elderly, the infirm and the disabled. Of course, we believe that doing the right thing is more important than budgets and statistics. God directs us to care for those in need and He will provide everything we need to do so. However, in the pragmatic world of Canadian politics, some lives are seen as expendable and others are deemed useful for their emotional value.

Why have Canadians become so complacent about inflicting death on the elderly yet so justly concerned about preventing death among troubled youth who also apparently have concluded that they are experiencing "intolerable suffering"? We've been lied to. We've been fed a narrative that ailing Canadians are being hooked up to machines—against their wills—to keep their hearts pumping and their lungs expanding while they endure excruciating pain. That's the oft-repeated public narrative. We've also been told that the Supreme Court, composed of nine mortal human beings, each with his or her own moral flaws, is capable of making decisions for 35 million Canadians. We've been told that court decisions are final, irrevocable and infinitely wise.

We've conveniently forgotten that Supreme Courts have been wrong before (like in 1929 when they decreed that women were not persons). We've carelessly forgotten the constitutional provision of the Notwithstanding Clause (Section 33 of the Charter) that allows Parliament to set aside SCC decisions for up to five years. Instead, we've let these nine individuals throw out laws, throw out babies and keep the bathwater (as in the 1988 decision that denied personhood to babies) and throw out the moral values upon which our nation's laws and civilization depend.

When it comes to the tragedy of suicide among young people (both on and off reserve), we also need to look below the surface. And we need to do it quickly. In Attawapiskat and on other reserves, suicide is not an isolated event, although even those who join themselves in suicide pacts are, arguably isolated and lonely individuals. Pulling young people back from the brink is about more than providing education, jobs and clean drinking water—as important as those things are to a healthy emotional state. As we speak, armies of well-meaning psychologists and grief counsellors are preparing to descend on these troubled communities. What new hope will they offer to these precious young people whose hope for meaning and purpose has been replaced with false hopes and distorted dreams?

It seems obvious that people who are contemplating ending their lives need real hope so they can summon courage to go on—to face the challenges of life, whatever those are. Young people living in a democratic country with their lives ahead of them and with opportunities for employment, marriage and personal achievement beckoning, should not be gasping away their youthful energy in dark and shrinking nightmares of despair. "Mental health", the rallying cry of sincerely concerned politicians and bureaucrats should itself be analyzed. In a healthy society, healthy emotions should be the norm and troubled and despondent young people should be the exception. Across the country, however, un our cities and on reserves we have robbed youth of their natural hope, blinded them with a postmodern cultural bias and condemned them to a worldview devoid of an eternal perspective.

We've taught children, both indigenous and non-indigenous, that the God who created them in His own image and for His purpose no longer exists and cannot meet their needs or answer their questions. We've taught them that life has no particular value; we use tax dollars to kill over 100,000 preborn babies each year. Those who miraculously survive the abortionist's knife are supposed to nurture self-esteem and find personal purpose in a meaningless existence. We expose them to night after dreary night of brutal TV "wrestling" matches between hotheaded and arrogant fighters, endless variations of police shootouts and violent and gruesome killings, prurient and selfish sex acts, displays of homosexual "comedy" and a pathetic array of accusations and denials of assaults, drug use and fraud.

We want students to make responsible decisions for themselves about all manner of things from sexual activity to career choices to not inflicting self-harm. At the same time, we tell them they are only advanced animals with no eternal purpose. On the reserves, especially, we talk about our respect for the Elders and then in the broader society we discuss how we can help our elders kill themselves. We encourage them to stay away from drugs and excessive alcohol consumption. Then we discuss how to legalize marijuana and punctuate our sportscasts with beer commercials.

Our society, both native and non-native, is in a serious identity crisis and we find ourselves lost. We want autonomy, self-government and freedom from rules and restrictions. We want the freedom to do whatever we want but we don't want consequences for our poor choices. We want to spend but never pay. We want all the joys of life without the pain of childbirth, the challenges of growing up, the discipline of work, the sacrifices and commitments required in marriage and family life. We idolize youthful strength and vigour and ignore the loss of strength and ability that sometimes come with old age. "Reality" TV has created a fantasy world where only the strong, the beautiful and the wealthy can achieve purpose and happiness.

And now our government has allowed the Supreme Court to thrust us down the rabbit-hole of diminishing returns in regard to the value and sanctity of human life. Debate is taking place on C-14 but with an urgency and haste born out of an undeserved awe of the Supreme Court. Some "progressives" say the proposed law does not go far enough; they want minors included and those suffering from poor mental health (yes, like the troubled youths in Attawapiskat). Others worry that failure to pass a law—any law—by June 6 will plunge Canada into an unregulated Wild West show of doctors killing patients (as if that weren't already happening in secret). Being pushed into a bad decision by nine Supreme Court bullies would be a tragedy. We expect courage of politicians.

Now is the time to stand up for human life, its purpose and meaning. Not only the young people of Attawapiskat but all Canada's aging seniors need to know that their lives have value. It's time to return to the "principles that recognize the supremacy of God and the rule of law". As Canadians, we sing: "God keep our land glorious and free!" If we mean that, if we truly want to experience that freedom, we'll have to find the courage to tell it to the young people in Attawapiskat and across this country. Our aging seniors need to be reminded that our God has a plan and purpose for their lives, even when their strength is failing.

We Canadians do need to make a pact, not a suicide pact like C-14 but a solemn covenant to restore to our nation an awareness that all our freedoms, our children, our mental health, our clean water, our democracy itself are gifts from the hand of our loving Creator. If we will renew our covenant as a nation established on His principles and acknowledge again that "He shall have dominion from sea to sea", we can see hope spring up anew in places like Attawapiskat . . . maybe even in Toronto and Ottawa!

April 20, 2016

Bill C-14, was introduced to the House on April 14, 2016 by the Hon. Jody Wilson-Raybould, Minister of Justice. After being rushed through the House and Senate, it received Royal Assent on June 17, 2016. In the first year under the new "assisted suicide" law, approximately 2,000 Canadians were killed by physicians. Doctors whose consciences will not permit them to participate in medical killing are still fighting for the right to practice medicine without violating their consciences.

Conservatives Resume Planned Parenthood Funding

"Buddy, can you spare $6 million? I won't use it to buy liquor, honest...." Chances are, you've been asked—at least once in your life—to "...help a guy out. I'm hungry. No, I won't buy a bottle; I just want a sandwich. I haven't eaten for days." When the unhappy person standing before you reeks of alcohol, it's easy to presume one or two things:

- This person recently had enough money to purchase alcohol in some form.
- This person may be unemployed or unemployable due to excessive consumption of alcohol, perhaps on a regular basis.
- This person may be seeking money for the purpose of purchasing more alcohol.
- This person may be self-deceived and unwilling or unable to be brutally honest about his or her aspirations, eagerness to change or to seek employment.

Regardless of the specific circumstances and the moral angst many of us may feel at such a time (wanting to help but not wanting to enable more self-destructive behaviour) any rational person can quickly reason this way: assuming that the penniless person asking for help is genuinely hungry and not just, well, thirsty . . . any loonies, toonies, quarters or dimes we may give—even if used only for food—allow that person to devote any other funds that may be acquired to the purchase of drink or drugs.

That means that "compartmentalizing" our personal charity in no way reduces the likelihood that the individual in question will continue to pursue destructive personal choices. Even buying a meal for such a person—while funnelling our little contribution into "food"—enables the reallocation of any other resources to the purchase of enslaving substances which tend to keep the person self-deceived, unemployable and dependent on the good will of others.

Now about that $6 million...International Cooperation Minister Bev Oda is at it again and her Conservative Party leader, the Rt. Hon. Stephen Harper is giving her leeway to pander to the radical feministas at Planned Parenthood. Their funding ($6 million over 3 years) has been restored as long as they "don't use if for abortions". Life lesson alert for the Conservatives: if you give Planned Parenthood $6 million it will help them promote their worldwide agenda of abortion, contraception and the early sexualisation of children who later become their clients. Planned Parenthood is the biggest abortion provider in the world. They are smart enough to take money from the Canadian government, put it into an account called "non-abortion" and move other funds into their "abortion" accounts. In short, they are philosophically abortion–oriented. Everything they do supports abortion and access to abortion. If we help them print a brochure, we are helping them provide abortions. If we fly their staff to a meeting in Tanzania (where abortions are illegal), we are helping them provide abortions in India where they are not.

We wouldn't fund the mafia if they wanted to host a "Children's Day" would we? Even with assurances that none of the money would be used to commit crime? We wouldn't fund a KKK rally in Cincinnati if they promised to avoid mentioning racial issues at that event would we? Giving money to an abortion provider who promises (wink! wink!) to not use the money for abortions is no more credible.

It's time we held this government to a higher standard. The games played around this issue are not only hypocritical and deceptive but they insult the intelligence of Canadians. ANY money given to Planned Parenthood will contribute to the annual slaughter of the unborn around the world. If that's what the Conservatives want, they should be honest and tell prolife Canadians that they are not and never will be prolife. They support abortion and abortion providers.

If, however, they desire to actually protect innocent human life with their long-awaited majority, they should remove Bev Oda from her position, rescind this duplicitous grant to the largest baby-killing organization in the world and take their place in history. I'm not holding my breath but I'm willing to be surprised.

September 22, 2011

Protecting Children from Radical Bureaucrats

The short article below is the text of a press release issued on July 30, 2015. I leave the text intact.

CHP Leader calls on Harper to protect children from radical bureaucrats

Responding to yesterday's announcement that Health Canada has approved the controversial abortifacient drug RU-486 (mifepristone), Christian Heritage Party Leader, Rod Taylor, says it's time for Prime Minister Harper and Health Minister Rona Ambrose to rein in bureaucrats who are implementing a radical social agenda with the apparent consent or approval of the government.

"This is just the latest breach of public trust that puts children at risk", said Taylor, "in this case, preborn infants, who are already under siege in Canada where there is no law to protect them right up to the moment of birth. The PM and the Health Minister surely knew this announcement was coming and if not they should have known. The debate over RU-486, which not only kills tiny babies but carries significant health risks for the unsuspecting women who use it, has been raging long and loud. For Health Canada to make this announcement on the eve of a federal election must be seen as a calculated move by this government to cater to the poor-choice lobby in hopes of retaining their collapsing grip on power. It won't work of course; it never does. Those who compromise principles for power and sacrifice lives for personal advantage will find no respect, even from those they seek to please."

The CHP leader said the Health Minister and the PM "certainly have a duty to protect children—born and preborn—from anything which puts their lives and health at risk". He expressed agreement with Mike Schouten, Director of WeNeedALaw, that the Health Minister should immediately issue an Interim Order suspending the decision of Health Canada. Taylor said that pro-lifers must hold the government to account if it will not act:

"The Minister cannot hide behind an arms-length approach. She has a solemn responsibility to protect children. The fact that 14 women have died in the US as a result of using RU-486 gives even more reason for Canadians to be alarmed and incensed that a government department designed to promote health should instead be used to implement death. Pregnancy is not a disease and RU-486 is not a cure. It is another money-grab by Big Pharma at the expense of innocent and trusting Canadians. We ask the PM and the Health Minister to act responsibly and prevent the tragic loss of life that will surely result from the public distribution of RU-486 in Canada".

Taylor also called on incumbent Conservative MPs and aspiring Conservative candidates to use their influence—publicly and privately—to have Health Canada's RU-486 approval put on hold. "Now is no time to remain silent", he said. "Across the country, government ministers and MPs are busy making very showy displays of handing out taxpayer money to a variety of causes and projects in hopes of generating voter support at the polls. For government MPs and Conservative candidates to turn a blind eye to this blatant abuse of power would be shameful. Speak up! Now is the time to take a stand in defence of life and justice!"

The Christian Heritage Party of Canada is the only federal party committed to the "protection of innocent human life from conception until natural death".

July 30, 2015
Note to Conservativea: Trying to please all voters by abandoning pro-life principles doesn't work. Remember Election 2015?

Cold cases: the NDP goes for the spotlight while ignoring 1.6 million missing women

For years, there has been a public outcry for an inquiry or a more thorough investigation into the disappearances of missing aboriginal women, including those who have vanished on the "Highway of Tears," Highway 16 west of Prince George, BC. Others have vanished from cities and villages and dark streets across the nation. Of course, women of other ethnic backgrounds have also been victims—many of them are known to have been killed by weirdos and perverts like Pickton but the number of unsolved cases of missing aboriginal women and girls is truly appalling. The usual number used is about 600 missing (mostly presumed murdered) in the past 20 years. First nations leaders say the number could be even higher; some say as many as 3,000!

My heart goes out the families and communities which are mourning for their missing loved ones. The failure of governments and police departments (with some notable exceptions) to investigate thoroughly and bring to justice the cowardly perpetrators of these deeds is certainly an additional wound to those seeking closure and comfort. I raise my voice in agreement that the situation is serious and calls for a serious inquiry.

However, in the midst of this tragic series of events and calls for help, I can't help noting one ironic twist in the rallying for an inquiry: Niki Ashton, NDP MP for Churchill has made a public demand for the Harper government to pre-empt a threatened UN inquiry by leading the effort to investigate the disappearances and murders of these 600 aboriginal women. We agree with her. But what about the 1.6 million (1,600,000) Canadian women and girls missing from our families and communities as a result of abortion?

The NDP as a group and Niki Ashton as an individual continue to turn a blind eye and a deaf ear to calls for an investigation into the personhood of the unborn child. The human baby in the womb (aboriginal and non-aboriginal alike) has no legal protection whatsoever in Canadian law. On this issue, Niki agrees with Stephen Harper. Neither of them wants any kind of inquiry nor any discussion in Parliament of the human costs of the willful killing of 100,000 little human beings in Canada each year. Women of every race are victimized by this atrocity. They are told "It's just tissue," but after their sons and daughters are ripped from their wombs many experience an unexpected sense of loss and depression. Breast cancer rates are rising and many studies indicate that abortion is a contributing cause but people like Niki Ashton don't want to discuss that.

The ironic thing is that in the case of the missing aboriginal women who have gotten MP Ashton's attention, many of these are—by now—cold cases, difficult to track and difficult to prosecute. The attempt should still be made. However, in the case of the babies killed by abortion, we know exactly how they died, where they died and who killed them. In fact, the government of Canada paid for them to be killed.

A total of 3.3 million little boys and girls have been the victims of this tragic social experiment since about 1970, approximately half of them girls. Maybe MPs like Niki Ashton should show a fraction of the interest in ending that killing spree that they do in grabbing the spotlight in a politically-correct call for a public inquiry into the disappearances of aboriginal women. Many of these little ones killed by abortion are aboriginal girls as well; their mothers are also victims. The unfeeling politicians who encourage them to make choices they will later regret are guilty of abandoning them to a system that is swallowing them up by the thousands.

Yes, we need to investigate the social breakdown that is stealing young women from the reserves and from the streets of our cities. But we also need to dig deeper to find all the missing children of Canada. There is something else missing in political circles: it's called honesty, moral consistency and a respect for human life.

July 5, 2012

Friendly Fire and Suicide: Two Tragedies and a Lesson for Pro-life Partisans

This week, the nation was saddened by Defence Minister Kenney's news release that Canada has lost a soldier in the war against ISIS. The announcement was made all the more tragic by the frank explanation that Sgt. Andrew Joseph Doiron was killed by "friendly fire" from troops which Canadian soldiers have gone into harm's way to protect and assist.

The tragedy of losing a loved one on the battlefield is never easy but that grief is compounded by the nagging thought that the loss was unnecessary . . . that it could have been prevented by people on our side. It occurs to me that there is a similarity between the emotions stirred by this tragedy and the grief and sorrow felt by those who have lost a loved one to suicide. Although Sgt. Doiron's death was unintentioned, the sadness of unnecessarily losing a member of the armed forces, dear to his family and friends, reminds us of the value we place on every human life.

I have experienced with others the heartache of losing friends to suicide. The often unanswered questions that trouble the family and friends of a suicide victim are not the kind of questions that go away quietly. They center around: Why? Why now? Why him or her? Why didn't he or she talk about it? Why didn't I see this coming?

A friendly fire incident must raise similar questions: Why didn't the shooters recognize their friends? Why didn't they confirm their identity before firing? Why weren't the protocols more stringent?

Shifting to a political perspective: over the years, the CHP has had its share of "friendly fire". We've had good social conservatives—people we admire—tell other people not to vote for us. We've had good members leave the party and pull their support because they've been convinced that we could never win. We've had close personal friends who have voted for another candidate (their 2nd choice) instead of for us because they didn't want to take a chance that a 3rd candidate from one of the "other" parties might get in. (As often as not, the candidate these folks voted for did not win anyway and the candidate they opposed still got in. In these cases, our friends who voted pragmatically not only failed to achieve the results they hoped for but also forfeited the use of their ballots to send a life-affirming message to all candidates, the media and the public.)

We've had close personal friends and supporters abandon the CHP because of a policy with which they didn't agree. It seems they've tolerated (in other parties) poor moral choices and poor party policies on social issues because they've thought they were the "least of two evils" and possibly had a better likelihood of winning.

Some critics have claimed that the CHP is a "one-issue party" because we are the only federal party willing to openly talk about abortion. Really, the problem is that abortion is a one-party issue. None of the other parties will touch it. We thank God that there are still some courageous MPs in the Conservative Party who refuse to be silenced by the power brokers in the PMO [written when the Rt. Hon. Stephen Harper was PM] and in the party machinery inner circle. Those pro-life heroes in the Conservative Party who stand bravely to defend the pre-born often face "friendly fire" from their own caucus, from those timid and politically-correct MPs and campaign strategists who assume a pro-life view is a liability and who place more value on votes than on lives.

On the other hand, we have had some members who have said that the CHP should focus only on the abortion issue and leave all other issues to the big parties. This also is friendly fire but it is a criticism we must respond to; while abortion and pro-life policy rank very high on our scale of values and deserve our diligent attention, Canadian law and culture is complex and any political candidate seeking public support must assure voters that he or she also has an interest in and answers for questions regarding the economy, healthcare, international trade, national defence, agriculture and transportation. The CHP does have policies on all these issues and we offer Canadians solutions based on unchanging biblical truths.

Let us in the CHP reflect on our responsibility to recognise our friends and allies. Let's be sure that we are not guilty of friendly fire on those who are our allies, on those who labour in the pro-life trenches. If we in the pro-life movement fail to achieve unity in our ranks, we not only become guilty of friendly fire, but we engage in collective suicide; not the personal tragedy of ropes and guns and pills but a corporate tragedy that condemns the pro-life movement to failure.

Meanwhile, it is still true that the CHP is the only federal party that promotes the protection of innocent human life from conception to natural death. We in the CHP still oppose assisted suicide and euthanasia which—if implemented—will certainly lead to doctors deciding (based on efficiencies and budgets) when people will die. We think it tragic that the Supreme Court has placed the elderly and the disabled at risk of "friendly fire" from those they trust . . . their own doctors. We believe in the supremacy of God and the rule of law. We invite all those who share our principles and our concerns to join us in the trenches.

We reflect on the tragic death of Sgt. Doiron and we honour his sacrifice on the battlefield. That type of sacrifice for a national cause was referred to by Abraham Lincoln as "the last full measure of devotion". We pray that he will not have died in vain but his efforts and those of our other brave men and women in uniform will help establish and preserve the kind of free society— at home and abroad— where all human life is valued.

March 9, 2015

Hard Hearts and Soft Heads

Human beings, made in God's image, are called to pattern our lives after Jesus Christ. He displayed both clear thinking and tender-hearted compassion. He showed that both are possible. In our troubled 21ˢᵗ century, when compassion is confused with foolish sentimentality, our society often goes in directions that are neither compassionate nor reasonable.

When a people depart from God, their efforts to create an ethical society are doomed to failure because without God, there is no standard for ethical behaviour. When the written Word of God, the Bible, is dismissed as fabrication, the immediate reaction is to try to fill the moral vacuum with whatever rules and regulations seem right to the most vocal citizens of the day. It doesn't work.

In Banff, CBC reported recently (1) that a large grizzly bear—which had already chased hikers and even charged a man pushing a baby stroller—is now the object of a petition by over 4,000 people calling for its protection. Human life is being given a lower value than the life of a bear! True, the bear has not killed anybody (yet) but it poses a serious threat. Wildlife officers, who have the legal responsibility to manage the magnificent animals and to intervene in human/wildlife conflicts, now are conflicted themselves. While they rightly insist that their first priority is public safety, they are being pressured by community members to protect the bear in spite of its aggressive behaviour.

Folks, this is lunacy of the first order. It is symptomatic of a society that has lost its bearings. The Bible is clear on this topic: Exodus 21: 28 - 29 says that if an ox (or any domestic animal) kills a man or a woman and the owner of the ox knew that the ox had been in the habit of "pushing with its horns" in the past, then the owner of the ox is held accountable because he did not take safety precautions to protect the public. In the same way, we expect wildlife officials to protect the public from animals for which they have been given responsibility, especially when those animals have already displayed aggression towards humans.

Apparently, some members of the public do not want to be protected. Stacey Sartoretto, one of the sponsors of the petition to protect Bear #148, ascribes equal value and rights to the bear as she would to humans. "She (the bear) is just as much of a local as I am . . . she deserves the same respect as everybody else". The CBC article notes that there are about 100 bears in the area. It also mentions that Bear #148 had already been live-trapped once and hauled hundreds of kilometres away. It found its way back to Banff in a couple of days. Must we "wait and see" whether Bear #148 finally kills someone before we act? Will we act even then?

I've seen a similar thing in Smithers, BC. A couple of years ago, a cow moose in downtown Smithers knocked an elderly person to the sidewalk in an incident videotaped and viewed on CBC. I wrote a letter to the paper suggesting that this particular moose should be turned into food to feed some of our homeless people in the soup kitchens of the area. Again, my point was public safety, recognizing that the animal was dangerous and had already shown aggression. The next week, another letter to the paper, written in response to mine, indignantly accused me of betraying my "pro-life" position. Again, this person equated the life of a moose with the life of a human being.

One more example: a few years ago, campaigning door-to-door in my own neighbourhood, I met a woman who came to the door holding back two large dogs. As we discussed the lives of preborn human babies, she quickly said: "They're not persons. These dogs of mine, they're persons".

These examples all point to the irrational disconnect that has permeated our society. If life merely evolved, if mankind has no higher purpose than other animals and no unique position in the order of things . . . if human beings were not created by God to glorify Him as sons and daughters . . . if we are not charged with the stewardship of this planet, if we are merely co-equal and meaningless blobs of temporal tissue, then our life would have no more value than that of a mosquito. In such a chaotic worldview, why would any life have value?

We know better. We know that we humans are created not only for a purpose but also for eternity. Human life has eternal value and to discount that value is to insult and offend the Creator.

Let's expand this topic just a bit. On September 1, 1939, Adolf Hitler issued orders that put two men in charge of euthanizing— putting to death—every person with an illness deemed to be incurable. He judged people with incurable diseases as having lives "not worth living". His campaign soon included those who were judged incapable of contributing to the economy: cripples, epileptics, those with mental illness or mental disabilities. Later, his ghastly edict was expanded to include Jews, Poles and dissidents along with the other countless casualties of the war. That's where a madman disconnected from God can lead a nation.

Today, we look back on Hitler's Germany we are appalled. We tend to think that a civilized country like Canada could never succumb to such brutality. Really? How is it that out of misguided concern for "choice", Canada has killed as many as 4 million babies in the last 40 years? How is it that out of misguided "compassion" for those who may be suffering in their final days, we suddenly fall for the rhetoric of a "life not worth living" and allow the killing of the elderly, the disabled and the depressed? Our "assisted suicide" bandwagon is still picking up speed; if we continue on this path, we'll find—as they did in Europe—that there are no brakes.

How is it that out of a misguided concern for "fairness" or "compassion", our nation has become a promoter of sexual perversion and gender confusion, exposing young children to lifestyles and practices which lead to behavioural addiction, sexual disease and dysfunction, self-mutilation and often suicide?

The answer is that we have allowed press-manipulated emotions to rule our decision-making without reference to eternal truth and the unchanging principles of God's Word. As in Hitler's day, emotions can sometimes be stirred by passionate speeches and behaviours, can sometimes be compelled by peer pressure and political force. Only when we return to a biblical perspective and let our words and actions be directed by an all-knowing, all-wise Creator can we hope to restore reason and true compassion in our nation.

July 18, 2017

http://www.cbc.ca/news/canada/calgary/bear-148-canmore-banff-park-grizzly-problem-encounters-captured-1.4189863

http://www.cbc.ca/news/canada/calgary/grizzly-bear-148-petition-alberta-parks-wildlife-aggressive-canmore-banff-1.4204776

Hiding the Truth

When governments try to cover up facts and statistics, it usually sends a signal that they are hiding something of which they are ashamed, something which could prove embarrassing or hard to explain to voters and taxpayers. When they cover up the cover-up, that signal gets even louder. The provincial governments of Ontario and British Columbia are hiding statistics on abortions and they're not eager to talk about it.

Effective Jan. 1, 2012, section 65 of Ontario's Freedom of Information and Protection of Privacy Act (FIPPA) was amended to exclude records relating to the provision of abortion services. There was no public announcement of this extraordinary change. In fact, there was no debate or discussion of it in the Hansard records before it was passed into law. It was simply approved by Ontario's Liberal cabinet back in the McGuinty era (which, come to think of it, isn't much different from the Wynne era). It's old news now, but how many Ontarians are aware of this very narrow exclusion: why should abortion be the only medical procedure for which costs, demographics, causes, outcomes, and trends are no longer available to the public? Patricia Maloney, an Ottawa-area pro-life blogger (*http://run-with-life.blogspot.ca/*) discovered the anomaly when seeking statistics through a normal Freedom of Information request. Her request was denied and she was told that the information she was seeking was not information the Ontario government would be releasing.

If we lived in Russia, China, North Korea, or Iran, we might not be surprised. The brutal dictatorships of the world have always practised truth-suppression. They've figured out that it's inconvenient when people "know too much". Taxpayers might object if they knew how many millions were spent killing babies. Folks who care about social issues and who have believed the old mantra about abortions being "safe, legal, and rare" might discover that they are *not* rare and *not* safe (not even for the mother and never for the baby). In 2010, the last year for which Ontario abortion statistics were made public, the Ontario Ministry of Health and Long-Term Care indicated that there were 18,330 abortions carried out in doctors' offices, 16,055 in private facilities, and 9,612 in hospitals, for a total of 43,997 abortions. By contrast, the Canadian Institute for Health Information (CIHI) reported only 28,765 abortions for Ontario in 2010. The discrepancy is at least partially a result of the fact that private clinics are not required to report this information. What's with that? Why can't we have accurate reporting of all medical procedures? (Unless, of course, abortion is not a "medical procedure?) If that's the case, why are we paying for it?

It's amazing to me, in a country where large numbers of people who are up in arms about the introduction of private health care for any other purpose, are quite content to tolerate the killing of babies in private clinics, using taxpayer-dollars, and with no accountability, even for properly recording the numbers, ages, and outcomes of these procedures. Taxpayer dollars which have been designated to treat disease and cure medical problems are being used not to cure illness but to kill little people . . . and we are not even allowed to know how much it's costing? This is disturbing and should be a topic for every radio and TV talk show host until this secrecy provision is exposed to the public and rolled back. It is estimated (at an average cost of $1600 per baby killed) that abortions cost Ontario taxpayers about $70 million in 2010 alone, the last year for which we have figures. I wonder how many hip replacements or ultrasound machines could have been purchased with that money?

Ontario is not alone in this conspiracy to conceal the social and economic costs of their "safe, legal, and rare" policies. In BC, approximately 15,000 babies are killed each year, now under a cloak of secrecy, with a very similar policy of truth-suppression regarding abortions. In 2001, the BC NDP government of the day, as one of their last acts before they were defeated, passed Bill 21, an amendment to the BC Freedom of Information Act, which disallowed public release of information on abortion. The BC Liberals who replaced them have done nothing to change this policy of trying to hide abortion statistics.

Well-known pro-lifer Ted Gerk, in concert with other BC activists, has made diligent attempts to have government reverse that decision but so far has not found enough politicians with the courage and moral integrity to address the cover-up of information. Where is our national public broadcaster (CBC) when it comes to exposing the deeds of darkness? Where is the public outcry over this outrage?

When people have all the information they can make better decisions for themselves and for their loved ones. If women were told the truth about fetal development and about the increased likelihood of breast cancer following abortion, there would be fewer abortions. If taxpayers knew what they were paying for and given an opportunity to redirect those funds to true health care needs, there would be fewer abortions. If the public knew that 60% of abortions are the result of coercion from a boyfriend or parent, they would be less supportive of the current abortion paradigm which rests on a deceptive misuse of the word "choice". The Christian Heritage Party is concerned about the abuse of power and the withholding of information from the public. Those who share our concerns must continue to press for transparency in the thorough reporting of publicly-funded "medical procedures".

December 16, 2014

"I didn't know I was pregnant!"

Stuff happens. Not all of us are noticers. Things can sneak up on you or slip on by. As a dear family member once said, "You never know what's going to happen when you get up in the morning". But really? Pregnant for 9 months and completely unaware? I have to admit, this stretches the boundaries of credulity. "The man"—as he is affectionately known by CBC—became an instant hero for extricating a baby from a garbage bag in the dumpster outside his Calgary home and was surprised to learn that he was the father of the child he'd rescued. His girlfriend apparently failed to notice the common signs of pregnancy and—when her unexpected baby was born she did the only logical thing any Canadian woman would do. She placed it in a garbage bag and threw it into the dumpster.

The whole incident bears a bizarre and faint resemblance to the story of Moses being pulled from the bulrushes by Pharaoh's daughter, later in a divine irony, to be nursed and nurtured by his own mother. Of course, Moses' mother was fully aware that she had been pregnant and the tiny floating basket was a desperate (and successful) attempt to save his life, not to get rid of a "problem". Despite the bizarre circumstances, we thank God that this modern rescue took place. Garbage bags and dumpsters just aren't good places for babies (although thousands have gone out that way behind abortion mills across this country).

Whatever ultimately comes from this incident, one is tempted to draw parallels to other current events. Two years ago, in the lead-up to that ill-begotten election of 2008, Mr. Flaherty and Mr. Harper had "no idea" we would not have balanced books in 2009, 2010, 2011, 2012, 2013, 2014 and so on. All their predictions were for "modest surpluses". But a strange thing happened on the way to the polls. It turns out (and this should be noted by those planning a business career) that spending more than you make results in deficits and deficits grow up into real debts. Who'd have known? And so today, after sinking another $80 billion into the hole, our finance minister and prime minister are projecting additional deficit spending until 2016. That should get us through two more elections and by then, who knows?

Similarly, when social planners began teaching teenagers and younger children "everything they had never even thought of asking about sex" they discovered—to their utter surprise—that this information prompted more sexual activity among youth, not less. More leaky condos—I mean condoms—resulted in more disease, more pregnancies, more abortions. Why didn't somebody warn us? I don't mean those narrow-minded Christians. I mean somebody with real credibility, like Oprah or Clinton or...Svend Robinson?

Surely we've learned something in the years since then. The school of hard knocks is a tough place to learn but at least you really earn that diploma! We want safer streets so instead of holding violent criminals accountable for their actions, we'll let lawyers and judges experiment on our communities by using the "revolving door" to let known offenders back out into the communities. That should work.

On the issue of free speech—we want all citizens to have freedom of expression so we will only restrict the freedom of those who hold to a biblical worldview. Why should they impose that on others? Meanwhile those who taunt, threaten and intimidate from Islamic pulpits or the offices of gay lobby groups or radical environmentalist organizations must be free to speak. After all it is supposed to be a democracy, is it not?

One more thing: certain alarmists are predicting financial chaos, social disaster, shrinking classrooms, multicultural friction, the collapse of social security and our ability to provide health care to all, even a loss of respect for human life itself. They claim that ignoring the warning signs of history may cause us to repeat the mistakes of the past and then suffer the consequences. Why do they think that the troubles that caused earlier civilizations to collapse could have the same effect on us? Don't they know we've found a cure for consequences? Anyway, if we just keep our eyes closed, maybe we'll find out it was just a dream! The alternative is nearly unthinkable. We might have to start doing things differently...

October 25, 2010

"Je suis PHC et je suis pro-life!"

While the world and many news anchors are still reel-to-reeling the reality of radical Islamist jihad and the wanton destruction of innocent human life vis-a-vis the Charlie Hebdo and related massacres, (with occasional references to the slaughter of perhaps 2,000 Nigerians by Boko Haram), I have been meeting with Canadians in Quebec who want to do something to stop the slaughter of Canadian babies currently tipping the scales at over 100,000 innocent human lives each year in Canada.

The mass killing of the pre-born is every bit as horrific on a case-by-case basis as the brutal slaying of the Charlie Hebdo journalist team or the ambush of police officers or the cruel murder of grocery-store hostages; it's just not being covered by the media nor mentioned by the world leaders who linked arms to show their unity on the democratic right to free speech. Here's the scoop: babies are ambushed in the womb. No advance warning. No chance to run away. If numbers matter, abortion outranks all other causes of deaths. I guess that's why BC and Ontario have stopped collecting and reporting abortion statistics. Those numbers are just so inconvenient.

Aside from the killing of the innocent, there's also a free speech issue. Not only is each individual baby deprived of the opportunity to ever say anything to anyone, those who seek to come to their defense are having their right to be heard taken away as well. Our friend, Mary Wagner, is behind bars today for having the audacity to hand out roses to women who are about to have their babies ripped from their life support systems in the womb. Apparently, Mary's offer to pray for these women is seen as going a bit too far. It tends to interfere with the orderly processing of death-clinic clients in an efficient and profitable manner.

70

That's why I was so encouraged to meet with men and women in La Belle Province who want to do something about the slaughter of the innocents - men and women who are not afraid to speak about the value of human life and our role in defending it. Today I was encouraged by several who are considering representing the CHP (PHC in Quebec) in the next federal election.

The words and actions of other party leaders and MPs have made the decision of party support very straightforward. Mr. Trudeau, whose father first made abortion legal in Canada, has now declared that no Liberal MP under his leadership will be allowed to vote for the protection of the pre-born. Mr. Mulcair, not to be outdone, has emphasized the NDP's stance on ensuring universal access to abortion-on-demand. The leaders of the Bloc and the Green Party still seem to think that the "choice" to abort somehow empowers women. And of course, Mr. Harper has stated repeatedly that he will not allow *any* legislation restricting abortion to be passed while he is PM. He's backed those words with action, too. By speaking against and voting against Rod Bruinooge's Anti-Coercion Bill (Roxanne's Law) and Stephen Woodworth's Personhood Motion, and by making sure that Mark Warawa's motion against gender-selective abortion never made it to the floor for a full debate, he has clearly shown that getting re-elected is more important to him than defending the pre-born.

That's a tragic choice but one our PM has made as an adult. 100,000 babies every year will never get to make a choice about anything. Even their mothers with their so-called "choice" are being used as puppets of the abortionist mind-set; statistics indicate that over 60% of post-abortive women made their fatal decision under pressure from a boyfriend or others. For them, the "choice" argument wears a little thin. Canadian voters still have a choice when they go to the polls. Canadians still have a choice about what political party they join and support with their finances and energy. Working together before an election, those who wish to show solidarity with the preborn can link arms and work together for the protection of innocent life.

Canadians can still choose whether to mark their ballots in defense of innocent human life or in support of the status quo. The Christian Heritage Party will do its best to provide pro-life candidates where the other parties fail. I thank those men and women in Quebec and across Canada who are stepping forward to protect the innocent. I hope many more will join with them and in solidarity say, "Je suis PHC (CHP); je suis PRO-LIFE."

January 20, 2015

This article was written in the wake of a horrible terrorist attack in Paris where radical Muslims gunned down the editor and several reporters working for Charlie Hebdo, a newspaper which had dared to criticize Islam. Around the world, vigils were held and displays of solidarity with the victims. "Je suis Charlie Hebdo" became something of a battle cry for a time. My article hints at the hypocrisy of defending some innocent victims of mindless slaughter but not the many, many victims of abortion.

Family, Marriage and Gender

In the beginning He made them male and female. Matthew 19:4

For this cause shall a man leave his father and mother, and shall be joined unto his wife and they two shall be one flesh. Ephesians 5:31

Bullying? Sexual Harassment? Call it Out but Call it Sin.

In recent years, the destroyers of innocence have run a number of side-campaigns aimed at disarming and/or vilifying promoters of traditional family values. One such campaign has displayed a disproportionate focus on the word "bullying", most often used as a code-word—a kind of red herring—to legitimize homosexuality and other unhealthy sexual behaviours. In most cases, the victims of "bullying", at least the ones the MSM likes to talk about, are poor, misunderstood, adolescent males who are confused about their gender.

In spite of the fact that research indicates a far higher incidence of real bullying against young people who are unusually fat or skinny or tall or short, the usefulness of the "anti-bullying" campaign has clearly been as a victim-centered appeal to normal, well-intentioned people of all ages and classes to "call off the dogs" of meaningful discussion, (er, I mean "spiteful homophobic hatred"). They call on us to "get used to the new normal"—that is, to a daily experience where there is no longer such a thing as "normal" and where those who still cling to outmoded notions of traditional morality do their best to hide it.

The series of events which led to the tragic death of Amanda Todd are unusual in that they don't appear to be associated with homosexuality, lesbianism or gender confusion. The public outrage over the mean-spirited abuse she suffered through social media is vaguely reassuring. We want to believe that this is a one-time random failure that can be "fixed" by a multitude of townhalls and memorial services. One is encouraged that—in spite of the brutal treatment Amanda received from one online sexual predator in particular and the crude and thoughtless trash talk and physical violence she suffered from her peers—at least the vast majority of Canadians are still able to be shocked and capable of compassion.

The internet was used, along with peer pressure and the emotional vulnerability of youth to coerce this sensitive girl to do things she didn't want to do, including ultimately the taking of her own life. Now there are vast numbers of concerned citizens of all ages who "want to do something" to prevent a re-occurrence of this lonely and deeply painful death and who have mobilized in various ways to educate young people and change the behaviours of both victims and perpetrators. I suppose one should be grateful for that outpouring of emotion and resolve . . . I suppose it could be worse. I suppose all this might have happened, for instance, with no decent folks left to call for reflection.

In the wake of this tragedy, though, I want to be sure that some elements of this story are noticed and not forgotten, because if we truly want to protect other children from this chilling and desperate descent into lonely despair and hopeless self-destruction, we need to understand all of the elements of Amanda's story. The following pieces of the puzzle may all have contributed in some way to the events that so marred Amanda's life. Think about what an obstacle course—in our country—adolescent life has become for young people who just want to grow up normal, accepted and loved.

Here are the challenges:
- Broken homes: Many young people in our broken culture struggle with self-esteem and a "longing to belong", to have things make sense and to experience a complete bonding with both their parents and the sense of security and approval that we were all meant to enjoy. In addition, the nurture and protection that the family was designed to

provide is lacking for so many young people today, making them vulnerable to both physical and emotional attacks.

- A hyper-sexualized culture: From the time that an infant can process images, the relentless assault of sexual imagery on his or her senses—of nudity, sensuality and wanton pleasure-seeking—can confuse any young person, whether a victim or one seeking gratification. The school system follows up on the daily fare of entertainment and marketing media with earlier and earlier attempts to engage young children in discussions of their sexuality. While blissful ignorance of the sexual nature of human relationships within the family structure is neither possible nor desirable, the constant bombardment of information about sexual activity and behaviour along with the innuendo that "everyone's doing it" can wear down the defenses of even a disciplined young mind. When so many are drifting without an anchor, choices can be made, the consequences of which can never be undone, like 12-year old Amanda Todd's peer-pressured exposure of her breasts to a webcam.

- A lack of purpose and understanding of mankind's divine dignity: For years—at school, in many homes, in the thrall of the TV and even in liberal churches—young people have been defrauded of a deep and abiding faith in God and of the perspective that they are made in the sacred image of God, that God watches over them and that they have a responsibility to seek to please Him . . . and that when they do so they can expect His favour. Amanda Todd had a sense of being abandoned and of having nobody that loved her. The lies of the age we live in had hidden from her the truth—that God loved her and sent His Son so that she could have an abundant, joy-filled life; she was deprived of that confidence because those around her, those who might have been her friends or mentors, had themselves believed the lie that humankind is just a herd of purposeless creatures with no destiny and no loving God who cares for them.

- A violent, self-pleasing, aggressive and malevolent culture: It's not the unbelievable cruelty and selfishness of her seducers and tormenters only that needs to be exposed and challenged. It's a whole culture—especially the youth culture which has been groomed into self-absorption in recent decades—a culture that soaks up "reality" shows like "Survivor" and disrespectful and mocking talent shows like "Talent" and "Idol" where the losers are paraded, prodded and dismissed with pithy and sarcastic epithets. Shows like "Dragon's Den", where aspiring businesses are boosted or sunk (with a deadly combination of vitriol and humour). It's the "wrestling" shows with excessive and gratuitous violence. It's "America's Funniest Home Videos" where the audience roars with laughter as people fall off their bikes, run into trees, get scared out of their wits. And of course it's a careless culture of "choice" where 100,000 babies are deliberately killed (in Canada) each year by abortion and comfortable and compromised MPs arrogantly spout off about "choice".

Add to the mix a few sadistic pedophiles and emerging technologies which invite graphic interplay and anonymous addictions and you have a recipe for disaster. Poor little Amanda Todd wandered unsuspectingly into this morass and all of us wept for her tragedy. But if we are going to fix this problem, protect young people from predators and set a higher standard for respectful and compassionate behaviour, we're going to have to dig a lot deeper than "cyber-bullying". We're going to have to repent for failing to preserve for our children a respect for human morality and the God to whom we owe our existence.

October 18, 2012

On October 10, 2012, Amanda Todd, a 15-year old student in Coquitlam, BC, took her own life after being tormented and blackmailed over an extended period of time by an online bully and sexual pervert. The tragic details of her shaming and ultimate suicide are here:
https://en.wikipedia.org/wiki/Suicide_of_Amanda_Todd

Across the country, multitudes were deeply moved by her story and the emotional pain she suffered. Aside from the thoughtless and cruel actions of her tormentor, the early sexualisation of children in this country has made many more children vulnerable to abuse. Clamping down on online bullying is important but we must intervene much earlier to protect children from ideas and attitudes which result in the objectification of women and girls and the proliferation of pornography and sexual abuse.

Cross-Dressing "Conservatives" Expose Themselves in the House (Oh My!)

While the mainstream media offers diversions to the public—such as Jason Kenney's apology following his non-apology (for using gutter language in his dismissive misfired missive about Alberta's deputy premier Thomas Lukaszuk)—many in the country missed a much more significant bit of news from the House. Fifteen "Conservative" MPs voted in favour of Bill-279, a bill giving special rights to transsexual / transgendered people and viewed by many social conservatives as likely to expose children to further attacks on their biological sexual identity.

The bill passed second reading as a direct result of the support it received from the so-called "Conservative" MPs. In addition to the fifteen who supported it, another sixteen were either absent or abstained, including the Prime Minister, Foreign Affairs Minister John Baird and MP James Moore, Minister of Canadian Heritage. Both Moore and Baird have supported the advancement of the "gender agenda" in the past.

For those Canadians who care about these things, especially those who have held out hope for a renewed protection of family values and a return to standards of public decency, this abandonment of such a key area of public policy should come as a shock. But do people even notice? Has the absurdity of a "Conservative" government doing the dirty work of leftist social re-engineering caught the attention of those who worked so hard to get them elected?

Words should mean something. When politicians masquerade as something they are not, it should ruffle some feathers. It should open some eyes. Even if what is so glaringly obvious is not a pretty picture.

We pay for the mutilation of bodies—"gender reassignment surgery"—in many ways. It takes precious health care dollars. It distorts reality for our young people and, if the proponents of this bill have their way, it will put women and young people at increased risk of assault. Those who have rejected the natural, healthy relationships for which we are designed in favour of gender confusion have thrown out the anchor, the compass and the map.

Now we are paying for another "reassignment": that of politicians who appeared to be "Conservative" but, after being elected, found they were in need of a "new political persona." Perhaps they fall into that vague category sometimes referred to as "two-spirited." We used to call that "double-tongued." In order to clarify the state of affairs for Canadians, it might be more honest if those "Conservatives" who have abandoned the values that were mistakenly assigned to them in the past, to simply complete the transition, cross the floor to the NDP and have an "outing." They've already exposed their agenda.

June 14, 2012

http://www.lifesite.net/news/15-conservatives-who-helped-federal-transsexual-bill-pass-2nd-reading

Divorced from Reality

Two wrongs don't make a right. When you're in a deep hole, you don't get out of it by digging deeper. A few weeks ago, Canada experienced corporate angst and apoplexy when it was discovered that our "same-sex marriage" laws are woefully inadequate (be still, my heart!) when it comes to divorce. This became painfully evident when two lesbians, one from the UK and one from Florida—who had come to Canada to be joined forever in "wedded bliss"—found themselves unable to obtain a legal divorce. Oh, the indignation of it all! The violation of personal dignity!

I must admit, my first suggestion for correcting this inequity (or is it iniquity?) would have been to issue a generous one-size-fits-all divorce for all same-sex couples. Why wait for reality to sink in? Why wait for the long, complicated list of reasons why? Simply send a notice to the many unfortunate participants in this cruel joke called "same-sex marriage". Let them know that Canada has seen the error of its ways and will no longer hold them accountable to maintain a lifelong commitment to the fraud, the charade of marital status between two of the same. Indeed, since marriage has always been about the joining of opposites, the forced cohabitation of two of the same is rather like trying to force the positive poles of two magnets together. They don't naturally attract; they repel. Without a proper legal arrangement for the respectful, tolerant, mutually beneficial dissolution of one's lifetime vows (made in all sincerity and based substantively on the latest proclamations of the MSM), a "partner" in such cases may not only repel but may in fact, be forced to rappel. "Rapunzel, Rapunzel, let down your hair, so I can rappel and go elsewhere."

Alas, such a solution would have been far too easy. The angry accusations of the Opposition called for justice to be done and this terribly "unfair" shortcoming of Canada's world-class homosexual and lesbian marriage law be rectified. (Yes, the shortcoming being that foreigners who came to our shores to hook up inconveniently—but permanently—were being denied the opportunity to break their vows if they happened to reside in a Troglodyte realm where their vows were not taken seriously). I know, it sounds confusing, but then abandoning God's design and thousands of years of human social experience does bring with it a bit of confusion. Mortals cannot be expected to understand these things.

Instead of going back to the drawing board and scrapping a social experiment doomed to failure, the Conservative government chose to put a patch on it. Last week, Justice Minister Rob Nicholson announced that the government would correct this glaring omission; and so they did. It's amazing how quickly an embarrassing problem can be solved with an embarrassing solution. Where there's a will, there's a way!

So the Conservative majority government of Mr. Stephen Harper can now be hailed as the saviour, not only of homosexual and lesbian marriage, but also of divorce! If we were in the business of adding to the Scriptures—which we're not—we might suggest this catchy couplet: "What God has not joined together, let not man not separate!" Double negatives are "genderally" frowned upon but in this case, making sense of the ridiculous may be the only way to deal with the confusion of state-man-and-mandated temporary permanent unions. Besides, it's a triple negative . . .

In short, the government that presumes to sanctify the unholy finds itself obligated to respond to the latest nuanced wrinkle of political correctness while trying to stay out of the bedrooms of the nation (and now of other nations as well). Meanwhile, the well-beaten trail between the courtrooms and the classrooms of this nation reveal a whole new source of legal fiction and friction. Here's an idea: next time some caterwauling lobby group wants the government to pronounce a blessing on its misguided agenda...try saying "No."

January 2012

Ignoring God's laws gets complicated. Same-sex marriage was legalized by Parliament in 2005 but in 2012, the issue of same-sex divorce became a problem. Here's a National Post article explaining the problem:
http://nationalpost.com/news/canada/justice-minister-looks-to-clarify-law-so-same-sex-marriages-can-be-undone-in-canada

My spoof above simply pointed out that it would be a lot simpler to do things God's way. For the record, God makes no provision for same-sex marriage. He also says that He hates divorce.

More of the Same: PM Defends Same-Sex "Marriage"

In spite of the expected accusations to the contrary, Stephen Harper today articulated clearly his position on the nagging issue of same-sex marriage, falling back on his recurring abortion rhetoric that "...we have no intention of reopening or opening this issue". The mystifying aspect of his stance is that he claims that "...we had a vote on this issue", referring to a vague request during his first year in office when—with a minority government—the hostile House was asked whether they wished to revisit the issue of same-sex marriage. The House said "no"; case closed. Really? Where is the leadership in caving in to a misguided, unreasonable and self-serving lobby after a single failed attempt to open a discussion? If Wilberforce had given up after his 1st, 2nd, 3rd, 4th, etc. attempt, Britain might still have the slave trade.

Everyone who's followed the debate over the years knows that the passage of same-sex marriage in 2005 was only successful because the Liberals and NDP were whipped (some before the vote and a few brave souls after). It only reached the House in the first place because of illegitimate court rulings and special treatment for that paragon of virtue, jewel thief Svend Robinson, who first introduced the bill. The indecent assault on the Charter by unelected judges set the stage, the leftist media (including taxpayer-funded CBC) violated listeners ad nauseum with their tales of sad and sorry homosexuals who "only want to live 'normal' lives with the same rights as everyone else" and Parliament bravely stepped up to the plate and voted against the wishes of the public who elected them. Since then, the news and entertainment media, the taxpayer-funded school systems and the human rights commissions have worked hard to convince Canadians that the current status quo is what they want. Their bullying tactics have been appallingly successful and "alternative sexual lifestyles" have now become the "new normal".

Back to the issue of political expediency and the true grit (no pun intended) required to challenge bad laws and pass good ones. Over the years, from its first iteration as the Reform Party and up through its somewhat compromised current edition, the Conservative Party as a whole, and Mr. Harper as an individual, have promised to eliminate the wasteful and repressive long-gun registry. We agree with and applaud that stance. Hold the line. Don't flinch. Do what's right. Fail once? Try again. And again. What makes this issue different? After all, marriage between one man and one woman is the bedrock foundation of our Western society and social institutions. Why does this Prime Minister not have the backbone to stand up for marriages, for families and for children?

If the goal of attaining power is to simply retain power, Mr. Harper's limp excuse for not challenging the status quo might be seen as justifiable political expediency. If, however, seeking the privilege of leading this nation is to improve the prospects for a morally-cohesive society, established on fundamental principles of justice, free speech and strengthened families, Mr. Harper's promise to "not reopen or open the issue" is a failure of moral fibre. Of course, Mr. Harper is answering a question people aren't asking. Reopen the debate? It was never closed.

January 13, 2012

Background: On the campaign trail in 2005, Mr. Harper promised that he would create legislation defining marriage as between "one man and one woman", the same definition we support. It never happened, even when he presided over a Conservative majority for 4 years.

Update: In September 2012, the National Post went so far as to label the Harper Tories as "Warriors for Gay Rights" (see the article here): http://nationalpost.com/news/canada/warriors-for-gay-rights-the-conservatives-have-become-unlikely-lgbt-supporters

On May 28, 2016 the Conservative Party convention delegates officially voted to remove from their policy book the plank in support of traditional marriage between one man and one woman. https://www.theglobeandmail.com/news/politics/conservatives-end-official-opposition-to-gay-marriage/article30197721/

O.P.P. conducts major porn bust—and misses the "big fish"

Last week, the Ontario Provincial Police arrested 80 individuals in connection with child pornography and other illegal activities including the sexual abuse of children. Kudos to the O.P.P. May they continue to root out this evil and may they be successful in prosecuting the offenders. I just wish they would go after the big fish—the ones who are systematically exploiting and abusing children in the public schools of Ontario. People like Premier Kathleen Wynne and Education Minister Liz Sandals, with their explicit and controversial sex-ed programs, are turning Ontario's public schools into recruiting centres for early childhood sexual activity. The odious curriculum, forced on children from K-12 against the wishes of many parents is nothing short of sexual abuse.

When the original author of Ontario's reviled sex-ed curriculum, Ben Levin, was convicted last year of "making child porn and counselling to commit sexual assault", most common-sense Canadians assumed that the curriculum he helped design for his own devious purposes would be discredited and discarded. Who would dare to promote such garbage in the public schools after the curtain was pulled back to find a dirty old man at the controls? Ben Levin was the Deputy Minister of Education under Dalton McGuinty and was held in high esteem by lesbian Premier Kathleen Wynne—that is, until he got caught. That's the one unpardonable sin for those in power. It's embarrassing when a key player is (pardon the inference) exposed.

Ontario's curriculum claims to arm children with knowledge to "keep them safe". It does nothing of the sort. How do children fall under the influence of pimps and pornographers? What leads them into becoming victims of sexual assault and exploitation? One factor is "early sexualisation", that is, creating in them at ever earlier ages, a fascination with all things sexual and a curiosity and desire for sexual experience . . . long before those desires can be satisfied in a meaningful and mature lifetime marriage commitment. Once "desensitized" to the issue, young people can be trained to discuss sexuality and their deeply personal feelings in a casual and public setting. Many of them will be turned against the moral values of their parents and some will become activists for the cause of "sexual expression".

Like their accomplices and business associates in Planned Parenthood, Kathleen Wynne and her pals realize that the best way to encourage early sexual activity (resulting in a profitable cycle of pregnancies and abortions and creating a generation of non-married potential sexual partners) is to get young children thinking about sex and gender. Ontario's sex-ed curriculum purports to empower and protect young people by imparting knowledge about the human reproductive system and the ethics and principles of consent. It asks the question "What does consent look like?" What hypocrisy! The Premier and the Education Minister never got consent from parents to teach this garbage! They act as if 12- and 13-year old girls and boys can handle explosive and explicit sexual images and concepts without defilement and without compromise. "Just say no!" they offer to young people as a deterrent to unwanted sexual advances. Yet when parents, by the thousands said "NO!" to Premier Wynne's sex-ed program, she just ignored them.

Premier Wynne and her committed core of child abusers should be investigated for the harm that has already been done and is continuing to be done to children and young people. Parents send their children to school to learn to read and write and to equip them for future careers. Prostitution, pornography and pimping are not careers. A good sex-ed curriculum (age-appropriate) should teach abstinence until marriage and fidelity in marriage. Students should be taught biological reality, not sociological fantasy. Gender orientation memes should be dropped and the two actual biological genders created by God—male and female—should be honoured as the basis for all family relationships.

To the O.P.P., keep at it! Expose evil. Uncover the works of darkness. Bring perpetrators to light. But understand that until the promotion of heightened sexual interest and perverted desires is banned from Ontario's schools, until the graphic display of sexual content is curtailed in our media and the internet, you will be fighting a losing battle. We can't have both graphic and immoral sexual imagery in our schools and a generation of young people with wholesome and enduring morals. We have to choose.

The Christian Heritage Party promotes chastity, sound morals and lifelong committed marriage between one man and one woman. We see that parents have been given the primary responsibility as educators of their own children, especially in matters of faith and morality. Elected officials and bureaucrats must be re-educated to understand their roles. They have been entrusted by parents, voters and taxpayers to serve, not to dictate. We must work to win back the classroom as a place where children are taught knowledge and skills, not destructive ideology.

May 2, 2016

The distortions of gender confusion continue to trouble parents across the country, not only in Ontario. BC has its version—SOGI 123—and Alberta's wicked NDP government is using the most shameless bully tactics to force private schools to adopt its sexual philosophy. May God give us courage to stand in the gap for them and future generations!

Some Are More Equal Than Others

George Orwell's *Animal Farm* contained this famous line, memorable for its ludicrous, oxymoronic slogan: "All animals are equal but some are more equal than others". It would be laughable if it weren't such an accurate picture of our current government's attempt to appear just and fair as it imposes its unfair and biased gender agenda on the Canadian public. The really tragic aspect of this deception is that many Canadians are falling for it. We must sound the alarm—loud and long—if we are to prevent the crippling loss of free speech, common sense and healthy community attitudes towards the family.

Last week, the House of Commons passed Bill C-309 at Second Reading, a bill which would officially declare the first week of October each year as Gender Equality Week. Only one MP voted against it and that was Brad Trost. We applaud him for his courage and regret that there were not more MPs willing to take an unpopular—and likely misunderstood—position based on principle.

Why, you may ask, would he oppose a bill which ostensibly seeks to advocate for equality? The answer is found in the lengthy list of "whereas" justifications for C-309. At first blush, the bill would seem to be another step in the long struggle for equal pay and equal opportunity for women, causes which we all would support. On closer examination, however, this bill (like so many government actions of late) is a shallow cover for yet more gender-based activism. Any excuse will do for yet one more outraged complaint about the supposed mistreatment of those who refuse to accept the biological gender assigned to them before birth.

The preamble to C-309 rambles through a long list of complaints about the struggles faced by women in the workplace but sprinkled throughout are phrases that reveal its true intent. *"Challenges faced by . . . individuals of minority gender identity and expression" . . . "transgendered and visible minority women". . . "issues related to gender identity and sexual orientation, particularly transgender women in visible minority groups" . . . "challenges Canadian women and individuals of minority gender identity and expression continue to face"* and so on.

The list of issues which are meant to explain the importance of C-309 goes on to highlight inequities in regard to race as well as to gender. While decrying the oppression it claims all women in Canada experience, it gives extra attention to "First Nation, Metis or Inuit" women, making this bill about racial equality, another cause about which I'm sure we're all concerned but which seems not directly related to the purported topic of the bill.

One background statement in the list mentions that there has been a "disproportionate rise in the number of female inmates in Canada's correctional institutions". Do the bill's proponents want to establish quotas there as well? If there are increases in the arrests and convictions of females, perhaps there are behavioural trends that are at fault. Perhaps, women and girls being constantly assured that they can and should assert their right to be just like men in every way are becoming more prone to social misbehaviour than they were in the past? Perhaps society's general departure from good morals has affected women more than men? At any rate, it seems very unlikely that the increase in female incarceration is any kind of malevolent or malicious program instituted by white males to further create hardship for Canada's women.

The boringly repetitive and detailed list of grievances also mentions that women are "underrepresented as participants and leaders in sports and physical activities". Really? How many of us would like to see a couple of 300-lb defensive linemen landing in a heap on a newly-empowered woman carrying a football? Can it be done? Sure. Are there women with the talent, skill and desire to succeed in male-dominated contact sports? No doubt. Is it a desirable goal to introduce a quota system into hard-hitting professional sports so that women don't feel "underrepresented"? I say no. Sports are of course an area where talent and ability—and yes, sometimes strength and size—are supposed to open doors of opportunity. There are plenty of opportunities in the sports arena for those with the skill and perseverance to find them. They cannot be created by putting quotas on "representation".

The bill's preamble goes on to lament that "a lower proportion of Canadian politicians are women". Stop right there. Every citizen of voting age is entitled to step forward and offer himself or herself to the voters. Of course, there are cliques and "old boys' clubs" which favour some people over others. There are many reasons why some succeed in gaining electoral support. It may be money, education, worldview, language skills. It may be stamina, passion or looks. It may be ethnic background in certain areas or business experience or family connections. But don't tell me that Canadian society as a whole is against a woman's right to seek office. "It just ain't so".

These tired complaints would be merely annoying if they were not being relentlessly used to erode society's long-standing and well-deserved reverence for the traditional family and the dignity of both men and women, those who take their places in society with gratitude and enthusiasm. We honour mothers. We honour fathers. We believe that every individual—male or female—has a right and a responsibility to find the opportunities that God has provided for him or her and to achieve the highest level of success possible.

Of course, we believe in equal pay for equal work. That crosses all lines of gender, race and creed. We believe in equal opportunity. We believe in respect for all and the rule of law. But let's not allow misguided social policy activists to twist the equal treatment of men and women into yet another lever in regards to "gender identity". The attacks against the biological reality of male-female differences take many forms. For several years, Canadians were taught to make "bullying" Public Enemy Number One. Not any kind of bullying. Not the ordinary, hurtful schoolyard bullying about being fat or having big ears or out-of-date clothes. No, the big target was homophobic bullying. Because the battle was never about bullying; it was about making homosexuality more acceptable. Well, the "anti-bullying" crusade got old; the new poster child, the new cause celebre is "transgenderism". Again, the clamour and commotion is a false front for promoting gender confusion among schoolchildren. Bill C-309 is just another example. Don't take the bait. Read between the lines.

Feb 6, 2017

Real Women of Canada have also published a well-researched article which puts the lie to many of the false claims being made by the proponents of C-309. We appreciate their work.
http://www.realwomenofcanada.ca/gender-equality-week/

We also thank MP Brad Trost (Saskatoon-University) for defending our children. We need more MPs like him. Help us keep politicians honest and protect Canadian children from the confusion of legislated gender dysphoria.

C-309, called An Act to Establish Gender Equality Week, passed 2nd Reading in the House on Feb 1, 2017 and later passed 3rd Reading.

Throwing Marriage Away: Why Conservative Delegates Chose Divorce

By now, most Canadians have heard the news: delegates to the Conservative Policy Convention in Vancouver (2016) have removed from the party's policy book its declared support for traditional marriage between one man and one woman. This decision sends a clear message that the party endorses other kinds of "marriage".

Many saw this coming but others were blindsided by the 2-1 delegate division on this important issue. The question is: why have party delegates taken this policy off their books and what are the implications for Canadian voters?

In the title, I used the word "divorce". I didn't mean divorce between a husband and wife, although no-fault divorce (an oxymoron if ever there was one) has had, and continues to have, a most devastating effect on our children and young adults, our social structures, our communities and our economy. No, I was talking about a divorce between the pragmatic element of the Conservative Party and those in the party who still believe in "conserving" that which has value.

The media likes to call these two groups the "fiscal conservatives" and the "social conservatives". In their view, it is possible to hold fiscally responsible positions about debt, spending, entrepreneurship and government intrusion, while rejecting pro-life positions on abortion, euthanasia, and traditional Christian values in regard to marriage. I question the practical application of this kind of division. After all, the so-called "fiscal conservatives" of Mr. Harper's 9-year reign added over $150 billion to the national debt and allowed the size and cost of government to grow. Mr. Harper promised to do nothing to regulate abortion (and kept his word) but he also promised to run balanced budgets and failed to do so.

More importantly, I question how those who hold "socially conservative" views can continue to enthusiastically support a party which has decided that the family unit composed of a husband, wife and children should no longer be considered the norm and essential to the well-being of our country. Some principles are just too important to be bartered away for votes or public acclaim. The sanctity of life, the core value of the traditional family unit, personal freedoms to speak, worship and associate—these things define our lives as individuals and as a nation. To abandon them for perceived partisan advantage is not only cowardly but suicidal.

Same-sex marriage (the most obvious alternative to traditional marriage) was foisted upon this country under a Liberal government in 2005. At that time, most Conservatives spoke and voted against it. Liberal MPs were whipped to vote for it and it passed (barely) without general public consensus. Its legal antecedent came from the Supreme Court's faulty decision in the 1995 Egan case in which the court pretended that "sexual orientation" (a phrase not found in the Charter) "should have been included" and based its decision on its own predilections, not on historical facts nor the will of Parliament.

Since then, the public has been deceived into thinking that we have no choice but to adapt our policies and principles to the will of the Supreme Court. That view has carried on into other spheres, most notably the descent into madness of approving the killing of patients by their doctors (Bill C-14, now being debated in the House). Of course, it's not true that nine unelected judges have the moral or legal right to create new laws or throw out old laws at their whim. Our parliamentary democracy is based on the "supremacy of God and the rule of law" . . . at least that's what the Charter says. Judges who elevate their own opinions above those of God do so at their peril. Politicians must have the courage of their convictions and resist evil.

"There is a way that seems right to a man but it leads to death". This profound statement tells us that when, as individuals or as a nation, we look for an "easy way out", we sometimes make choices that have unintended and disastrous consequences. That will surely be the case if Canada adopts physician-assisted suicide. It will also be the case for the Conservative Party if it continues to seek broader public support by adapting itself to the low moral standards of this age. The victory celebrations that took place on the convention floor when delegates opted to endorse same-sex marriage ring very hollow when we consider that true marriage and the traditional family—building blocks of any strong society—have been abandoned.

The Christian Heritage Party has always supported and always will support the family model designed by God our Creator: one man and one woman joined in a lifelong commitment, with or without children. When circumstances result in single-parent homes or "blended families", God will be there to help those parents provide the best home they can for their children but His gold standard is still the two-parent home with a father and a mother. Our nation will prosper when more of our citizens—and the politicians who represent them—recognize and defend this God-ordained pattern for marriage and family.

Following this weekend's sudden shift in the Conservative Party's definition of marriage, many long-time Conservative members are contacting us and sharing with us their disappointment at the progressive decline of traditional family values in the party they once called home. Some have taken out memberships with the CHP and have committed themselves to helping us maintain our principled and consistent stand in the midst of confusion and compromise. We appreciate every fellow citizen who recognizes the implications of societal change and what it will take to restore morality in this country. God's standards have not changed.

May 30, 2016

https://nationalpost.com/news/canada/government-does-not-have-a-place-in-your-bedroom-conservatives-vote-to-accept-same-sex-marriages

Uniform Diversity

"We support diversity; on this topic, everyone must agree with us!" That seems to be the battle cry at the university today. Of course, the implication is that diversity is wonderful but diverse opinions are dreadful.

That's why—at most western universities today—the consensus of opinion is "politically correct" . . . and safe. With few exceptions, most professors and their students link arms around the sacred cows of "women's choice" (ie. abortion-on-demand), "diversity and equal rights" (ie. homosexuality, lesbianism, public nudity and explicit sexual content in elementary classrooms), "climate change and environmental concerns" (ie. banning or taxing of fossil fuels and promotion of costly and inefficient alternate energy), "science" (ie. papers and books promoting a causeless, accidental universe, a meaningless human existence and a non-moral code of ethics), etc.

You get the idea. Lots of talk about a rich culture of multiple worldviews and sharing of ideas; in reality, a droning mantra, a "call to worship" at the throne of locked-in, case-hardened, exclusive and unquestioned dogma. The consensus may grow, may change, may shape-shift over time but whatever form it takes at any moment, that iteration is—at that moment—held to be unassailable truth and those who question it are tried, condemned and punished.

Wikipedia, in its explanation of what a university is supposed to be, says this: "An important idea in the definition of a university is the notion of academic freedom". Wikipedia's definition of academic freedom is this: "Academic freedom is the conviction that freedom of inquiry by faculty members is essential to the mission of the academy as well as the principles of academia, and that scholars should have freedom to teach or communicate ideas or facts (including those that are inconvenient to external political groups or to authorities) without being targeted for repression, job loss, or imprisonment."

Sadly, that is not the experience of many professors today. The university—even in the West—has become a prison and sometimes a graveyard for any thought and expression which could be called "diverse".

One needn't look far for examples:
- Ben Stein—in his movie *Expelled*—has done a superb job of documenting the academic intolerance for professors who would dare to talk about Intelligent Design in their classrooms. Intolerance for any God-talk has resulted in professors being denied tenure, losing access to research facilities and for some, losing their jobs.
- Jordan Peterson, professor at the University of Toronto, has been called on the carpet and pilloried for refusing to play the "pronoun" game. The new demands for public adherence to a new set of pronouns for use in referring to new "genders" which people have invented for themselves have put Dr. Peterson on the front lines of a battle for freedom and he (thankfully) has refused to cede one inch. We need more men and women like Dr. Peterson who will stand for freedom and true diversity of thought.
- The Canadian Centre for Bioethical Reform (CCBR) has run into (and stood up to) numerous attempts to stop them from spreading their important and impactful information, including photo-evidence on university campuses. It's tragic that the pro-life message is often resisted not only by administration and faculty but by fellow students and student unions. Apparently, the fight for Free Speech on campuses like Berkeley in the 1960's has not resulted in a

lasting heritage. Like most freedoms, it seems that freedom of speech must be fought for again and again.

This intolerance, of course, does not restrict itself to universities but also descends with a cold chill to high schools . . . like the Catholic high school in Alberta, where a young lady recently found herself in a firestorm for her comments comparing the slaughter of the preborn to the Holocaust.

On the international stage, the notion of freedom of speech and freedom of religion finds its fiercest battle in countries dominated by sharia law. In those countries, there is not even a pretence of tolerance for diversity of opinion. Those who turn from Islam to follow another religion—or no religion—are simply killed. No questions asked. The sad part of that in the West is that people who even say what I just said are in turn rejected by many universities, either by students, faculty or both. In a videoclip from Prager University (one of the exceptions) Hussein Aboubakr tells of his own rejection by students at other universities where he was invited to speak. (see footnote)

What is the answer? Keep speaking. Keep telling the truth. Pray that God will grant open ears, open hearts, open eyes, open minds. Stand up to the bullies. Only the Truth can set men free.

April 30, 2017

September 27, 2016, Professor Jordan Peterson of the University of Toronto released the first of a three-part video series, entitled "Professor against political correctness: Part I: Fear and the Law". His refusal to use the pronouns invented by the LGBTQ crowd got national attention and pressure from the university. He has continued to stand strong and his boldness has inspired many others to stand firm against the tyranny of political correctness.

You can listen to his opening lecture here:
https://www.youtube.com/watch?v=fvPgjg201w0

Here's the clip from Prager U:
https://www.facebook.com/prageru/videos/1394199187289600/

One Seared Conscience Demands Another

The darkness hates the light; that's all there is to it. Jesus explained this two thousand years ago and, of course, it's as true now as it was then. "Those who do evil hate the light and do not come into the light for they fear their deeds will be reproved." John 3:20 Misery loves company and those who do not want to change their beliefs and practices want everyone else to change theirs. When noble men and women—still sensitive to God's whisperings and the guidance of their own consciences—take a stand and refuse to participate in an evil act, evildoers will try to regulate, legislate, intimidate and coerce them into cooperation.

In one of the more recent examples of this abhorrence of the light and of moral uprightness, the UK General Medical Council has just issued the draft of a new guideline regarding "personal beliefs and medical practice." In it, the Council warns doctors that they must prescribe contraceptives, refer patients for abortion, perform gender reassignment surgery and in every other way imaginable, they must be willing to violate their own consciences and "go along to get along." To do otherwise might imply that there is a higher law or a moral code and could unintentionally convey the idea that those who kill babies, mutilate sexually those born into one of the two biological genders or who inject old people with life-ending drugs are "morally misguided," perhaps even "wrong." Such an insinuation must be avoided. The only doctor who could possibly be wrong would be the one listening to his or her conscience instead of to the Council.

Sounds like another council of a couple thousand years ago, which—for the same reasons—wanted the early disciples to "stop preaching in the name of Jesus." Those council members felt that the promotion of Christianity might indicate that they—the ones who put him on the cross—were somehow guilty, perhaps even wrong. Of course, that would never do. However, the disciples of that day asked the high priest and the council this question: "Do you think it would be better to listen to you than to listen to God?" The answer to that question was rather self-evident.

However, nothing is self-evident to those who are self-deceived. I had the privilege of speaking last week with my MP, the Hon. Nathan Cullen (Skeena-Bulkley Valley). Nathan was a contender in the recent leadership race to replace NDP Leader Jack Layton. When the dust settled, Nathan was named Opposition House Leader and so, presumably, has influence with new Leader Thomas Mulcair and the NDP caucus. I had hoped, of course, to convince Nathan to support MP Stephen Woodworth's Motion 312 (which called on Parliament to establish a committee to examine the question of when human life begins). I was disappointed, but not surprised, when Nathan told me that he and his NDP colleagues intended to vote against reviewing Canada's 400-year old law, yes, the law which fails to defend human beings in the womb. However, as we discussed several other topics (the new Transgendered Bill, the gold-plated MP Pension plan and MP Brian Storseth's C-304 (which would protect freedom of speech by removing Sec. 13 from the Human Rights Act,) I was given Nathan's opinion on "conscience rights," which both shocked and troubled me.

I brought up the firing of marriage commissioners in Saskatchewan who had refused to perform marriages for same-sex couples. I thought it would be obvious to anyone who cared about personal rights and the freedom to act according to the dictates of one's conscience that this was a gross violation of human rights. I thought it proved conclusively that the concerns expressed in 2005 were justified, when Nathan and others voted for same-sex marriage, that is, the concerns that Christians would be compelled to violate their consciences or suffer punishment by the state.

Nathan, however, said that no violation had taken place since "churches" were not compelled to conduct homosexual marriages. The fact that men and women with deep personal convictions, based on their religious views, could not refuse to participate in evil did not bother him at all (of course, he and I have differing definitions of "evil"). While he suggested that some leeway might be allowed for existing commissioners, he said that men and women applying for those jobs in the future would have to acknowledge that homosexual marriage is the law of the land and therefore the office of marriage commissioner would require their cooperation. Mr. Cullen may be able to put his conscience on ice while performing his civic duties, may be able to shut his ears to the truth and turn a blind eye to the killing of the unborn, etc. but for those who know and love the God of the Bible and who "tremble at His Word" (ie. they believe that He speaks today and that He really cares about whether we do things His way or not), partial or limited obedience is not an option.

For the record, Mr. Cullen was not alone in his unwillingness to even consider the issue of the beginning of human life. Prime Minister Harper also voted against it and was joined by 67 other Conservatives, including most of the Cabinet of his majority government. We are deeply troubled by the unwillingness of the PM to support this important motion presented by his own loyal backbench MP, Mr. Woodworth.*

What is the conclusion of the whole matter? "Fear God and keep his commandments". Our consciences demand that we defend innocent human life and the sacrament of marriage between one man and one woman AND that we defend the right of all people to refuse to defile themselves by violating their consciences and the clear teachings of God. It seems pretty easy to understand. But

105

then, "the fear of the Lord is the BEGINNING of wisdom" (Prov. 9:10). Without the fear of the Lord there is NO wisdom.

May 31, 2012

On September 26, 2012, the Hon. MP Stephen Woodworth's Motion 312 (the Personhood Motion) was defeated in the House by a vote of 203 to 91.

*If Mr. Harper and his inner power circle in the Conservative Party thought they were playing it safe by avoiding this critical issue of abortion and the recognition of the reality of human life in the womb, they were mistaken. Their crushing defeat at the polls in 2015 had not much to do with the issues of life but it did close the window of opportunity to enact any life-saving legislation. The opportunity was squandered. I reflected later on the truth of Jesus's statement: "Whosoever shall seek to save his life shall lose it; and whosoever shall lose his life shall preserve it". Luke 17:33 As always, my hearty thanks go out to the many Conservative MPs of the time who acted in good conscience and voted in support of Motion 312! They will never lose their reward.

The 'Bawdy Politic': Who's Buying the Lie?

While most Canadians are scrimping and saving, some are "pimping and craving". The average hard-working man or woman is legitimately employed in some productive business that serves the nation but a small segment of society is engaged in a lifestyle choice that degrades women and children, destroys marriages, supports criminal activity and spreads disease. Prostitution has long been understood as an evil to be controlled but—as previously reported in the CHP Communique *Sex Trade* (Jan. 8 2014)—the Supreme Court of Canada has thrown out all laws regarding pimping, operating 'bawdy houses' and communicating for the purpose of prostitution. They have given the Government a year to write new laws and the Government is asking for your advice in addressing that vacuum.

Time is running out. Your MP and the Prime Minister need to hear from you on this issue. In 1988, the Supreme Court struck down the last vestiges of abortion law in Canada and no government since has had the courage or the principles to pass new legislation. If we fail to act now, the same thing may happen with prostitution in Canada. It already is a scourge, destroying young lives and increasing the tragedy of domestic and international human trafficking. If Parliament allows the Supreme Court ruling to become the status quo, our nation will reap the whirlwind in social ills, violence and crime.

In recent years, Canadians and others around the globe have become easy targets for mindless manipulation. The media and leftist social engineers latch onto a simple phrase which they repeat ad nauseum until students from daycare to university take up the chant. On the topic of abortion, the phrase is "choice"; on sexual orientation, it's "tolerance" and a war against "bullying". When it comes to the euthanasia debate and assisted suicide, they pretend that receiving a lethal injection gives you "death with dignity". Nightly broadcasts—in Canada emanating from our stately, revered and taxpayer-funded public broadcaster, CBC—and in tired text reprinted thousands of times in ink and cyber-twaddle, define a problem for which society must accept the "obvious" solution. The solution: fall in line, abandon your traditions and morally-based views and show your enthusiasm for the new reality. Their reality.

The new reality that social engineers, out-of-touch Supreme Court Justices and bawdy house operators want you to embrace regarding prostitution is that "making it legal will keep these girls safe". Don't you believe it! Nazi and communist propagandists have long realized that a big fat lie, repeated often enough, will be believed. Canadians are not being taught to think; they are only being told what to think.

March 7, 2014

On this important issue, the public did respond and the government did ultimately pass legislation that put more pressure on pimps and johns. We are grateful that people took the time to write and that the government of the day listened to the concerns of family-minded people. Below: CHP, ARPA and EFC articles:

http://www.chp.ca/2014/sex-trade/

http://arpacanada.ca/attachments/article/1388/English%20version %20RespectfullySubmitted%20Prostitution%20Sept%2012%2020 11.pdf (PDF)

http://www.evangelicalfellowship.ca/Bedford-Decision

Justice

Let justice run down like waters;
righteousness like a mighty stream.
Amos 5:24

The struggle of today is not
altogether for today . . . it is for a vast
future also.   Abraham Lincoln

Fraudulent Reporting of Canadian Crime Stats: The Emperor's Clothes Have Not Been Reported Stolen

StatsCan has just reported on Canadian Crime Stats for 2012. As usual, with a few notably excepted cities, the statistics show a drop in Police-Reported Crime (note the descriptive moniker). As well, the CSI (Crime Severity Index) is also down, according to the reported numbers. How many of you feel safer now than you did 5 years ago? Again, what do these numbers mean?

This category of Police-Reported Crime needs to be thoroughly examined. I have not had the time or opportunity to research this question in depth but I want to know: what gets reported? Canadians deserve to know what crimes are included in the numbers which are showcased for us each year—numbers intended to prove that the culture around us is getting more responsible and less likely to vandalize, steal, threaten or assault.

I recently watched a SUN News clip of an interview with Alissa Golob who was threatened by an angry storeowner on a downtown Toronto street because of her prolife activism. She called the police but they refused to come and investigate the incident. Her movie camera showed the man swinging at her and saying, "This is violence!" I would hazard a guess that that is one incident that failed to show up in the Police-Reported Crime Statistics. How many incidents of vandalism go unreported (at least by the police) each year?

What about the 491 Canadian babies born alive after attempted abortions and left to die by neglect or the actions of medical staff? A formal request to have these homicides investigated by the RCMP has been met with stony silence. I'm guessing these individual violations of the criminal code never reached the status of "Police-Reported Crimes" either.

What about the many "Occupy" invasions or the blocking of rail lines by Idle No More protestors? They may have actually made it into the record books at some time but since there have been decisions made to not prosecute, these major disruptions of normal access and transportation schedules must have been viewed as very benign inconveniences, barely falling into the category of crime. In my own small town we have had countless incidents of vandalism, graffiti, damage to signs and other private property. Admittedly, some of these never even get reported <u>to</u> the police, let alone, <u>by</u> the police. Folks are becoming so used to ugly graffiti and so cynical and hopeless about anyone ever being caught, convicted or punished that they often don't bother to call the police.

How about white-collar crime? Is that included in these statistics? At what point? Only on conviction? Are the actions of Mike Duffy and Patrick Brazeau et. al.—which are under investigation as criminal acts—being counted somewhere in the stats?

And what about the Crime Severity Index? Brutal, violent crimes, including gratuitous violence against children and the elderly are not on the decrease. Ignore, if you must, the 100,000 deaths of innocent babies each year in Canada by abortion. Politicians and police officers do. But it seems each week we hear of another mother who has strangled or drowned her baby. Gangsters and drug lords are shooting it out week by week in our cities. If a gangster falls in the forest where nobody can see, is it not still a crime? Of course in Vancouver we supply needles and equipment to drug users so their crime of illegal self-mutilation is now considered therapy. This must be having a helpful impact on our crime stats . . .

It's marvelous that StatsCan is bringing us all this good news about crime stats going down. But who is tweaking the results to make it look like we're winning the war on drugs? Who is downplaying the vicious cycle of pornography-prostitution-pimping-violence-gambling-gangsterism which has turned our once quaint cities into terror traps by night? It looks good for the RCMP to be able to claim crime is down. If they would say, "convictions are down", I'd believe them. But when we are told "crime is down" I'm afraid we've all read too many newspapers to believe that one. When I can leave my doors unlocked again, when young girls can walk to their bus stop again and not have to be escorted by their parents, when I can stop replacing vandalized property and when the trains can run on time, maybe I'll believe crime is down. But today, when StatsCan and the RCMP claim crime is down, it's just one more unreported case of fraud.

July 25, 2013

The StatsCan report which got my attention can be found here: http://www.statcan.gc.ca/pub/85-002-x/2013001/article/11854-eng.pdf

Insanity is doing the same thing over again, the same thing over again, the same thing over again...

Predictably, recent headlines declared that the Colorado shooter (Batman's Dark Knight mass murderer) and BC's woe-begotten child abductor, Randall Hopley, are both going to be "assessed" regarding their mental state.

In Hopley's case, the request for an assessment came from the Crown as they want to put him out of commission "indefinitely" by having him assessed as a "dangerous offender." In BC protocols, an assessment to determine whether an individual is a dangerous offender takes 60 days. This is something that would take the average Canadian, especially the father or mother of a three-year old child about 60 seconds. However, his defence attorneys are so confused by the "complexities" of this case that they don't think he should be termed a dangerous offender. Their reasoning? Because, although he kidnapped the youngster from his bed and held him captive for four days, he did return him alive and relatively unharmed.

What does the "rule of law" mean, in a case like this? Where does Christian compassion for both victim and perpetrator fit in? We were all praying for little Kienan Hebert while he was the hostage of Mr. Hopley. And we all cheered and breathed huge sighs of relief when he was returned unharmed to his parents. But that doesn't erase the enormity of the crime committed by Hopley nor give any assurance that he would not do the same thing again, nor that, in other circumstances, he might not act out his social dysfunction with much more serious results.

CHP Canada maintains that the "rule of law" requires that laws apply equally to all citizens and that, under a just God, the state has a responsibility to enforce laws and apply penalties that fit the crime and promote safety for all law-abiding citizens, especially children due to their physical limitations and their social and emotional vulnerability.

The Hopley case is characterized by several other bizarre elements: CBC refers to the search-and-rescue efforts of policemen, trackers, and volunteers as the "biggest manhunt in BC history." For all that, Mr. Hopley managed to elude discovery for four days and to then return the child to his own home (the scene of the crime) without being apprehended. From this we may conclude that there are gaps in other systems beside the court system. Also, the fact that the abduction occurred last September and the need for an "assessment" was determined today (nearly a year later) proves once again that our legal system is wretchedly inefficient, that costly and frustrating delays are hindering justice for both victims and perpetrators and that current approaches are not designed to curb crime or protect victims but to satisfy an arbitrary set of rules and maintain a malignant status quo.

In the case of the Colorado shooter, the defence is seeking a psychiatric assessment in order to have their client declared not guilty by reason of insanity. As I wrote last year, regarding the Norwegian mass murderer, Anders Breivik, CHP Communique *Of Course He's Insane!*, we do no favours to the criminally insane by withholding from them the legal consequences of their violent misdeeds. Instead of restoring calm and helping victims and perpetrators to come to terms with a tragedy and to recognize the potential of evil in a confused and tormented heart, we add to the burden by policies that seem to reward good and evil behaviour equally.

These are not isolated cases but this approach of psychiatric assessment in lieu of justice has become the typical response of defence lawyers. As I write this article, the newswires report that Trevor Kloschinsky, the man accused of killing Alberta peace officer, Rod Lazenby, will have his mental state "reviewed by a psychiatrist."

We all remember with shock and horror the Greyhound bus murder and decapitation trial and the "supervised walks" granted to Vince Li, the troubled man who used a butcher knife on a sleeping fellow-passenger.

In another case, the recent killing of Jun Li followed by the mutilation of his body and the mailing of his body parts by big-name homosexual model Luka Magnotta has gripped the hearts of Canadians with fear: fear of similar grotesque attacks and fear that not only our justice system but our whole society is out of control.

There is a proper time for a psychiatric assessment and for efforts to help mentally ill people cope with their confusion. There is a time for reaching out in sincere compassion to those who do not seem able to accept the realities of life—the big world and their small part in it. The time for caring action, for sincere attempts to build relationship and to help troubled individuals adjust to reality is before they commit murder, mayhem, and destruction. They need to know that a loving God has created them for a purpose and has great plans for their lives. Once a murder has been committed, once a child has been kidnapped (or worse), the criminally insane perpetrator may still receive love and forgiveness but he must do it from behind bars. His confusion (sometimes brought on or exacerbated by his own actions) may be a contributing factor in his moral failure but it must never become an excuse.

In a just society, the law must stand firm without showing favouritism for the mentally ill. Insane laws create serial killers and make a mockery of justice. Let's set a standard for the Western world. Let's give people—both victims and perpetrators—the dignity of being responsible for their actions and the just reward of reaping the harvest of their deeds, whether good or evil. Failure to do so will condemn a generation to more confusion, more crime, and more despair. We can do better.

CHP Canada policy states that: "There should be no pleas of temporary insanity. The spiritual and emotional disturbances which led an offender to commit a crime should be addressed as part of the redress or rehabilitation measures handed down at the time of sentencing."

Aug 14, 2012

Longer Sentences for Some Offenders, a Pass for Others

Prime Minister Harper has just announced proposed changes to federal legislation which will mean longer sentences and consecutive sentences—rather than concurrent ones—for sexual predators convicted of molestation of children, particularly multiple victims, and for those convicted of child porn. While more time behind bars for sexual criminals does not immediately make the world a better place, it does increase the deterrence factor of sentencing and it does keep sexual predators away from children for more of their time on earth. We applaud the Conservative government for showing their teeth in defense of children and most Canadians will welcome this verbal commitment to confronting the sexual abuse of children. However, the PM should go much farther than he has.

Abuse of children in Canada begins at much younger ages than that which is targeted by this new legislation and it comes in many more forms.

Firstly, the killing of 100,000 innocent preborns each year in Canada by abortion—with the approval of the government and paid for by tax dollars—is clearly the single largest abuse of children in this country . . . and the PM continues to promise to do nothing about it. He says that he "cannot understand" what causes men to sexually exploit children and to commit the heinous crimes against them which his new legislation will address. I agree with him but I also "cannot understand" why the killing of the innocent preborn is tolerated and paid for in a nation that claims to abhor violence and bullying.

Secondly, in schools across this country, children are being sexually exploited—at ever younger ages—by a barrage of explicit sexual content in curriculum packages increasingly focused on

117

homosexuality, sexual experimentation by teens and pre-teens and introspective approaches to sexual orientation, a topic not even pondered in classrooms 50 years ago. This assault on children's innocence and natural curiosity in their formative years has driven the expansion of the abortion market for teens, has lowered the ages for both victims and perpetrators of sex crimes, has fueled an explosion of sexually-transmitted diseases among youth and has led to a disoriented, dysfunctional, dissatisfied generation that now needs to be both protected from—and punished for—crimes against the young and innocent.

On the world stage, Foreign Affairs Minister John Baird has weighed in against Russia's new laws which are aimed at protecting children from homosexual propaganda. Say what? A law protecting children from exploitation is bad because it mentions homosexuality? Instead of criticizing Russia, we ought to be protecting our own children from the flood of filth which has fed the trend toward carnality in Canada.

We support the PM's tough stance on child predators. However, if we really want to protect children, Canada will have to protect them also from the social engineering experiments of humanist educators and the callous greed of the abortion industry.

August 30, 2013

The Tougher Penalties for Child Predators Act, C-26, was introduced on February 6, 2014 and received Royal Assent on June 18, 2015. We thank those responsible for acting to protect children from defilement and harm. You can track the bill's journey here:
http://www.parl.ca/LegisInfo/BillDetails.aspx?billId=6434291&Language=E&Mode=1

Pimping from the Bench

On March 27, the Ontario Court of Appeal ruled that the law against "living off the avails of prostitution" was a violation of the rights of prostitutes and they pushed the legalization of prostitution to new and unheard-of depths. Where society once understood its responsibility to care for the vulnerable, to promote long-term, committed relationships rather than casual, drive-by, flow-through, throwaway sex (which demeans and demoralizes one of God's great gifts to humanity), today, our acceptance of gutter language and gutter behaviour results in decisions which replace our natural modesty and dignity with animal instincts, a drive for pleasure, money and control.

By failing to uphold the laws against selling one's body, the court has effectively become a pimp, pushing another wave of misguided and helpless young women into a life from which they may never recover. The court ruled that prostitutes should be able to legally hire "bodyguards." These "bodyguards" for the sex trade would not be noble and courageous volunteers like those men who keep the head of the President or the Prime Minister. No, the aggressive, lazy and useless types who will latch onto such easy "work" will be the type of violent, dominant and demanding leeches who hang out in bars, leering and looking for a fight or a pick-up.

It's tragic and shocking to see the learned judges of this land siding with the crude and self-flaunting women who brought this ridiculous case to their bench. But more tragic still is the sinking feeling one gets when one realizes how few in our society even see the problem. When the masses allow themselves to be numbed by the dumbing-us-down, taxpayer-funded media—so that questions about elevating the poor and unfortunate are framed in the context of promoting the sale of women's bodies—

we are already reaping the results of a couple of generations weaned from common sense, decency and respect for mankind's intended purpose and character.

Polls from across the country indicate a large segment of society, if not an outright majority, have been conditioned to accept the distorted views pontificated by the court. Selling one's soul is even worse than selling one's body. This court has invited Canadians to do both. By promoting the degradation of women, they have both prostituted themselves to the spirit of the age and set themselves up as "bodyguards" for the flesh market. The young girls (and boys) who will be drawn into the vortex and destroyed will pay with their wasted lives but the pompous politicians, lawyers and judges who are "living off the avails" will continue to collect their fat pensions. Pimps with dignity.

March 29, 2012
Following the Ontario Court of Appeals ruling in 2012, on December 20, 2013, the Supreme Court of Canada threw out Canada's laws against "keeping a bawdy house, living off the avails of prostitution and communicating in public for the purpose of selling sex".
http://www.cbc.ca/news/politics/supreme-court-strikes-down-canada-s-prostitution-laws-1.2471572

The Court gave Parliament 1 year to write a new law. Thankfully, Parliament went to work and passed new legislation, focused on pimps and johns. C-36 received Royal Assent November 6, 2014.
http://www.parl.ca/DocumentViewer/en/41-2/bill/C-36/royal-assent

Maximum Punishment, Minimum Security

On September 14, 2013, René Charlebois pushed open a door at a minimum-security prison in Laval, Quebec and walked away. Charlebois, a "full-patch" member of the Hell's Angels said to be close to notorious "Mom" Boucher, was serving time for—among other things—second-degree murder, conspiring to commit murder, trafficking narcotics, trafficking Schedule I and II substances and participation in a criminal organization. Did I mention he was being held in minimum-security?

Meanwhile, at the Vanier Centre for Women in Milton, Ontario (a maximum-security prison), Linda Gibbons and Mary Wagner are being held for repeatedly seeking to <u>save</u> lives. They have made it a habit to peacefully protest abortion by entering the so-called "bubble zones" surrounding abortion clinics to offer counsel and comfort to women contemplating abortion, to those who are booked for the procedure or are recovering from the trauma of the loss of a baby.

Anyone see a problem here? I do. Can anyone honestly say they see any justice here? I certainly don't. The ridiculous juxtaposition of these two scenarios taking place simultaneously in the Canada we love boggles the mind.

In my little backyard greenhouse, I have a maximum-minimum thermometer which records the highest and lowest temperatures each day. We have maximum speed limits and minimum wage laws. The concept of maximum-security and minimum-security prisons is that those who have committed the most violent crimes and are considered the most dangerous should be kept under the closest supervision and control; the rationale is that those who have committed minor crimes or are considered non-violent and who do not pose a threat to public safety can be allowed some limited freedoms within the walls of the penal institution where they are being held. From the examples above, it appears that the courts have used the prison system to punish the worldview represented by the two gentle women being held at Vanier and have assumed (in their ignorance) that the basic goodness residing in the bosom of mankind will keep a hardened criminal like Mr. Charlebois from breaking out. Give your head a shake.

To make the point even more dramatic, Mary and Linda have committed no crime against society. They have put their lives and freedom on hold to alert their fellow Canadians to the tragic loss of life and dignity that has resulted from Canada's moral vacuum in the area of abortion. The cowardice of self-serving politicians who will not lift a finger to defend innocent human life is on trial. So far, the courts have used their power to cover up the sins of our self-serving culture and to remove these fearless witnesses and defenders of life from public view. It won't work. Those who pontificate in the courts of this land will themselves one day stand before a just and righteous Judge who will not be so quick to wink at the shedding of innocent blood.

September 23, 2013

Three days after this article was written, René Charlebois took his own life as police converged on his hiding place. More on that here:
https://www.thestar.com/news/canada/2013/09/26/escaped_hells_angel_kills_himself_as_quebec_police_close_in.html

Both Linda Gibbons and Mary Wagner have been in and out of custody several times and continue to defend the lives of innocent babies. Here's one article about the two pro-life heroines. https://www.therebel.media/faith_goldy_june_29_2017

Motives, Intents and Situational Ethics in the Wilderness

Last week, an Alaskan visitor fishing along one of BC's northern rivers startled a mother grizzly bear with at least one cub. As we all know, a mother bear is a force to be reckoned with when she feels her cub is threatened. So it happened on that fateful day and our visitor was badly mauled. He experienced broken bones and serious injuries to his head but by the grace of God, he was able to escape and hike out to his truck. For that we can all be truly thankful. Not every such encounter ends with a reprieve.

What troubled me however, when I read the news report, was the response of the wildlife branch, which announced that they were "not actively pursuing" the aggressive grizzly mother. The reason: "her actions were deemed to be defensive . . . " In other words, the fact that she mauled a man to within inches of his life is irrelevant because we understand that her response was a natural response for a startled grizzly mother.

What's wrong with this picture? A couple of things: first of all, a dangerous wild animal has attacked a man and gotten away with it. I'm sure if the man had died that wildlife officers would be attempting to find and destroy the bear to prevent further tragedy. But now that this bear has tasted blood—has fought with a human being and won—isn't it conceivable that she may be even bolder at the next encounter? While she didn't kill this fisherman, neither did she run away when she saw him. Fishing and hiking in grizzly country is always potentially dangerous but bears are unpredictable and how an individual bear may respond to an encounter is not an exact science. This one attacked; might she not do so again?

Secondly, we're applying a psychological evaluation to a non-human and basing our approach on our best guess as to motives and intent. In our judicial system, intent has some legitimate role in a judgment because we are dealing with human beings and the basic principles of justice. When dealing with the elements of our surroundings, including flora and fauna, oughtn't our actions to be based on the best outcomes for the human community? Grizzly bears are not endangered. I certainly appreciate their part in the ecosystem, their unique beauty and power and their symbolic representation of the wild and wondrous creation of which we are a part and for which we are stewards. Nevertheless, to ascribe motives and to defer consequences (i.e. to make the mauling of a man a "non-culpable offense") when that man has nearly died seems too much like giving the animal kingdom a voting representative at the table of human discussion.

The Bible has something to say about the moral responsibility which rests on the owners of dangerous beasts; they are instructed to destroy an animal which has injured a man and threatened his life. If your ox has gored a man and you do nothing to prevent it happening again and if it happens again, you, the owner, are responsible. The Fish and Wildlife branch of government has the primary responsibility of overseeing the interactions between mankind and the wild beasts around us. They know this bear has mauled an innocent human being. If this bear does this again, F&W is responsible. If a person dies as a result, they must be held accountable; the same goes for parole boards which release murderers who go out and do it again.

Scripture says, "Let a bear, robbed of her cubs meet a man; that's better than running into a fool and his folly . . . " Bears are not, nor can they be, held accountable in an eternal sense for what they do but sometimes they must face consequences in this life. Human beings, on the other hand, must take responsibility for their actions. Those who have been placed in charge of wildlife matters must learn from the past and avoid foolish decisions. We are able to reason and we are held accountable for our actions, both in this life and the one to come.

September 28, 2012

I couldn't find the original article but here's one describing four other grizzly attacks in BC in September 2012.
https://bc.ctvnews.ca/hunter-mauled-by-grizzly-in-fourth-b-c-bear-attack-in-10-days-1.2562261

Exodus 21:28, 29: paraphrase: If your ox has had the habit of pushing with his horns and you don't keep him under control. . . if he kills a man, you're in big trouble. Your life for his life.

Of Course He's Insane!

When Anders Breivik ordered the fertilizer he presumably used to blow up the Prime Minister's office in Oslo, when he purchased the ammunition he later used to systematically murder scores of teenagers on Otuya Island, when he wrote in his journal about his plans to wreak destruction and when he self-identified as a "martyr", he was insane. Logic and strategic planning are not necessarily the exclusive domain of the well-adjusted. Sane people—by any definition of the average citizen of any civilized country—do not put on a police officer's uniform and mercilessly and methodically begin shooting young campers.

Why does it matter? Because Breivik's lawyer is questioning the "sanity" of his client and seems likely to attempt to defend him (ie.remove his guilt) on the premise that his brutal multiple murders were not really his fault. This tactic is used endlessly in defending those who commit horrific atrocities and it should stop here and now. We know this man is insane. No psychiatric assessment is required. The fact that we're even discussing it makes me wonder if the lawyers, judges and politicians of our "civilized" societies are still sane or do we need to build new wings on every mental institution to accommodate a new class of "certifiable" professionals?

In Canada, we have the case of the Greyhound bus murderer, Vince Li, who savagely cut the head off the young man seated near him—for no apparent reason. Our compassionate legal system has deemed him "not guilty by reason of mental illness". I agree that Mr. Li is insane. I don't need to read the report. The average Canadian—shall we say "normal"?—simply does not cut off the head of a fellow passenger on sudden impulse. Does that excuse the crime? Shall we overlook brutal murders or excuse them on the basis of "mental incompetence"? Perhaps only those brutal murderers whom we could classify as "well-adjusted" should bear responsibility for their crimes?

Mental competence does not require a moral compass but a society without standards will become a society without recourse. A woman drowns her children in the tub. A father goes berserk— whether wildly or quietly—and kills his own children. The mental confusion is tragic. The outcome of these actions is nearly unbearable, even for those not linked by blood or relationship. Shall we then become insane ourselves in order to try to understand the inner agony of the murderer? Shall we also put so little value on the lives of their pathetic victims that we all but whitewash the crimes?

What about our fellow citizens who may still be subject to the restraint of conscience and the threat of punishment? There are many in our society who have a grudge against someone. By failing to hold any killer accountable, by allowing any murderer to hide behind a psychiatrist's label, by refusing to exercise the duty of the state to protect its citizens against the shedding of innocent blood, we invite insanity into our streets and into the corridors of our schools.

Can any sane person think that Adolf Hitler was well-adjusted? Or the murderous brigands who cooperated with him in their savage attacks against the Jews? How about Stalin, the egomaniac and demon-driven tyrant who was personally responsible for the deaths of 30 million of his own countrymen? History holds such men accountable and so it should. They acted on a larger stage than the blonde Norwegian who calmly shot young people trying to swim away from Otuya Island but surely—if insanity justifies his insane acts it also justifies theirs?

No, this is insanity itself: to begin to justify evil because of mental confusion. Our courts and lawmakers have a responsibility NOT to be confused and NOT to send confusing signals. They must defend innocent human life by punishing the guilty or they sentence a whole generation to insanity and insane acts. Once evil is justified, there is no restraint and a society with no restraint will wander in ever-widening circles looking for the boundaries of its own existence. "Thou shalt not commit murder" applies to all and the state cannot commute a just sentence without losing its own bearings in a world gone mad.

July 27, 2011

On July 22, 2011, Norwegian Anders Breivik went on a killing spree in Oslo. He killed 8 people with a home-made bomb and shot 69 others, mostly young campers. He planned to kill more but was prevented from doing so. His court appearances consumed a great deal of time, money and public attention, especially around the topic of his sanity and guilt. In the end, he was sentenced to 21 years. As a prisoner, he made formal human rights complaints about his treatment while incarcerated.

Police Protection for Pimps and Prostitutes?

When the world goes crazy, there seems no end of the crazy solutions to self-inflicted problems.

Addicted to harmful, illegal drugs? Get the government to open a designated shooting-up gallery so that you can pursue your destructive, illegal habit without having to use dirty needles and most of all, without having to repent and change.

Caught a bad disease from using and abusing multiple sexual partners of either gender? Demand the government provide expensive drugs so that you can mitigate the damage and enjoy the dissipated lifestyle a little bit longer.

Unintentionally pregnant? How inconvenient. Must be the condom manufacturer's fault, certainly not yours for seeking sexual fulfillment with a variety of partners. That's an easy one: kill the baby (the taxpayers will pay for it). If anyone challenges you on this decision, have him thrown in jail.

Confused about who you really are? Can't get no satisfaction? Try changing who you are. Get the government (ie. taxpayers) to pay for a sex change. Why let God define your gender? Who does He think He is anyway?

Just trying to make a little change by working the streets? Surely you deserve the protection of the state. After all, isn't promiscuity some kind of Charter right? For far too long, policepersons in Canada have been hindering the "personal development and career choices" of prostitutes and pimps. It's time to demand that the government protect you and your right to full employment. Just because parents of teenaged girls want to spare them the anguish of sexual slavery, a debased image of themselves and a narrow and shrinking worldview that sees humanity as a purposeless, sensually-driven mass of writhing tissue, why should that keep you from doing whatever you want, whenever you want, with whomever you want?

This is the craziness of our age and our debased culture. Prostitutes who once knew they were doing wrong and selling themselves like pathetic cattle on the streets, now demand that we applaud their lifestyle choices and adjust our laws so that they can ply their trade freely, without a blush of shame and able to call for police protection if one of their morally bankrupt clients should get violent or refuse to pay. Here's what legal-prostitution activist, Anna-Aude Caouette had to say as her ludicrous case was making its way to the Supreme Court: "Criminalization means that, as sex workers, we have no access to the legal system or police protection".

What a world we live in! It's bad enough that prostitutes and drug addicts see the world through a confused moral framework. The real tragedy is that so many highly intelligent, highly-paid officials of Parliaments, courts and media give these twisted views the coverage, the accommodation and the support that turns them into laws and practices that affect us all.

As I've quoted before, "The fear of the Lord is the beginning of wisdom". Proverbs 9:10 If respect for the Creator God is the beginning of wisdom, that means that those who reject God have NO wisdom. Intelligence is not the same as wisdom. Intelligent persons can build a bomb, kill a baby, shoot up heroin or waste their short and nasty lives in a prostitute's bed . . . but wise people will avoid all that and spend their lives following the path of Truth and Justice, seeking to please God and to nurture healthy family relationships. A wise society will not give credence to craziness but will provide protection for what is good and punishment for evil.

Let's stop pretending that there is no difference between good and evil.

June 13, 2013

After Madame Bedford won her case at the Ontario Court of Appeal on March 26, 2012, that decision was appealed to the Supreme Court. The article above was written before the Supreme Court judgment threw out Canada's laws against the keeping of a bawdy house, living off the avails of prostitution or communicating in public for the purpose of selling sex. A new law, C-36 was passed in 2014.

Punishing the Victim

There's a childhood tale of a lad fishing in a bucket and hoping to catch a whale. It may not seem reasonable to an adult (the population of whales swimming in buckets has been drastically reduced in recent years) but to a child "all things are possible". Also, necessity—as has oft been noted—is the mother of invention. Where there is no ocean, no whaling boat and no crew at hand, one does the best one can with existing resources. One fishes in a bucket because at least there is water.

We accept that kind of thinking in children but we expect more from our police forces, our prosecutors and our judges. Childish thinking may be guiding those who have accepted the responsibility for keeping Canada's streets safe. Criminals do not usually wait around for the police to show up. They flee into the night. They leave no phone number or forwarding address. The police are left to wonder: How can we catch them? If we do catch them, how can we prosecute them? If we do prosecute them, how can we keep them in jail? What if they resist? What if they hire a lawyer who will invent clever excuses for them? What if the media take up their cause, endlessly questioning the manner of the arrest, the likelihood that the victim had unnecessarily provoked the attack, the uselessness of prisons for rehabilitation, the underlying causes of antisocial behaviour? How can we maintain our reputation as those who diligently pursue justice?

Unlike the criminals who tend to disappear, a victim of violent crime, like the child's fishing bucket, is often easy to find. The victim is easy to arrest, easy to vilify and easy to condemn. The victim may report himself to the police. The victim may provide evidence useful to the prosecution. The victim is cooperative, talkative and available for questioning. At the end of the day, when the paperwork has been done (lots of paperwork) one can say that at least something was done. At least the victim had his day in court. At least someone was punished.

Sound ridiculous? So it is. It also describes the recent nightmarish experience of Ian Thomson, a heavy-equipment operator and a former firearms instructor in Port Colborne, Ontario. He has been charged with firearms offenses and threatened with jail time after he defended himself and his home from three masked men who were throwing firebombs at his home. Hard to believe but it's true.

Mr. Thomson, in good faith, reported the incident to local police along with surveillance video footage. One would have expected an all-out effort by the RCMP to find the attackers responsible and to put them safely behind bars. Instead, they took offense to Mr. Thomson's antiquated notion that a person has the right to defend himself and his property. They also took advantage of the video evidence he provided to turn their investigation on him, rather than on the mysterious intruders. Of course, Canada's Constitution has no explicit guarantee of the right to private property so some authorities conclude there is no right to defend it. And it might seem a bit over-the-top to recognize the right to self-defense when Canada allows the killing of 100,000 innocent human beings each year through abortion, the so-called "right to choose".

After all, these three masked individuals may have been merely exercising their "right to choose" to firebomb Mr. Thomson's house. If he had quietly stayed inside and allowed them to complete their destructive project, he could have been the object at least of countless sympathetic news stories as news anchors and journalists would have "tried to find answers" for his tragic and unnecessary death. There could have been a public memorial service and a few interviews with neighbours. Then the RCMP could have quietly gone back to their paperwork.

The disintegration of common sense, the lapse in judgment which calls evil good and good evil, the total lack of responsibility taken by those who are pledged to enforce the law and to protect the innocent—all this must end! If Canada is to survive as a civilized nation, our people, our police forces, our court system, our politicians, our educators must all begin to recognize and uphold traditional values of decency and common sense. We, the people, must demand that the law punish the guilty and protect the innocent. When good citizens, acting in good faith, use reasonable and appropriate tools and behaviours within their means to protect life and personal property, they should be honoured, not humiliated and harassed.

If we fail to understand these things, we become a nation of enablers, our citizens become afraid to get involved, our policemen become afraid to do what they signed up to do and the lower element that lurks in dark places become emboldened to do anything they feel like because they know there will be no real consequences. Surely we have enough reasons and enough reasoning ability to empower all reasonable people to use reasonable force in the struggle to establish and maintain a reasonably just and free society.

January 25, 2011

You can read about Mr. Thomson's ordeal here:
http://news.nationalpost.com/2011/01/20/man-faces-jail-after-protecting-home-from-masked-attackers/

The Collapse of Reason and Conscience in the Trinity Law School Dispute

There are so many things wrong in the unfolding saga of the efforts to crush the Trinity Law School, that it's hard to know where to begin. The revelation yesterday that the Province of BC—through Minister of Advanced Education, Mr. Amrik Virk—is considering "revoking" its 2013 approval of the law school before it can open its doors is just one more example of the increasing arrogance and hostility towards adherents of the Christian faith.

Universities are supposed to be places of open inquiry and freedom to explore. To deny that freedom to law students who choose to study at Trinity—knowing beforehand the standards of personal chastity and religious conviction the school requires of its students—is absurd.

The refusal of law societies in three provinces to accept the credentials of future graduates of Trinity is nothing short of bigotry. No reference is made to the expected quality of education. Rather, the insinuation is that students who profess the Christian faith and who agree to live by its principles would be somehow unfit to defend, prosecute or judge—a conclusion so mind-numbingly misguided that one can only wonder at the level of self-deception. The shallow excuses given to the public could not deceive anyone thinking clearly.

Courts of justice—which are supposed to operate in a fair and unbiased manner—are based on certain fundamental shared convictions. The Preamble to Canada's Charter of Rights and Freedoms (part of our Canadian Constitution) begins with these words: "...Canada is founded on principles that recognise the supremacy of God and the rule of law..." That would be the God of the Bible, the Creator of heaven and earth. To summarily reject people who recognise His supremacy makes the entire basis of our justice system untenable. To treat Christian lawyers or law students as second-class citizens is to blatantly disregard the "rule of law" which presupposes that all must have equal opportunity and be judged by the same standards of right and wrong.

It is ironic indeed to have this collapse of sanity taking place under a department with the remarkable title of "Advanced Education". How is it an advance to dictate to a private institution, dedicated to higher learning, what solemn agreements it may or may not make with the students who aspire to acquire knowledge and wisdom within its gates?

We know that the pressure to accommodate shifting lifestyle preferences is powerful. Money and media have now combined with the power of the state to try to squeeze out Christian influence and mold after their own image every institution that might guide young lives or establish norms of social behaviour.

We call on Mr. Virk, the Province of BC and the Law Societies of BC, Ontario and Nova Scotia to admit they have made a mistake, apologise to Trinity and allow the university and its students and professors to get on with the business of studying and eventually teaching law. I recommend that those who have been creating stumbling blocks to the noble efforts at Trinity go back and study the law themselves. They will look long and hard to find any legal merit in their obfuscations. Loopholes are the refuge of manipulators but those who seek to establish true justice will find guidance in the original intent of our Constitution, the time-tested precedents of English Common Law and the timeless wisdom of the Bible from which they sprang and upon which they rest.

136

The Christian Heritage Party seeks to preserve our Canadian heritage of fundamental freedoms and equalities against the many assaults upon these God-given, Charter-affirmed rights.

November 24, 2014

In 2012, Trinity Western University (TWU) in Langley, BC, began planning a law school on its campus. In 2014, it faced serious opposition from the Law Societies of BC, Ontario and Nova Scotia, when the law societies said they would not accept the credentials of TWU Law graduates because of TWU's requirement that students attending must maintain biblically-respectful sexual behaviour while students. After a number of court appearances, the case was heard in the Supreme Court of Canada in December, 2017. As of this writing, all parties are awaiting the judgment.

Before going to print, the Supreme Court ruled against TWU and in favour of the law societies. This was a terrible decision and will have far-reaching impacts on freedom, conscience and justice in Canada. Stay tuned.

The Judgments She Wrote

Chief Justice Beverley McLachlin is retiring from her position on the Supreme Court of Canada. We wish her well in her retirement. We also wish she had never become Chief Justice where she has presided over so much that is evil. In combination with cowardly politicians and secular social engineers, the Supreme Court, under Beverley McLachlin's 17-year tenure as its longest-serving Chief Justice, has overseen fundamental shifts and a radical decline in moral standards in our society. We'll look at a few examples but first we should take a broader look at the role of the courts and the dangers of allowing nine unelected judges to set the markers and rules for 35 million Canadians.

CBC and other national news media have been quick to laud Ms. McLachlin's accomplishments but there are two things Canadians should remember as they look back on Ms. McLachin's record: Supreme Court Justices are neither infallible nor supreme. Yes, they constitute the highest court in the land but they are still human beings capable of making mistakes . . . and when it comes to human history and national character, the Supreme Court does not have the final word.

Our Constitution acknowledges in its Charter Preamble the "supremacy of God". When governments or courts or even societal consensus depart from the wisdom and guidance of Almighty God, He has ways of bringing us back again to the core principles and values upon which He has founded human societies and civilizations. When a court or legislative body orders behaviour that is contrary to His revealed will for mankind, it invites an appeal to the Supreme Ruler and Judge. Our God is a God of Justice and we can be assured that His judgments will ultimately prevail.

Let's look at a few of the more troublesome court decisions which have come out of Canada's Supreme Court under the leadership of Beverley McLachlin:

- In 2005, Chief Justice Beverley McLachlin, acting as the Deputy Governor General during the illness of Governor General Adrianne Clarkson, actually signed into law the Civil Marriage Act, legalizing same-sex marriage in Canada. Of course, this followed a series of lower-court decisions and the whipped vote of the Liberal caucus under Prime Minister Paul Martin. It also reflected McLachlin's minority opinion in the 1995 Egan case which added "sexual orientation" to Sec. 15 of the Charter. This judicial opinion has now become the prevailing cultural practice and is affecting education, law and public health.

- In December, 2013, the McLachlin Court threw out the law regarding prostitution. While Parliament was able to pass new legislation restricting prostitution, this was a symbolic attempt to remove one of society's longstanding moral restraints.

- In February 2015, The Supreme Court unanimously rejected the law against doctor-assisted suicide and called upon Parliament to write a new law, allowing the killing of terminally-ill people. The Conservative government of the day chose not to enact Section 33 (the Notwithstanding Clause) and in the Fall election that year, control of the House was passed to a Liberal majority. No protection of conscience rights was included in the law nor any requirement for meaningful and effective palliative care.

There is more—much more—that could be said about judgments which have negatively impacted Canada and which will be very difficult to change. However, not everything Chief Justice McLachlin has done was wrong. In several cases, she defended freedom of speech and no doubt one could find praiseworthy examples of sound reasoning. But if we reflect for a moment on the examples given above, we cannot join the crowd of left-leaning sympathizers praising her record.

The question is: how do we restore to their rightful prominence the Canadian values which activist judges like Beverley McLachlin have weakened and undermined? One can hope that the next Chief Justice will be directed by principles and understandings more like ours. It's chilling to think that Prime Minister Trudeau may appoint a successor who is also an activist judge, determined to reshape Canada according to his or her personal opinions and not according to enduring biblical standards of righteousness and justice.

It's time to rethink our model of helpless politicians and helpless citizens, content to follow the dictates of an appointed court. MPs and Senators must become willing to use the legislative powers they have, such as the Nothwithstanding Clause (Section 33 of the Charter), to protect Canadians from destructive court opinions. If democracy means anything, it certainly means that nine unelected judges do not have the authority to force elected representatives to act against their consciences. May God give our MPs, our Senators and our Justices a hunger and a thirst for righteousness. The challenges facing Canada are big but God is bigger.

June 18, 2017

Beverley McLaghlin, was the 17th Chief Justice of Canada, the first woman to hold this position, and the longest serving Chief Justice in Canadian history. She also served as a Deputy of the Governor General of Canada. She announced her retirement on June 12, 2017, effective December 15, 2017.

Canada's Justice System is Criminal

Because sentence against an evil work is not executed speedily, therefore the heart of the sons of men is fully set in them to do evil. Ecc 8:11

One of the valuable constructs of a civil society is the system of laws, mores, traditions, rewards and punishments by which it deals with its uncivilized members. Since the first recorded murder, mankind has been challenged by the need to agree upon acceptable boundaries for human behaviour and to find effective ways of holding one another accountable for staying within them—"colouring within the lines" so to speak.

Agreeing upon standards is what we call "lawmaking". It's much easier, of course, if we first agree that there is a transcendent set of principles—not open to discussion—which is a foundation for all man-made laws. The CHP endorses that opinion but that debate is beyond the scope of this article. The issue we would like to briefly address here is the search for tools by which laws can be enforced or upheld. Canada has a "rule of law" and an enforcement system, including the police (who observe, apprehend and lay charges), the courts (which assess testimony and evidence, compare proven misbehaviour with current laws and precedents and apply those to the situation under examination) and a range of consequences meted out to those pronounced "guilty" (prison time, community service, fines, shaming or nothing at all).

One way to judge the merits of the system is to measure its effectiveness. Do Canadians feel safer now than they did in the past? Are costs rising or falling? What about recidivism? (Not to be confused with revisionism). What about the injuries to and financial losses of victims? Is there an effective mechanism for making injured citizens whole? Or is it all about "harm reduction? (Accepting criminal behaviour as a necessary evil and adjusting society to reduce the potential for major harm to criminals). Are we simply redefining crime because we seem unable to seriously stop it?

Stockwell Day recently received flak from the opposition for challenging the glib media assertions that the crime rate has gone down (based on Statscan's Police-Reported Crime numbers and Crime Severity index). While the Conservatives' solution (spend $8 billion to build more prisons) may be faulty (more on that later), it seems that Stockwell Day was absolutely correct in his opinion that a large number of crimes go unreported.

The Statistics Canada report, Criminal Victimization in Canada, 2004, warned that two-thirds of crimes are not reported to police—including "88 per cent of sexual assaults." Criminal Victimization Surveys are currently conducted in Canada every five years.

"StatsCan victimization surveys show that only 34 per cent of crime—around one-third—is reported to police, so using this to define 'crime rates' is simply inaccurate," says Bernie Magnan, chief economist, The Vancouver Board of Trade.

Question: Do you think there might be something wrong with a 'justice' system where two-thirds of victims don't have enough faith in the system to even report the crimes?

As to the severity of crimes, Statscan assigns a value to each crime, based not on the type of crime but on the length of prison sentence imposed on the perpetrator. Maybe it's just me but it seems that sentences for violent crimes have been getting shorter and shorter over the years and actual time spent behind bars is often only a fraction of the sentence. If that is why the severity index seems to be going down while all around us hoodlums and vandals terrorize neighbourhoods and damage and destroy property with a seeming lack of concern for consequences, then it's time to change the system! First, we need serious and appropriate consequences for violent and sexual crimes. Secondly, the process of trial and sentencing must be streamlined to reduce costs, to accelerate the demands of justice, to provide timely deterrence and to restore confidence in the public justice system. Public safety and effective deterrence must be our top priorities.

Indeed, the lack of value placed on victims—their emotional and physical wellbeing and the restoration of their property—is no doubt one of the many reasons for the lack of reporting. The small likelihood of receiving timely and effective protection or of recovering stolen or damaged property coupled with the fear of reprisals—all of these can lead honest citizens to wring their hands and do nothing. Even the police can become discouraged, especially in cases of minor drug busts where they may risk life and limb only to have the case thrown out of court and see their smug and sneering local drug dealer back on the street after officers have wasted their time and effort making the arrest.

Meanwhile, the Conservative government (yes, the same people who just added $80 billion to the national debt over the past two budgets)—in an effort to "save money"—has abandoned the prison farms that have been part of Canada's penal system since 1880, saying that not many prisoners end up in farm work after their eventual release. As if there is no benefit to learning practical skills and developing regular work habits while away from the regular humdrum life of responsibilities and challenges that most Canadians face daily in school, home and the workplace! While in jail, prisoners whom you'd have thought had forfeited some of the rights and privileges of honest law-abiding

Canadians, are allowed to vote, to study to become lawyers, to have the use of modern athletic facilities but are not mandated into a work-for-restitution program whereby their victims may receive at least a partial repayment for their losses.

There are hundreds, perhaps thousands, of examples of inappropriate sentences but two for comparison should suffice. Karla Homolka, after lying in her plea-bargain, spent a mere 12 years in jail for her part in the brutal murder of (at least) three young women. Linda Gibbons, Ontario grandmother, has already spent 8 years behind bars [when this was written] for merely speaking to pregnant women about the value of the life of the unborn children they are carrying. She is behind bars today while Karla Homolka is "free to roam about the country".

As so many have pointed out, the "revolving door" justice system doesn't protect us. But the Tory government does not need to spend $8 billion on new jails. All they need to do is adopt our (CHP's) "Restitution and Public Safety" policy, which would empty more than half the jail spaces, while compelling non-violent criminals to pay restitution to their victims; that would give us lots of jail space for the violent criminals . . . along with a sentencing structure that would make eventual release dependent on evidence of a changed attitude. Voluntary reformation (meaningful change of heart) would reduce recidivism as it has done in the lives of many inmates touched by Prison Fellowship Ministry.

The issue of restoring justice to our courts and public life is both broad and complex. Our Lord came to set men and women free, not only from prison cells but from a life enslaved to sin and selfishness. When the Truth sets a person free, he is truly free!

August 22, 2010

Time Off for Bad Behaviour

It seems the old scheme some young folks used to employ (before the days of automatic dishwashers) still works today but the stakes are higher. In those irresponsible days of youth, some children discovered that if they broke a dish now and then, they might be considered hopelessly incompetent and never get trusted with that chore again. "Boo hoo. Please don't throw me into the briar patch!"

Today, there are CEOs of large companies, professional consultants and "ethics advisors", not to mention a few RCMP officers, who have been relieved of their duties—but not their paycheques—for a variety of complaints ranging from failure to be truthful with shareholders to pulling the trigger of a service revolver or the inappropriate use of a taser, leading to untimely and unnecessary deaths.

Maybe it's just me, but somehow the idea that a CEO accused of ripping off pensioners who have invested their life savings in shares in his company should drive off with a huge compensation package bothers me. That any consultant should be taking six figures home for a few months' work is a puzzle but that a consultant should take home nearly a half a million in severance after a short time on the job is pure robbery and greed. A severance package is supposed to show some appreciation for your level of commitment and to soften the blow of having to look for new work. Severance, particularly for those being dusted off with taxpayers' money, should not be an excuse for retirement or a ticket to plush villas and vanillas.

The worst thing though is when those sworn to uphold the law and protect the innocent actually become the perpetrators of

145

crime and sully the honour of their fellow-policemen through behaviour more fitting in those they put behind bars.

When honest men make an honest mistake, the public expects them to own up to it, face the consequences and show honest remorse. When police officers are embroiled in a controversy over questionable actions that have led to a tragic death, the public expects them to be relieved of their duties until an independent investigation can be conducted. The public does NOT expect them to sit back and receive their full salary for several years while the investigation drags out. Part of the problem is the "drags out" aspect—our embarrassingly inefficient justice system. Whether it is an internal investigation, a criminal case before the courts or a judicial inquiry, we need to find another gear. To delay justice for the guilty is bad enough. To keep innocent people on the hook and in limbo for years is unconscionable.

The other part of the equation is that if an officer is guilty of a crime, he does not deserve to be paid for doing nothing while that determination is made. If there is adequate reason to suspect illegal or inappropriate behaviour on the part of a policeman, it must not appear that he is being rewarded for his bad conduct.

Crime must have consequences even for those whose career is fighting crime. Investigations should be short, less than a month, no more than two. Guilty or innocent, punished or pardoned. After the ordeal, if an officer is acquitted or found innocent of the accusations, then he should be reinstated with back pay and compensation for any harm done to his reputation.

In our society, far too much is made of "weekends", "vacation" and "retirement". We have become faddists who endure work and school and live in constant anticipation of free time and

146

relaxation with commensurate loathing and anxiety for the inevitable "Monday morning" when we have to go back to work. This tragic cultural worldview keeps people from enjoying their best waking hours or performing at peak levels in the career paths they themselves have chosen. Mankind is happiest when he is productive and finds greater satisfaction in accomplishments than in slothfulness.

We all enjoy a well-earned rest from our labours . . . but when we bestow an undeserved but well-paid rest on those who have let us down and abused our trust, we send a message to every young person, every taxpayer, every criminal that the world is not fair and that keeping the law, working hard and playing by the rules will not be rewarded. Live for yourself, take what you can get, try not to get caught, enjoy your long trial. This is the opposite of the message we should be sending.

Rewarding evil leads to more of the same. If we keep this up we'll have to hire even more police officers and build more jails. Let's just use some common sense. Let's get to the bottom of things quickly. Let's exonerate the innocent and punish the guilty. That's the kind of example we should be setting for our young people.

March 17, 2011

Truthophobia: The Fear and Hatred of Facts

In recent years, the self-righteous condemnation of "hate crimes" and various "phobias" has been all the rage (no irony intended). The self-absorbed political oligarchs, talking heads and media gatekeepers have contrived to set up a hate-filled straw man whom they can blame as the source of all division and violence; attention has been cleverly shifted from the very real threats to public safety, civil order and personal freedom to this vague and sinister character who simply refuses to accept the new Canadian identity and values as defined by the elite.

It has been said that the first casualty of war is the truth. That we are engaged in an epic battle for the culture is obvious to most. What is at stake, and why, has been distorted by media spin and autocratic fiat so that great swathes of the population have lost the ability to discern between the genuine dangers we face as a society and the fantasies of self-informed bigots of whatever stripe.

Let's assume that there is such a thing as factual truth and that it can be known. Let's assume that people who know the truth will make better decisions than those who are believing a lie. Let's assume that in order to keep the multitudes from understanding the truth and making better decisions at the ballot box, those in power will use every means at their disposal to conceal the facts and distract voters from the real issues. It's happening. It's happening today. Those who hate the truth will not tolerate those who speak the truth. First they will insult. Then they will threaten. Then they will fine. Then they will imprison. And then . . . we all know (or have some of us forgotten?) what happened in Germany in the 1930s and 1940s. First there was a lie. Then there was a demand for uniformity of public opinion and the forced expression of agreement with the lie. This was enforced in the early stages through peer pressure, then threats, then imprisonment and torture and then . . . six million Jews were killed along with countless others. The Soviet Union later applied the same methods, covering the truth with lies, all the while printing the "news" (fake news) every day in *Pravda*. "Pravda" means "Truth". Over thirty million died under Stalin's lies, many of them simply for speaking the truths that Stalin and his henchmen did not want told.

Today in Canada, we are being told lies that masquerade as truth. Our children are being lied to in public schools. Those who tell the truth are being ridiculed, accused of hatred and racism and already they are being threatened with the loss of jobs, the loss of their homes and the loss of their freedom. Truth is fallen in the streets.

Let's look at three issues about which the ruling elites in government try so hard to suppress the truth. Why are they afraid of the truth? Why do they hate the truth? Because it interferes with their plans and contradicts their narrative.

They say: There are many genders and gender identities and to claim otherwise is hateful and bigoted.
We say: There are two biological genders, male and female. This is scientific reality. To claim otherwise is nonsense; teaching multigender theory to schoolchildren encourages dangerous experimentation which can lead to destructive behaviours, harmful behavioural addictions and dysfunctional human relationships.

They say: Islam is a religion of peace and deserves special protection. MP Iqra Khalid's Motion-103 is all about protecting Islam and offers no protection to Jews, Christians, Sikhs, Buddhists or others. They claim (without any justification) that a

149

current climate of hostility towards Islam requires this unprecedented partiality.

We say: In Canada, all citizens, not only Muslims, should be free to worship without fear, free to associate, to convert and to peacefully proselytize. It is not acceptable that Christians should be mocked and attacked by the secular media (as they so often are), while Islamists are protected from public mockery by 'special legislation'. We know that around the world, radical Islamists routinely torture, behead and mutilate Christians and Jews. While it is difficult to verify accurate numbers, thousands of Christians (some say as many as 90,000, some even more) are martyred around the globe each year, many by Islamists. To establish special protection in Canada only against speech critical of Islam is an insult to those of other faiths, especially the Judeo-Christian faith on which Canada was founded.

They say: Abortion is only a woman's choice and must be protected, promoted and justified. They don't want the pro-life message on campuses. They don't want pro-lifers near abortion clinics. They won't talk about the link between abortion and breast cancer. They won't talk about the censorship of abortion statistics in BC and Ontario. They say the preborn infant is not a human person until fully delivered.

We say: The unborn child is a living human being and is deserving of legal protection. We say that freedom of speech includes on the sidewalks in front of abortion clinics, that young women deserve to know about the link between abortion and breast cancer, that young men should not be allowed to coerce their girlfriends into killing their babies. We say (and most Canadians agree with us) that preborn girls should not be killed in sex-selective abortions, just because they're girls.

There are many more examples of truthophobia, the irrational fear of truth. There are many more ways that truth is being sacrificed for political correctness and partisan advantage. These are only a few. It's time Canadians demanded honesty from their politicians, from the courts and from the media. It's time Canadians demanded honesty in the classroom. Freedom of speech and freedom of conscience are at stake. Unless we vigorously defend these now, our prisons will become political tools for tyrants and all too soon, brave Canadians will again have to choose between martyrdom and slavery.

Now is the time to lift your voice for freedom, for common sense, for truth and justice. Truth is not something to be feared; it is something to be sought. "You shall know the truth and the truth shall set you free." John 8:32

February 21, 2017

There are many examples of this struggle to protect the truth and especially the freedom to speak the truth. Motion 103 (M-103) was pushed through the House of Commons and passed 3rd Reading on March 23, 2017. The motion sponsored by MP Iqra Khalid stressed the importance of protecting Islam and only Islam from criticism. It is currently being studied by a committee and many fear that it will be brought back as a bill making criticism of Islam a crime. It is a blatant attempt to promote Islam and could even lead to acceptance of Sharia Law in Canada.

To learn more, visit Canadian Citizens for Charter Rights and Freedoms (C3RF):
https://www.canadiancitizens.org/download-c3rf-brochure-motion-m-103
http://www.christianpost.com/news/90000-christians-killed-in-2016-1-every-6-minutes-study-172464/

Two Wrongs Don't Make a Right

In all societies, the pendulum swings, public sentiment changes and things once thought impossible become increasingly likely. Such is the case with Canada's broken relationship with the descendants of her First Nations. The shameful treatment of aboriginal people by European settlers and their successive governments has been documented extensively in recent years: how they colonized, occupied and expropriated land held for generations by the diverse people-groups now collectively known as Indians, Natives, Aboriginals, Indigenous Peoples or First Nations. From the loss of traditional territories to the introduction of destructive drink and diet, from scenes of violent conquest and the distribution of wasting disease to residential school tragedies and unfair discrimination in the polling booth, First Nations peoples have endured crippling abuse across a span of generations and most Canadians now know that. A variety of approaches to alleviating the accumulated harm of these centuries of mistreatment—all well-intentioned—have failed to satisfy the deeply-felt needs of First Nations. The clock keeps ticking.

This year the timer has gone off. Most Canadians recognize that there is a new urgency in the calls for serious talks and beyond that, serious action to find solutions for the broken and unsustainable relationship between Canada and her aboriginal citizens. Sparked by the apparent lack of consultation in the changes to the Indian Act and other legislation rammed through Parliament by the Harper Governments Bill C-45 (the 2nd Budget Implementation Bill), the streets of Canada have suddenly become the scenes of numerous demonstrations by the loose-knit group Idle No More. From an initial attempt by some chiefs to enter the House of Commons where they were rebuffed by Commons security guards, "spontaneous" protests have been held across the country which have been highly publicised by the mainstream media. In the midst of that, the dramatic efforts of Chief Theresa Spence of Attawapiskat to engage the Prime Minister and the Crown in fresh discussions have gotten more Canadians involved in the conversation, even though she has since been thoroughly discredited for her mismanagement of federal funds ($34 million per year to her community of about 300 homes). Nevertheless, her "hunger strike" on Victoria Island has been a visual rallying-point for thousands of First Nations people and sympathetic non-natives across the country. Although the outcomes are not yet known, a meeting between Stephen Harper and some representative chiefs has been scheduled and the timing and significance of this development should not be underestimated.

Just this week, a Federal Court has released its judgment granting greater recognition and unspecified new rights to non-status Indians and Metis, adding another 600,000 Canadians to the existing 700,000-plus status Indians currently recognised by the Government of Canada and the Indian Act. If this ruling stands, it will have enormous implications for these people and for other Canadians not included in this judgment. Will current financial commitments towards status Indians be extended to Metis and non-status? Will existing funding be further diluted? What about income taxes and sales taxes? What about government responsibilities in regard to health and housing?

Assembly of First Nations National Chief Shawn Atleo and the chiefs standing with him are calling for immediate transformation and the replacement (not repair) of the Indian Act with other legislative tools. Specifically, they are calling for full implementation of treaty provisions, many of which predate both the Indian Act and Canada's patriated Constitution of 1982. They have a good point regarding the failure of the government to abide by its own solemn treaties and agreements. C-38 and C-45 were pushed through Parliament with little opportunity for consultation or debate and the unilateral alteration of native voting procedures as well as the perceived removal of environmental protection from streams and rivers became the catalyst for this explosion of frustration and clamour for change. The crazy patchwork of legislation, negotiated settlements, outdated Indian Act provisions, treaties, resource agreements and other half-measures have muddied the waters but have not resolved the conflicts or settled outstanding issues. Soaring social costs and demoralising conditions have created a very complex situation and one that must be resolved quickly if Canada is to avoid protracted conflict and uncertainty.

There has been no shortage of ink and airtime devoted to Idle No More, Chief Spence's demands and the hastily-scheduled meeting of the PM and the Chiefs. There can be no illusion that five centuries of conflict, mistrust and disappointment can be resolved in four or five hours of talks. However, meeting is the first step. It would be easy for critics on all sides to point fingers, lay blame and set goals or demands that are unattainable. Such antics may make good ratings for the cable networks and may win hearty approval from the folks who are on side but will not help move the practical issues of housing, employment, health, education and culture forward.

The PM and the Chiefs have a golden opportunity to renew the understandings and the expectations reflected in our Constitution, our treaties and our laws. They must agree to change the things that are holding us back from achieving the ideals on which we agree. They must seize the moment and work together to achieve full equality of opportunity for all Canadians. May God the Creator give them wisdom, grace, humility and courage to address complex issues, seeking justice under the banner of grace. As the great Chief Cornerstone once said: "Do unto others as you would have them do unto you". Luke 6:31

January 10, 2013

In November 2012, the Idle No More movement was birthed, at least partially in response to Bill C-45 and possible implications of changes to environmental regulations and how those changes might affect First Nations. Wikipedia's version of the events and timeline is here:
https://en.wikipedia.org/wiki/Idle_No_More

Chief Theresa Spence of Attawapiskat became a voice for the movement and began a highly-reported hunger strike on Victoria Island on December 11, 2012.

21-Gun Salute!

With the successful passage of Bill C-19, *An Act to amend the Criminal Code and the Firearms Act*, Mr. Harper's Conservative government has delivered on a long-standing promise and they deserve credit for completing this task.

There will always be naysayers who equate guns with violence and who think that a focus on punishing criminals is a regressive approach to crime; in their opinion such an approach is lacking compassion and narrow in perspective. The opposite is true and those arguments have been made many times in many different ways. The NDP's knee-jerk resistance to C-19 was as predictable, boring and tiresome as its stance on most other issues of consequence. "If it moves, shoot it! If it keeps moving, regulate it!" For today, anyway, I say "Bravo!" to MPs Candice Hoeppner and Vic Toews who kept doggedly pushing this bill in spite of the broken-record objections of their critics. And a tip of the hat to Prime Minister Stephen Harper for keeping his promise . . . (on this issue).

Now a word on the budget and the notion many of us share: that a "Conservative" government should actually be pushing to achieve a debt-free Canada, which would mean getting out of deficit much more quickly than we are. A golden opportunity was missed on budget day—to establish a realistic pension plan for MPs, one that would be fair to taxpayers and hard-working citizens . . . but that is a topic for another day. Today we thank those who have worked so hard to cut the wasteful spending on the registry and we raise a toast to common sense and perseverance. Well done!

April 5, 2012

On April 5, 2012, Bill C-19, An Act to amend the Criminal Code and the Firearms Act, received Royal Assent and became law, undoing the expensive, intrusive and ineffective Long Gun Registry first brought in by a former Liberal government. The battle over gun control continues to rage with "progressives" blaming guns for violent crime. The CHP endorses responsible firearm ownership and use. Violent crime, whether committed with fists, knives, cars, shovels or guns is a result of lawless attitudes. We need to restore respect for the lives and property of others.

The Arrogance of Entrenched Power

David Stephan and his wife Collet have been sentenced to, respectively, four months jailtime and three months house arrest for "failing to provide the necessaries of life" for their 19-month old son, Ezekiel, who died of meningitis in March, 2012. That's when the Stephans treated their son, the youngest of four, with natural remedies, not realizing that he had bacterial meningitis. By the time they called for an ambulance, it was too late. What began as a family tragedy has now become a court judgment on personal choice, parental rights and a state-imposed bias in favour of government-sanctioned allopathic medicine.

The Stephans were tried by jury in April of this year and found guilty for not seeking timely help from a medical doctor. They thought their son had croup and sought advice from a naturopath. In the end, the failure to properly diagnose and treat the meningitis led to Ezekiel's death. On June 24, they were sentenced by a judge. Although Justice Rodney Jerke acknowledged that the Stephans were "caring parents and neither intended to put the boy's life at risk", he passed sentence on them for relying on their own instincts and bypassing the commonly-accepted practice of bringing children to medical doctors for diagnosis and treatment.

Crown prosecutor Lisa Weich, who was seeking a much longer sentence for the Stephans, claimed that the crown was trying to provide a "voice for Ezekiel". More on that later.

Our hearts are moved with compassion for these loving parents who—following the dictates of conscience and their understanding of the standard approach to medicine—took their responsibilities as primary caregivers seriously and attempted to provide natural nutritional therapy for the child they loved. Let's look at a couple of the assumptions made by judge and jury. We cannot in this short article address in detail all of the many conflicts between "industry-standard" medicine and "alternative therapies", but we wish to focus on the "one size fits all" approach which would take decision-making away from parents on many levels and what that means for all of us.

We all appreciate the medical profession and most of us have been greatly helped, from time to time, by the accumulated knowledge of doctors, by prescribed medications and procedures. Had I not received medical intervention on several occasions, I might not be alive today . . . but do medical doctors always succeed? Do doctors ever make errors in judgment? Do medical errors in judgment ever result in unnecessary deaths? The answer, of course is that doctors (and judges), like all people, make mistakes. Sometimes those mistakes cost lives. One author, a medical doctor himself, says that medical errors are the "third-leading cause of death in the US".

In a PBS interview, Dr. Martin Makary of Johns Hopkins University School of Medicine details the research he's conducted that indicates as many as 250,000 Americans die each year as a result of medical error. The concept is not new. "Iatrogenesis" refers to adverse or unintended health outcomes caused by physicians, pharmacists, nurses, dentists, psychologists, medical laboratory scientists and therapists. Iatrogenesis can also result from "alternative" medical treatments If trained professionals can "make a mistake", why are these parents singled out for their error in judgment?   In this case, it should also be noted that meningitis is sometimes fatal, even when treated by a medical doctor. It has many possible causes, including adverse vaccine reaction, has an often-vague, unspecific symptom picture which can result in misdiagnosis early in the disease and diagnosis is considered difficult in children under 2 yrs of age. Modern

159

treatments have reduced mortality rates to less than 10% which means that doctors on average lose less than one meningitis patient in ten. If that one happens to be your child, you will have the same grief in loss as the Stephans but without the legal trauma. In Canada, medical doctors, paid through our universal healthcare system (ie. taxpayer-funded), not only make occasional errors but some of them "make a living" killing babies!

Each year, over 100,000 preborn children are deliberately killed by abortionists. Yet when this couple try (unsuccessfully) to restore their child to health, they are punished. Something is awfully wrong here. When Crown Prosecutor Lisa Weich claims to be a "voice for Ezekiel", I have to ask, "Why do you not seek to be a voice for the 100,000 who are deliberately killed each year?" Many medical procedures or drug regimens accepted as standard care within our public system carry "unintended consequences". Some of these are well-known; others are suspected. Most such claims are denied by those who profit from the procedures or from the drugs. For instance, multiple studies indicate that abortion in a first pregnancy dramatically increases the risk of breast cancer. This information is denied to most young women considering abortion.

Another example is the risks associated with vaccinations; many Canadians are concerned about a suspected link between childhood vaccinations and the onset of autism. An adverse reaction to vaccination can even be meningitis, but rarely is the perpetrator held accountable. These concerns are routinely treated as baseless fear-mongering by—guess who?—the pharmaceutical companies. Further to this, many people die during cancer treatments; some die from the treatment, not from the disease. We all make the best choices we can under trying circumstances. In hindsight, we sometimes make mistakes. In other areas of criminal law, "intent" is key to culpability. In this case, failure to follow the crowd was deemed criminal. The personal tragedy of losing a child was compounded by public shaming and punishment.

With the passage of C-14 earlier this month, the Canadian medical profession entered a new era of medical malpractice. Doctors now have become dispensers of death potions to those who request them. So far, several Colleges of Physicians have closed ranks and have demanded that doctors within the system either participate in ending the lives of their "eligible" patients or at least refer them to another doctor who will. This violation of conscience is being challenged in court but once again, it raises the contrasting image of doctors deliberately killing while parents trying to protect their children are judged for failing to consult a doctor. Where is the rational logic? Where is compassion? Where is the understanding of the parents' role in determining what is best for their children? This is a hazardous world. We have each had "close calls" with death or disaster due to a momentary lapse in attention or judgement. By God's grace, things usually end up alright, but most of us carry deep regrets for some ill-timed act, misjudgement of a situation, or a neglected need. There is a time to extend grace and understanding to those who are already bearing the burden of loss.

The Christian Heritage Party stands by the family, not only this family but all families who seek to raise their children according to their own standards and beliefs. Professionals are not always right. Judges are not always right. Doctors are not always right. When the government usurps the role of parents and forces children to submit to government-prescribed medicine, education, gender agendas or secular religion, that government is out of line. Many parents will not agree with the Stephans' approach to medicine. All parents, however, should oppose the compulsory imposition of a narrow point of view of medicine on parents who have been given their sacred responsibility by God. Alternative approaches to medicine should not be universally condemned because of one treatment gone wrong any more than we should judge standard medical procedures based on mixed outcomes. All evidence should be examined before jumping to conclusions.

Please stand with us in defence of parental rights, the sanctity of life, marriage and personal freedom.

June 27, 2016

PBS interview with Dr. Martin Makary of Johns Hopkins University School of Medicine:
http://www.pbs.org/newshour/bb/is-fatal-medical-error-a-leading-cause-of-death/

Media Bias

Thou shalt not raise a false report.
Exodus 23:1

"A lie repeated often enough
becomes the truth."
Joseph Goebbels, Propaganda Officer
for Adolf Hitler

A Compass That Points Only Left

I would like to register my complaint—in the strongest possible terms—to the CBC's "Vote Compass" page, which I viewed recently during the Alberta provincial election. It is unconscionable that the taxpayer-funded CBC should purport to be serving voters while using its pretension of "unbiased" election coverage to herd voters into its own narrow selection of choices.

Firstly and most importantly, in the Alberta election just concluded, CBC offered voters only choices and information related to six of the registered parties and leaders involved in the election. There were nine registered parties running candidates but you'd never have known it by visiting "Vote Compass". To pretend to be giving voters reliable information while leaving one third of the registered parties out of the discussion was nothing short of deceptive. For voters who actually accepted CBC's advice and gave their vote to one of the six parties without even being aware of the other parties or the candidates running for them, this so-called "compass" actually may have led them away from choices they might otherwise have made. In this way, of course, it constituted a non-monetary political contribution to each of the six parties which it did include.

Secondly, by asking a series of leading questions, biased in their wording, this "compass" subtly encouraged those who answered the simplistic multiple-choice questions to identify with parties on the so-called left wing of the spectrum. This is the kind of ploy used by advertisers and perhaps by the marketing gurus of various political stripes. It should not be the modus operandi of a news service paid for by all taxpayers of every political persuasion.

Thirdly, it is a clumsy political tool. The questions themselves revealed more about the collaborators behind "Vote Compass" than about the character and integrity of the party leaders. Of course, it didn't even touch on the personal values, skills or ideas of local candidates, nor could it. However, intelligent voters have always weighed the personality, experience and passion of local candidates and—in a free society—should continue to do so. Voters who expected the CBC "Vote Compass" to tell them how to vote may have gotten more than they bargained for and but the distortion of the political process hurt all Albertans and, in the end, will work against the best interests of all Canadians.

Candidates, voters and political parties need to be protected from charlatans who—entrusted with power and influence—use that power to control information. We need a media ombudsman who will hold press and broadcast entities accountable for deceptive and misleading reporting, polling and gimmicks like "Vote Compass". If purporting to report on candidates, all candidates and all parties should be represented. To exclude smaller parties and less-well-known candidates is to assume that small things can never get big or that ideas once scorned can never gain acceptance. The NDP in Alberta are evidence to the contrary.

Today, I write because of this distortion of process that was at work during the Alberta election; but in a few short months Canadians across the country, including Albertans, will be voting in a federal election. CBC's simplistic, cookie-cutter, "one size fits all" approach must not be allowed to narrow the field to its own small selection of chosen parties. There are 17 registered federal political parties and the CBC has not been given a mandate to pick winners and losers. Let the voters do that and give them all the information they need so that they can do so intelligently. The CHP believes there should be a level playing field for all candidates and political parties. Ideas should not be blocked by the electoral process. News agencies—especially those funded by the taxpayer—must not selectively cover elections and twist the process to suit themselves. We need a media ombudsman during elections, who is required to respond within 48 hours to unfair electoral practices. This would ensure that unfair practices are stopped quickly and therefore level the playing field for all parties and for Canadians.

May 12, 2015

Peering into the future

"Hindsight is 20-20". At least that's what people like to tell themselves. "I may not know the future but at least I can see what went wrong in the past". The so-called "Monday morning quarterback" is the proverbial couch potato who can sit back and—knowing what the defense did wrong and what special circumstances affected the outcome of the game—describe the perfect plays he would have run if he had been the quarterback.

There are two problems with the assumption that we would have done better than a particular quarterback or, for that matter, a particular politician "if I had been in his shoes". One problem is that we are not in his shoes. Using the quarterback as an example, we did not look up to see two 300-lb. men bearing down us at full speed as we scrambled in the backfield, looking for a receiver. He did. We have the advantage of multi-angled slow-motion replays. He did not. We don't have to guess what the other men on the field are about to do because they have already done it. The second problem—staying with the quarterback allegory—is that the past means different things to different people. The quarterback may see that he held onto the ball for too long. The guards and tackles may see that they failed to defend the pocket. The receivers may realize (or maybe not) that they were too predictable or too slow and that they failed to give the quarterback a target he could safely hit. The coach will be blamed for poor strategy or even for hiring the wrong people. Even the referees will be blamed for poor calls.

In the political realm, it is even worse. Unlike the goalposts in a football stadium, political goalposts sometimes move. We live in an age where not only the future is mysterious but even the past is difficult sometimes to assess. The national mainstream media claim to be reporting on current events—what we normally call "the news"—in an objective manner but their extreme biases are so blatant and pervasive that the opinionated reporting of last week's news is already tainting the historical perspectives which should guide us in next week's decisions. The old saying is that "he who does not remember the past is doomed to repeat it". We have a responsibility to remember the lessons of the past and apply them to our future; but first we must understand what really happened. Otherwise, we will be making bad decisions based on false assumptions about the past. Modern technology has made it very easy to record the past; it's also made it very easy to create a false past, something too many in the mainstream media have mastered.

Take an example or two: the misrepresentation of the Charter of Rights and Freedoms and the dehumanization of the unborn. Canadian courts—aided and abetted by a complicit mass media and a cowardly Parliament—have created a myth about the very recent history that led to the legalization of same-sex "marriage". The historically-verifiable facts that "sexual orientation" was not a Charter-protected status and that the courts did not have a legal basis for "reading it into" the Charter are not known to most Canadians. They have accepted the myth, the lie, that justice demanded the inclusion of same-sex partnerships under the umbrella of "marriage" which otherwise is defined by the union of opposites. But the media is the message and the dominant media moguls of today manipulate the narrative to suit their proclivities.

Most Canadians have believed the lie that the Constitution guarantees the right to a taxpayer-funded abortion. Even the Supreme Court in 1988 did not say that it did. However, that is the narrative that the chattering classes found convenient to promulgate. "Right to choose" is an empty phrase, if not carefully defined, but it allows political advantage to those who use it as a brutal lever to squeeze votes from the misinformed. Many Canadians still do not know that there is no legal protection for the unborn for the full nine months up to the very moment of birth. Most Canadians are unaware of the 491 infants who were born alive after "botched" abortions but who died later through neglect or infanticide. This kind of information is not made available by the media mavens of our day. It might interfere with their stranglehold on public policy.

So looking backwards over the past year, the past decade, the past century, what wisdom can we gain to make better decisions going into the future? We must recognise that "he who controls the past controls the future". We must take responsibility to understand "current events" (rather the recent past) for ourselves. When choosing our news sources ("who should we believe?"), we need to seek wise and honest men and women, in fact courageous men and women, who will speak the truth and not merely spout the latest politically-correct dogma. Dogma and propaganda have been with mankind since the beginning. Lies about the past have ever been used to affect outcomes in the future. The Pharisees lied about Jesus to manipulate Pilate's judgment. Hitler lied about the Jews to co-opt the German people into his plans.

It is incumbent on us to find good sources of news and commentary, fresh springs of wisdom and insight that are not merely polluted wells or broken cisterns, spewing out misinformation and falsehoods. Check out *Lifesite News* (http://www.lifesitenews.com) for a multifaceted view of the challenges to human life and dignity. Another source of alternate news is *the Rebel.media* . . . and there are many more good blogs and news sources if you go looking. And if you really want up-to-the-minute perspectives on today's events—with a clear window on human nature and guidance for the tough choices we all face—check out the Bible. King Solomon's Book of Proverbs has not yet been crushed under the bus of political correctness. The unchanging truths about God, the world He made and mankind's role in it are a reliable anchor for us as we are tossed about by the storms of life. For a fresh outlook on tomorrow and the new year ahead, it's good to know that the mercies of God "are new every morning" Lam. 3:23, that He will "never leave thee nor forsake thee" Heb. 13:5 and that "He is a rewarder of them that diligently seek Him" Heb. 11:6.

We can face the future with confidence if our trust is in Almighty God, maker of heaven and earth. 2013 has no surprises for Him. No "fiscal cliff", no "rumours of wars" can unhinge his plans for us or shake us loose from His hand if we listen to His voice: "Let not your heart be troubled; ye believe in God, believe also in Me". John 14:1

January 3, 2013

CBC Misses the Big One! . . . Again.

I could hardly believe it. Our national broadcaster (CBC) has a website which I check regularly. I know that they have an embarrassingly heavy bias on "social issues" and that their bias is painful to experience, but I go there anyway because they do have an extensive (and expensive) network of reporters, researchers and technologies that allow them to discover and follow Canadian stories, big and small. Over the years, CBC has shown an inordinate interest in anything associated with the words "human rights". Up until now.

On Wednesday, Feb 15, 2012, Bill C-304 passed its second reading. "What's C-304?" you may ask. Apparently CBC (at least its online version) has not yet asked that question. Or, more likely, these news sleuths have analyzed the discussion around C-304 and don't like it. But just because they don't like it doesn't normally mean they don't cover it. In this case, CBC opinion-shapers probably have not figured out what to do with this decision. MP Brian Storseth (Westlock-St. Paul) tabled Bill C-304, "An Act to amend the Canadian Human Rights Act (protecting freedom)" on September 30, 2011. Two days ago, the House of Commons voted 158 to 131 to pass Bill C-304. MP Storseth's bill would stop or reduce the constant attacks against free speech which are perpetrated and supported by the pernicious Section 13 of the Human Rights Act. Under this section, good, morally-upright, common-sense Canadians have been charged and penalized for questioning things like Canada's out-of-control immigration system and the wisdom (?) of allowing unhealthy sexual behaviours to dominate the education of our children.

For those keen on learning more about C-304, you may search in vain on the taxpayer-funded website of CBC. You may have to visit alternate information sources. But the changes made by

171

eliminating the oppressive and unfair Sec. 13 will benefit all Canadians and are a welcome breath of fresh air. No more will manipulative and self-serving troublemakers who populate the ranks of misguided sex activists and the crafty stealth supporters of radical Islamist Jihad groups be able to pummel law-abiding citizens with spurious taxpayer-funded accusations of "human rights violations", merely for pointing out inconvenient facts. Forced out of the shadows, these activists will have to rely on the courts—where truth is a defence and there are rules of evidence.

Since I favour cutting costs for taxpayers, I recommend that CBC-online close down one or two expensive departments lay off some of its highly-paid staff and pick up the news from *ARPA*, or *Roadkill Radio* or *No Apologies*. On its front page today, CBC talks about Paul McCartney giving up pot-smoking, Sears' price-cutting measures and the unhealthy result of eating a grossly huge hamburger. Yet the defense of Canadians' freedom of speech by a plucky MP from Alberta received no mention. Before C-304 passes into law, CBC will figure out a spin and come out swinging (in a thoroughly-neutral, unbiased manner no doubt—wink! wink!). But for now, they seem not to have noticed that Canadians, including MPs have said "Enough!"

Freedom of speech, freedom of the press, freedom of conscience and freedom of religion are too important to leave to elite, taxpayer-funded broadcasters like CBC. I hope their radio and TV coverage has been better than their web presence but I spent so much time looking for it online I didn't have time to turn on the tube. Everyone who cares about freedom: write to MP Brian Storseth, the PM, the Justice Minister and your own MP. Tell them to finish the job and deliver us from this evil Section 13. There may still be some sanity in Ottawa!

February 16, 2012

Dog Days and a National Bias

Well, the inquiry is underway and the dead huskies who once pulled sleds for a living are now being "exhumed". Nowadays, if an animal needs to be put down—let's say an angry bear—it is no longer simply shot with a rifle; it is "euthanized" . . . with a rifle. However, when a large number of dogs, once considered the private property of their owner, are killed unceremoniously (with a rifle), there are calls for an inquiry, new laws and pledges to ensure that "this sort of thing must not happen again".

Fast forward to one of Canada's private clinics (you know, the only kind of private clinics approved by the NDP) where hundreds or thousands of living human babies are torn limb from limb or sucked into grisly vacuum machines or poisoned with salt. (True, though these private clinics are funded by our health care dollars, they don't actually provide health care, just killing.) Look around you, note the blood and tragic grief. Then go home and pay your taxes. Like it or not, your taxes are funding these macabre businesses. And no, your reward will not be in heaven for your sacrificial donations to this house of horrors.

Now check the papers again. Where are the calls for an inquiry? Where are the voices raised against this uncivilized behaviour? Well, it's hard to find in the papers or on the tube. Because you not only fund abortions; you also fund the news media, the sombre-toned voices of those arbiters of truth, the CBC anchors and announcers who determine (for your own good and that of society) what you must watch ad nauseum and what you must be protected from. Sled dogs and corporate greed: now that's a story with legs! Dismembered babies and conscienceless greedy physicians: that story would cause unnecessary disruption and trauma to the little survivors of the abortion holocaust. Thousands on Parliament Hill? Erase the tape; there must be another angle to Manitoba's flood that we could run . . .

In Ottawa today, reliable inside sources tallied the March for Life participants at a record-breaking 15,000. No mention of it on the CBC online news site. No mention of it tonight on the CTV site. Numbers, if reported at all, are consistently understated by the downstream media.

While BC introduces the toughest animal cruelty laws anywhere in case any of the huskies shot at Whistler "did not die instantly", Canadian taxpayers shovel out millions against their will to pay for infants in the womb to have their arms and legs ripped off. Canada has no laws whatsoever regulating the killing of a human baby in the womb. The Canadian Supreme Court deems the unborn to be "non-persons". Meanwhile, the killing of "non-eagles" while still in the egg is a punishable crime. And while the arrogant NDP crowd that accused the government a few weeks ago of "contempt of Parliament" for refusing to disclose all the costs of prisons and jets, is perfectly comfortable refusing to disclose to British Columbians how many abortions are performed each year in BC, on what ages of women, for what reasons and with what complications. You can pay but you can't pray—at least not in the "bubble zones". Ask Linda Gibbons, the grandmother still in custody in Toronto for praying and counseling with women in front of these private clinics paid for with public dollars.

You can try to figure it out but the easiest thing to do is accept that we live in a confused society. Having recognized the madness which has afflicted the West and which blinds our media, take a deep breath, roll up your sleeves and determine that you will live the rest of your life trying to wake Canadians up. To go on in this murderous confusion is to condemn future generations, not only to an untimely death at the hands of the abortionist but to a life of self-deception and hopeless utilitarian hedonism for those who survive the womb.

May 12, 2011

Freedom of Information—Balancing the Bias on a "Who Needs to Know?" Basis

Many say that we live in the "Information Age" although—depending on who writes the news—it could be called the "Misinformation Age". The ability of news reporters, anchors and networks to define the debate, phrase the questions about which the public is expected to ruminate and highlight the answers that they think best serve the public interest is well-known, at least by those within the circles of influence.

A glance at the US Presidential race which has already begun and the coverage given to those potential Republican nominees deemed "electable" by the press is illuminating. The high scores for Herman Cain, for instance, in the grass-roots "straw polls" bears no resemblance to the miniscule airtime he is given by the networks or press chains. If the MSM can "help" Americans choose the Republican nominee in 2011, they can also shape the outcome of the real race against Barack Obama in 2012.

Canada's media operates in a reliably similar manner. Although Canada—nationally and provincially—operates in an ostensibly multi-party system, CBC, our taxpayer-funded media giant can be counted on to relegate the parties with whom they disagree and the issues which they would prefer that Canadians not examine to "the back of the bus". Current elections underway in Ontario are a case in point: on CBC's website, it appears that only four parties are running. Pictures of four leaders appear there. No mention is made of Phil Lees, the leader of the Family Coalition Party. Why not? He doesn't rate as newsworthy by the movers and shakers at CBC. His policies don't interest them and his getting a fair hearing from the voters is not their goal.

When it comes to access to information, left-wing activists, their vocal representatives in Ottawa and Victoria and their state-funded media friends are "incensed" if any elected representative or government bureaucrat, military person or business person ever refuses to disclose all the information they have on any topic, even if that disclosure imperils the security of the nation or government confidentiality. Failure to disclose is always assumed to be arrogant, undemocratic and an obvious sign of guilt. Words and phrases like "cover-up" or "lack of transparency" become the talking points until those beleaguered individuals are brought to heel and made to cough up.

However, when the activists seeking information are prolife and those withholding it are status-quo, abortion-on-demand hospitals and "health" agencies, the shoe is on the other foot and it doesn't fit very well. You can then count on the MSM to side with the "defenders of privacy". In 2001, shortly before their long-awaited collapse at the polls, the BC NDP government of the day introduced Bill 21, which put an iron curtain on the release of information regarding abortions in BC. The excuse of "protecting privacy" is so ludicrous it would be funny if it weren't for the pathetic seriousness ascribed to it by the militant, pro-abortion government of the day and their vocal comrades in the MSM. The pro-lifers seeking access to information were not looking for names and addresses of patients or doctors. They wanted to know things like:

- How many abortions occur each year in BC?
- What are the ages of those undergoing abortion procedures?
- How are different cultural groups represented in this destructive practice?
- How many repeat procedures?
- What types of abortions are performed?
- What are the gestational ages of the infants killed by abortion?

- What complications occur?

This request for information has not had the support of the MSM but it should have. If information is important and if Canadians "deserve to know" things, surely this area is one worthy of scrutiny.

Note that the Liberal government of Gordon Campbell that ascended to power a few months after Bill 21 was passed has remained just as tight-lipped on this issue. Not one of the pro-abortion policies of the BC NDP, not the bubble zones nor the funding nor the promotion of abortion have been curtailed in the least in 10 years of Liberal rule. Campbell's cabinet refused to open the books and release any of the information requested by the prolife community. Christy Clark has done no better.

But hey! We can find out which Defense Department helicopter Peter Mackay took from his fishing lodge and when he uses a government jet for personal business. Why? Because that information might embarrass the Tories (and it should). But information should be a two-way street and all those calling for transparency from others should demonstrate it themselves. The censorship surrounding the abortion industry, the health risks associated with gay sexual practices, the abuse of power by judges and human-rights tribunals—these should all be on the radar screens, the broadcasts and the front pages of the MSM and the demands for disclosure should apply to all government statistics, not just the politically-correct ones.

September 29, 2011

"Just the Facts, Ma'am; Just the Facts"

With a nod to Joe Friday, the classic characterization of a police detective from the early radio and TV show, <u>Dragnet</u>, I'd like to approach a few modern mysteries with the line of questioning frequently attributed to him. (Apparently the oft-quoted phrase above was a truncated version of his original "All we want are the facts, ma'am"). It would be so refreshing if some of today's news services (?) would remember that simple bit of advice. It seems everyone is pushing an agenda and when the "facts" can be used to support that agenda, they use them. When the facts seem to contradict the agenda's premise, they ignore them. The really frustrating use of facts is when they are thrown in, "bait-and-switch" style, to support conclusions for which they provide no real evidence.

There are many examples of this but I refer directly to the unproven theories (bandied about as facts) of the origins of life, the development of species and the periods of time during which certain deduced events are hypothetically surmised to have occurred. In a world where supposed journalistic high-achievers such as writers for the *New York Times* and other widely-read papers and magazines cannot seem to agree on the origin of an individual human life, (ignoring all the medical and scientific discoveries and high-tech imaging now available) these writers and pontificators seem bound by an inner compulsion they cannot disobey to declare unequivocally that they now know— beyond a reasonable doubt—how and when a dinosaur, which no living human has ever seen, nurtured its young.

I remember as a boy being fascinated by the depictions and deductions of scientist-writers in the prestigious *National Geographic*. The unearthing of a few stone artifacts and bits of bone were the backdrop for detailed discussions of stone-age life.

179

Since no photographs were available of early villages or of mastodon hunts or sabre-toothed tiger depredations, these were recreated by "artist's rendition" for the pages of *NG* and mingled with other stories and real photos of real people and animals living today. The quality of the photos from around the world and the credentials of the contributors lent credibility to the theories that invited a respectful confidence in the veracity of the conclusions.

In those early days, though, the articles often included the words "may have", "might have", "possibly", "some scientists believe" and other caveats that at least hinted to the reader that the latest discoveries would be supplanted by others and the latest theories were still—at best—theories. Today's pseudo-journalist feel no such compunction. After all, Believing is Seeing! Why introduce doubt when readers, young and old alike can be persuaded to conclude that theories are proven facts and prehistoric dates of millions of years can be verified simply by reading it in a journal of record?

Just this week, January 23, 2012 to be exact (as determined by the latest radioactive dating methods) CBC News, in its online version, published details of a recent fossil find and—in a stunning show of confidence for the conclusions of the scientists who made the discovery, spouted their theories as if proven in a court of law.
http://www.cbc.ca/news/technology/story/2012/01/23/sci-dinosaur-nesting-site.html

"A Canadian-led team of international researchers has unearthed the 190-million-year-old nesting site of the prosauropod dinosaur MASSOSPONDYLUS—predating previously known nesting grounds by 100 million years—at an excavation site in South Africa." This was the bold pronouncement of the CBC post. No reference to "some scientists say" or "according to some paleontologists"; the 190-million year date fixed for these particular eggs is stated as if it were recorded by an eyewitness scribe whose job it was to preserve these "facts" for the benefit of 21st Century mankind. Everyone knows (at least they used to know) that there are differences of opinion about the accuracy of various fossil-dating techniques. To make a categorical statement about an event presumed to have taken place 190 million years ago is to pretend that all scientists agree. That is to substitute theory for fact. It is unacceptable in a court of law and it is unacceptable in the pages of a supposed non-biased publication.

Now I want to give due credit to the amazing work of these bone-diggers. After seeing the photographic evidence I am absolutely convinced that they have made an interesting and an important find. Those are facts and I was happy to learn a little bit more about the amazing world in which we live and some of the amazing creatures that once walked upon it. But please! Every thinking reader knows that the intent of declaring unknowable and exceedingly large time frames to be facts is to try to make our universe more compatible to Darwin's theories and our populace more willing to place its trust in unthinking evolution and random chance. To mix facts and fancy in a "scientific" story is to use propaganda tactics and to insult the intelligence of readers. It also insults the intelligence of the Intelligent Designer, the only One who knows when the mysterious *Massospondylus* actually laid its eggs.

People have strong feelings about the origins of the universe, the origins of life and the origins of man. The effort to induce people to subscribe to one's pet theory by padding a few discoveries with a lot of speculation and calling it "science" is, at best, misguided and, at worst, devious. CBC, *National Geographic*, the *New York*

Times, the Knowledge Network, etc. should know better than that. "All we want are the facts".

January 27, 2012

Media: Traction, Subtraction and Retraction

When following a news story, it's good to go to the experts who can weigh in for accuracy. Thus, when 19,600 prolife marchers converge on Ottawa, any self-respecting news agency would certainly go to a math expert—say the RCMP—to get an accurate count. Their rough guess: 10,000. That's a good scientific model to follow. I suspect that if the RCMP had failed in their duty, another "unbiased" observer could have been dug up to give an opinion. "Then they suborned witnesses..." comes to mind...

Let's look on the bright side; with close to 20,000 marchers declaring their support for the protection of innocent human life, at least the media couldn't actually pretend there was nothing happening. They were forced to mention the event, even adding this unusual caveat, that the march "shut down traffic". So, besides interfering with "a woman's right to choose" pro-lifers can now be known as a group that routinely interferes with Ottawa traffic. If only the RCMP and the news media were as concerned with other types of traffic, like the "graphic traffic" in porn, drugs and bodies. But hey! I guess when newswatchers the world over are relying on you for "accurate counts" of peaceful marchers, some other responsibilities may suffer.

Meanwhile, the media wars across the globe seem intent not only to record but to form public opinion on all manner of topics. And there is no dearth of topics.

The Canadian public is forced—with the family of Tori Stafford—to relive the grisly chain of events surrounding her death and even to take sides on the proper administration of justice. The annual deaths of more than 100,000 equally innocent young lives are not mentioned by the same team of "thorough" reporters.

183

The selfish demands of rioters in Montreal and their callous disregard for the rights of their fellow-citizens (such as in the actual, as opposed to the imagined, shutting down of the subway system by smoke bombers, violence, property damage, etc.) are treated as an issue for thoughtful contemplation. After all, there are "two sides" are there not? The lowest tuition rates in the country are no excuse for those who think their extended childhood years should be absolutely free.

A side-trip to Syria where real bombs are used instead of smoke bombs reminds one that our anarchy is still in its infancy. No doubt there are legitimate issues there as well but the same callous disregard for innocent bystanders becomes a licence to kill if not restrained by public opinion, honest journalism and an evenly-applied rule of law. Syria is no haven of democracy. It would be difficult to align oneself with either side there as violence and bloodshed have become standard fare and at any point it is difficult to know what is true, who is guilty and how a nation can recover its footing.

In Canada, with our protection of the innocent (of those already born, that is) and freedom of the press, we have no excuse for sloppy, biased journalism. Truth-telling journalists are not being shot down in our streets. They may, however, not be welcomed by those doing the hiring at CBC. Truth itself is the victim and Canadians (who are so quick to claim Access to Information) are given more opinion than fact when they turn on the news.

My congratulations to the March for Life organizers! Thank you for your accurate count. Math is supposed to be a "hard science," not a flexible discipline. The numbers are growing and the media is noticing. Keep up the good work!

May 11, 2012

Much Ado About Duffy

When people refer to the "news networks" they're being generous. They are networks but the "news" is still whatever the editors, publishers and producers want the voting public to think about. Over the past several weeks, Canadians have been tormented with endless regurgitations from the Mike Duffy trial. Those who want the Harper government to fall—including most of the admittedly left-wing media as well as the obvious parties in the best position to benefit, the Liberals and NDP—have done their best to squeeze every drop of anti-Harper sentiment from the sorry saga of Mike Duffy's allegedly fraudulent expenses and Nigel Wright's generous but unwise gesture of paying the senator's $90,000 tab. All efforts now are to expose the PM and those closest to him as participants in the scheme. At the end of the day, it's only a story if it can be proven that Mr. Harper lied to the public and an admission of that nature seems less than likely. Still, the "newshounds" keep trying.

Is there nothing else going on worth talking about? The amount of money and the depth of the scandal are really insignificant when compared with other stories that neither the media nor the leaders of the big parties want to talk about. Some of those stories implicate Mr. Harper in a much more serious way than does the Duffy-Wright affair and yet Tom and Justin and their friends in the Big Media are giving him a pass. What should the media be talking about?

Well, if the abuse of taxpayers' money is the issue, why not talk about the $6 million payment to Planned Parenthood that took place on Mr. Harper's watch? That's more than 60 times the Duffy $90,000 and it went to an organization now shown (in the States) to be guilty of dismembering live babies and selling their parts. Where's the journalistic interest in exposing that truth?

185

How about the $400,000 that went to the Toronto Gay Pride Parade? Yes, it's an old story but much more interesting than repeated questions about "who was in the room?" when Mr. Wright put forth his plan to save the Conservative Party image.

Why is no major media reporting daily on the national debt that has grown to nearly $620 billion under a Conservative government? Surely the $79 million interest payment that Canadian taxpayers shell out every single day might be a topic for further discussion?

Then there's the 2010 document "Gender Identity in Schools" that came out under Conservative Health Minister Leona Agglukaq. This document has been used by provinces like Ontario and Alberta as justification for their horrendous programs of student indoctrination regarding sexual orientation. Canada Family Action's Doug Sharpe has called on the Prime Minister and current Health Minister Rona Ambrose to make 19 amendments which would render that document less harmful but so far there has been no public response from the government . . . too busy with the Duffy fallout I suppose. Meanwhile, Canadian children are at risk from these misguided government guidelines but no major media seems to care.

More recently, Health Canada (or is it Stealth Canada?) gave its approval for the abortifacient drug RU-486 to be distributed in Canada, a drug which kills babies and has been implicated in a number of deaths of women in the US. Did Mr. Harper know this was coming out just before the election or was it bureaucrats who wanted to embarrass him? Did the Health Minister know? She should have. Where is the CBC news team on this hot story? And why is there no move on the PM's part to block this drug rollout?

Before that it was Gardasil, which the Conservative government chose to pay for, acquiescing to the sexual agenda of Planned Parenthood and others, the agenda which assumes that all young people will engage in premarital sex so therefore we should just make it safer for them . . . instead of teaching them the values of abstinence and fidelity.

Most recently, it was the early dropping of the writ which will definitely increase the election costs for taxpayers, followed immediately by the PM's assertion that it would be the parties, not the taxpayers who would be paying for it. That was a patently untrue assertion and it was made on national TV, not in some murky "backroom". The tapes are available, the math obvious. Why is the endless Duffy discussion not displaced by the revelation that the Conservative Party has created for itself an opportunity to spend an additional $25 million on the fall campaign and send taxpayers a bill for half? (The other parties could do the same, if they had the cash).

Oh, don't get me wrong. I think it's important that our PM and those who work in his office are trustworthy. If the Duffy-frenzy finally results in a confession that the PM deliberately misled the public, then it will be hard to find much sympathy for him. But right now it seems that Canada is having a bad dose of 'reality TV' which, like most fantasy entertainment, is unreal, boring and unworthy of our time. Give us something worth thinking about and something that will inform voters on the big issues.

Of course, when none of the party leaders and no major media want to discuss the killing of 100,000 babies every year or the subversion of our next generation, it's hard to get past the dreary headlines we've seen over the past couple of weeks.

The Christian Heritage Party will discuss the hard issues even if the big parties and the media don't want to. Help us put the important issues back on the front page!

August 24, 2015

This was written just after Prime Minister Harper dropped the writ for the gruelling 11-week federal election in the fall of 2015. A year before, his government had passed changes to the Elections Act which allowed parties and candidates to increase spending by 1/36 for every additional day of the campaign (normally 5 weeks). In effect, the 11-week campaign allowed parties to spend more than twice what they could have spent during a normal campaign period and the larger parties could count on being reimbursed by taxpayers for 50% of their costs. In addition, it meant staffing Elections Canada Returning Offices for more than twice the number of days. In a press scrum, following the election announcement, Mr. Harper refused to acknowledge the increased cost to taxpayers. The 11-week campaign was a flop and the Liberals won a strong majority.

https://us5.campaign-archive.com/?u=2509f1b59d27f8337d34126d3&id=c505b83230&e=761ac5b351

"The Current" Holocaust Deniers

On a recent CBC podcast of "The Current" with Anna Maria Tremonti, I listened to her rabid attack on home-schoolers, followed by a CBC-produced "skit" that further exposed this identifiable group to hatred and contempt.

Ms. Tremonti was conducting "interviews" (heavily weighted with her own bias) around Alberta's contentious inclusion of Human Rights legislation in its approach to home-schooling in the province.

As she interrogated Paul Farris, head of the Home School Legal Defense Association, she repeatedly pressed him to specify what subjects could be negatively impacted by the application of Alberta's Human Rights Act in a home-schooling setting. She was not satisfied with his response that it could be "anything". No doubt, hoping to force him to say something negative about homosexuality or other sexual orientation issues, she kept up the attack until she heard the word "history" which suddenly invigorated her probing. Over the course of the interview and bringing in a couple of other voices decidedly unfriendly to home-schoolers, she attempted to connect today's home-schoolers and their possible approach to history with Alberta's much-ballyhooed Jim Keegstra (a public-school teacher in the '80s who is said to have taught his students that the Holocaust was a myth).

In this bait-and-switch, Ms. Tremonti exposed her narrow bias and selective interpretation of "human rights". She asserted, for instance, that the teaching of history has to do with hard facts, not opinion. Which facts? And by whose judgment are facts established beyond the scope of opinion? What about historical facts like the names of the first man and first woman in the human race? What about the Exodus of over three million

Israelites from their slave-holding adopted home of Egypt? What about the death and resurrection of Jesus the Christ 2,000 years ago? Are these things even talked about in the public school system or are students in that system being given a sterilized version of history, devoid of some of history's most poignant facts? How about recent history?

How about the ongoing Holocaust of Canadian babies through taxpayer-funded abortion? After all, three and a half million (probably more) have died in Canada in the last 40 years. Although the controllers of information (like the CBC) are trying their best to hide these facts and figures from Canadians, these are still facts that can be proven today. If public schools will not teach high school students the facts of life and death in Canada today, should not parents at least have the right to do so in their own homes? What about the numbers and the significance of prolife protestors gathered in Ottawa each year? CBC has historically tried to ignore these types of events or to spin them out of significance but home-schooling parents certainly have a right to tell their kids the truth about history, even including current events.

In attempting to link home-schoolers to Holocaust-deniers, Ms. Tremonti needs to be sure that she and her CBC colleagues aren't modern-day Holocaust-deniers themselves.

What about the fact that practicing homosexual men have a lifespan 20 years shorter than that of heterosexuals? That's a fact not taught in public high school and a fact that does not support the current popular theory that homosexuality is a benign lifestyle choice. Would Ms. Tremonti prefer that home-schooling parents not be allowed to disclose this provable fact to malleable minds?

What about Jesus' claim that He is "the Way, the Truth and the Life", and that "no man can come to the Father" except through Him? Christians regard this as a fact but it doesn't quite fit with the humanist, multicultural idea that there are "many paths to truth".

Ms. Tremonti returned several times to attacking home-schoolers' rights to teach their own children by referring to the small percentage of the population they represent. She asked Jacquie Hansen, VP of the Canadian School Boards Association, "Doesn't it bother you that a group representing only 1.3% of the population could impact legislation?" To her credit, Jacquie Hansen stood up for "diversity" in the broadest sense—that Albertan parents should be allowed to hold opinions and pass them on to their children, even if those ideas are not shared by a majority of Albertans. In fact, she defended (very well) parental rights, correctly declaring parents to be the "first educators" of their children.

I wonder if Ms. Tremonti has ever used the same logic (about the majority in society being imposed upon by the minority) when comparing the lopsided results of lobbying done by the small percentage of homosexuals and lesbians in Canada? . . . or the infinitesimal percentage of the general population represented by transgendered people? Those claiming this identity are now pressing for special rights that would trump the privacy and security of women and girls in public washrooms, changerooms and shower facilitie. Has Ms. Tremonti ever complained that the aggressive advocacy of this minority group could negatively and unfairly impact the lives of the vast majority of heterosexual Canadians?

At the end of the interviews, the ebullient (does that word come from the same root as "bullying"?) Ms. Tremonti cut off the

191

closing comments of Jacquie Hansen but then informed the podcast listeners that they were in for a "final word" on the question of home-schooling. Then at taxpayers' expense, we are subjected to a very rude fictional satire of an imaginary home school. The home-schooling parent/teacher is made to look stupid, angry, frustrated, incompetent, mentally-abusive and immoral. Her teenage son is portrayed as bored, disrespectful and doomed to failure in life unless he can escape the prison of home school. This segment is so arrogant, rude and unfair that in a just society, CBC should be making public apologies to all home-schoolers and offering the public some real facts about the high success rates of home-schoolers, their academic achievements (statistically speaking), their maturity levels, social adjustment, creativity and entrepreneurship, etc. However, we can't call Canada a "just society" while it allows the killing of 100,000 innocent human beings every year nor can we expect fair treatment from the self-appointed social engineers at CBC.

I just ask readers to do their own fact-checking. CBC has long functioned as a thermostat rather than as a thermometer and interviews like this one are not intended to inform but to influence. Congratulations to the parents of Alberta who have won a rare victory and "Thank you!" to the Alberta government which has made a wise and timely concession to justice, common sense and the God-given role of parents. Shame on CBC for their nasty attempt to find fault with those who have not accepted them as the sole arbiters of truth.

November 26, 2012

Partisan Politics and Electoral Issues

In great conflicts, each side claims to be doing the will of God. Both may be . . . but one must be wrong, for God cannot be both for and against the same thing at the same time.

Abraham Lincoln

I'm more concerned about Right and Wrong than about Right and Left.

Rod Taylor

A Little White Lie

When the Story broke that Bev Oda had inserted "one little word" into a document in order to justify the denial of $7 million of government funds (read "taxpayers' money") to Kairos, the predictable outcry from the Opposition calling for her head on a platter was played out against a backdrop of denial and apparent disinterest on the government side.

Of course, the question of whether Canadian taxpayers should be funding Kairos (or other charities) is not the issue. The salient point is whether Ms. Oda deliberately deceived the House and if so, the significance of that deception.

Other deceptions—not only of the House, but of the entire tax-paying and vote-casting public—have taken place in recent memory. (That is, if anyone remembers and if those deceptions have not been expunged from recorded history.) In 2008, during the illegal federal election, our Prime Minister assured the public that the Conservative government had no intention of running a deficit. That changed abruptly the day after ballots were cast.

When same-sex marriage was being discussed and ultimately passed by the House (which had promised in 1999 to NOT EVER change the definition of marriage) the concern that the religious and conscientious objections of citizens who still believe in marriage according to the original design was brushed off with blithe assurances that religious exemptions would be protected. Last year, court rulings violating the religious and conscientious objections of Saskatchewan's marriage commissioners were nearly ignored by all but a few brave MPs. Where was Mr. Layton's passionate commitment to accuracy in that regard?

There is a scandalous departure in Ottawa from anything resembling principles. The Bible extols the virtue of a person who "swears to his own hurt and does not change". In other words, a man (or woman) should keep his (or her) word and stand by it, even when the result of that faithfulness means some kind of loss (finances, popularity or promotion).

Around the world, there are cultures which put less stock than we do on truthfulness and honesty. One well-known tribe in Papua New Guinea traditionally held in special honour those who had successfully made friends with their enemies, deceiving them into careless trust which would suddenly end with shocked surprise and a cannibalistic feast. When they heard the story of Judas' betrayal of Jesus, they initially presumed Judas to be the hero for his successful deception of a close friend. Likewise, Islam allows the use of "takiyya"(the telling of untruths to infidels) if it seems to benefit the advance of Islam. In the West, under the teachings of Judeo-Christian foundational values, most of us believe that truthfulness is always a virtue and lying is always a sin. The myth of the "little white lie" is tolerated in casual banter but not really accepted in serious searches for the truth. Under oath, in a court of law, witnesses are expected not only to tell the truth but "the whole truth"—a recognition that partial truth meant to mislead is nearly the same as lying. Not so under Islam, nor apparently under the situational ethics of the type of partisan politics now being practiced in Ottawa.

Current examples of deliberate deception in the political realm are much more numerous than those of outright lies. The Prime Minister wishes to be known as a family man and defender of families. He also wants to be seen as a tolerant non-fundamentalist. Thus he can win favour by keeping abortion out of foreign health care initiatives on the one hand while voting against Roxanne's Law on the other. Thus he can dribble out funding for Gay Pride through a department minister while personally voting against Bill C-389 "the Bathroom Bill". The fact that no resistance was offered to this shameful bill in committee, the fact that two hand-picked lieutenants (John Baird and Lawrence Cannon) and four other Conservatives voted for it is hoped to go unnoticed by distracted voters who say: "Well, he's doing the best he can with a minority government."

It is time that the people of Canada show our leaders what leadership means by themselves saying what they mean. When people vote, they should not send a mixed message to our mixed-message leaders. If the people of Canada want to restore traditional marriage, protect innocent human life and influence our government to eliminate the deficit, they should vote for the only party that clearly states those values as unchanging policy objectives. I speak, of course of CHP Canada.

Telling the truth ought to be more common in the House of Commons. Transparency and humility should be the attributes of those sworn to serve. It's so much easier to stick to the facts than to make up excuses. Truthfulness is its own reward and when one's actions are consistent with one's words it becomes far easier to take responsibility for those actions.

March 25, 2011

A Long Goodbye

Last Saturday the nation said a long goodbye to Jack Layton, Leader of the Official opposition and helmsman of the New Democratic Party's surprising upset in the 2011 federal election. The NDP went from small-player status in Parliament to a position of prominence. Mr. Layton's sudden announcement that he was stepping aside temporarily to deal with a new attack of cancer was eclipsed by the even more sudden news that he had died. His family, his caucus, party faithful from across the nation and indeed many Canadians joined together to honour his years of involvement in the political struggles of the nation.

The Prime Minister made the unprecedented gesture of offering a state funeral for Mr. Layton. In a matter of days, the Leader of the Official Opposition was elevated from his role as critic and scrappy (as well as politically astute) campaigner for a variety of socialistic causes to something like an icon of Canadian values and a paragon of virtue.

CBC and other news networks wasted no time in turning a gesture of respect and condolence into a pageant of triumph and near-worship of a man who—after all—was a champion of causes that many Canadians find repugnant. His unwavering support of abortion-on-demand, his insistence that same-sex coupling and other forms of sexual confusion should be celebrated and affirmed, his affinity for class-struggle as a form of social progress and his fearlessness in adding yet more entitlement options to a nation already carrying crippling debt—these were portrayed as evidence of his courage and commitment and Canadians across the country were encouraged to bask in the light of his setting sun and fight on for the changes he endorsed.

It's difficult in the days so close to his passing to speak of these things without seeming disrespectful or coarse. All of us know instinctively the propriety of honouring the dead and of treating their memory and their families with respect in their hour of loss. We were among those who prayed for his recovery from his illness and were saddened by the news of his departure. We continue to respect his passion and sacrifice for the things he believed in. But it is a tragic twist and an offensive intrusion to suppose that—out of respect for the man and his position—we must agree with the values he espoused. The left-leaning media and certainly the leadership of the NDP have taken unfair advantage of Canadians, and especially young Canadians, by placing a nearly-patriotic duty upon them for extending Jack Layton's legacy with no opportunity to review his opinions and sift them, separating the wheat from the chaff.

Jack left a letter for Canadians to read and it's not surprising that his letter should encourage all Canadians, and especially young Canadians, to press on with the goals of the NDP—both social and economic. It was a last effort, admirable in its own way, to influence society with the ideas he himself held dear. Throughout his life, he challenged assumptions and debated with those who held different views. It would be realistic to assume that if he were here today and the shoe were on the other foot—if a great leader of a party with whom he disagreed were being laid to rest—he would not therefore adopt the views of that party but would respectfully offer his condolences and then appropriately resume his efforts. We should do the same. To surrender our values out of misplaced respect does no honour to the dead but lowers the standard of greatness and transforms our beliefs from conviction to opinion. Opinions will not change the world, at least not for the better.

Let us allow Mr. Layton his place in history. He earned it. But let's not allow media manipulation to make him a martyr or an icon. The ideas worth living and dying for are the ideas that ennoble the human spirit and hold a cultural counterpoint to the dreary dungeons of yesterday's socialistic and materialistic slogans.

August 31, 2011

"Agree With Thine Adversary Quickly..."

I have always thought it unfortunate and unwise that the Opposition parties—both federally and provincially—feel compelled to oppose just about everything proposed by the government. It seems that "holding their feet to the fire" (deemed a solemn responsibility) has more attraction if it also embarrasses the ruling party and gives those in opposition a leg up in the next election. In that sense, it can be expected as par for the course that agreement will be the least likely path chosen by the opposition when new legislation is put forward or issues are raised.

Case in point, the recent deep concern for security expressed by the new Official Opposition over the heavy reliance on and implicit trust in various companies operating out of the Peoples' Republic of China which apparently have a finger—or maybe two hands—in sensitive Canadian telecommunications businesses. Although I am most frequently in opposition to the current federal Opposition (since last year's election the NDP and prior to that, the Liberals), in this case, I think they may be onto something. It only surprises me that they have suddenly taken up the cause of national security when their leanings have always been toward a "global village" with universal rules and shared access to all the planet has to offer . . . especially if it involves a new government program. But I digress. This is a topic worthy of discussion and I'm glad they brought it up. In short, I agree with them. There, I said it.

I also wanted to specifically mention two other policy positions with which I do agree: one item from the Finance Minister and one from the Official Opposition. I often disagree with either or both and so it is important that I acknowledge their acumen when they get something right.

Firstly, where I agree with Finance Minister Jim Flaherty: in the course of defending the government's horrible, omnivorous omnibus bill—the budget implementation bill—Mr. Flaherty received a lot of flak for his assertion that those currently unemployed should not be so fussy when looking for work. In other words, in order to legitimately claim EI benefits, he said that job-seekers should have to show that they really were unable to find paying work; they would no longer be able to claim that a lower-paying job was not suitable for them or was outside their skill and interest. I think the intent of his statement was to encourage people on EI to get busy, to be willing to take opportunities that come their way and to do all within their power to be a net contributor to the system.

I agree with that sentiment. I have been "between jobs" more than once. I have taken work outside my career goals. I have moved to new locations to find work and have sometimes done work that I didn't really like much. I think I have benefited from this varied work experience; eventually I was able to find better jobs at better pay and I was none the worse for wear. But I have seen other workers, even friends of mine, just sit home and wait for their EI to run out, rather than hit the streets looking for work. That's just plain wrong. EI is designed to cushion the blow of an unexpected layoff. It should not be considered as an extension of benefits owed to an employee based on his or her past efforts. As low as the EI payout is, it is far above the corresponding investment from the employee, if taken to its leveraged limit (32 weeks of benefits for 10 weeks of work.)

What Mr. Flaherty actually said is, "There's no such thing as a bad job. The only bad job is not having a job." This was a good snappy quote but not quite accurate. There are bad jobs. There are bad employers. There are back-breaking jobs not suited to every potential employee. There are jobs with inadequate safety and environmental precautions. Taken to the extreme, Germany once considered forcing unemployed women receiving EI to accept jobs in the "sex trade". Now that's a bad job. It also runs contrary to the notion of "choice". But in general, a car salesman could pump gas if he had to. A lumber grader could stock shelves in a grocery store until a better job came along. I've even heard of a doctor picking fruit . . . far below his pay grade and a waste of his skills and training. However, the basic idea that people should expect to work for their bread and butter and not to coast on EI is sound and will produce better citizens.

Now as to agreeing with the Official Opposition: the NDP, with its socialist philosophy and its tendency to reject any of the moral values I hold dear, is not often the champion of causes with which I agree. However, the NDP has found a soft spot in the Conservative's rigid armour and I agree with them that their point is valid. It's this: they object to the bundling together of a myriad of controversial items, including environmental issues, Old Age Security changes and policies and procedures around Employment Insurance into a huge omnibus bill. I share their concern. I have not had the time (nor have the MPs) to read this 420-page bill and respond to it intelligently. However, it seems a brutal method of ensuring passage of potentially controversial laws by sheltering them under a budget implementation bill. It presumes that all Conservative MPs will vote for the assorted items—whether or not they agree—because, being a budget bill, it becomes a confidence measure. If it fails to pass, the government could be toppled. Mr. Harper is gambling that none of his MPs will risk their political careers to vote against this bill, even if they do not support all of its provisions. I agree with the NDP, the Greens and the Liberals for asking that the bill be broken up, even if I would not necessarily agree with their motives.

Now, if all the parties would just work together to protect innocent human life in the womb, to restore traditional marriage and to eliminate the gold-plated MP pension plans, I would agree with them on those things as well. If not, I'll just have to hold their feet to the fire . . .

May 24, 2012

Most of the foregoing article speaks for itself. Essentially, I believe MPs and MLAs should work together where they can, agree where they can and accomplish all the good they can, "no matter who gets the credit".

C-16: Where's the Loyal Opposition?

Justin Trudeau and his Liberal cabinet continue to ram through their social agenda, leaving broken fragments of Canada's cultural heritage and democratic traditions in its wake. C-16 is Justice Minister Jody Wilson-Raybould's sledgehammer approach to ending freedom of religion as we've known it and implementing the Liberal gender agenda in churches, schools and other institutions. That bill is being imposed on Canadians with little chance to debate and no time for reflection.

Something as significant as C-16 should be openly discussed and members of the public should be encouraged to comment. There are many knowledgeable citizens, family advocacy groups and faith-based organizations with both interest and insight into the implications of this bill but their input has been rejected. C-16 passed 2nd Reading with little resistance and was returned with no amendments to the House by the Standing Committee on Justice and Human Rights. That committee held no public hearings and the concerned citizens' groups mentioned above have so far been denied the opportunity to voice their concerns.

One group, however, that should be putting the brakes on the Trudeau policy agenda is the Conservative caucus, still known as "Her Majesty's Loyal Opposition". To whom or to what are they loyal and what do they understand to be the role of the Opposition? It would be wonderful to imagine that all parties in the House were truly working together for the good of the nation but there is a time for the Opposition to actually oppose and not give tacit assent to an out-of-control government agenda. It seems that the Conservative Caucus under Rona Ambrose are so anxious to appear politically correct on some issues that they have forgotten their responsibility to protect the rights and freedoms of their fellow Canadians.

There are, of course, some notable exceptions like the thoughtfully-articulate MP Harold Albrecht, outspoken socially conservative MP Cathay Wagantall and Conservative leadership hopeful Brad Trost who have made known their principled opposition to C-16. Notably missing in action have been Interim Leader Rona Ambrose and Conservative Justice Critic Rob Nicholson. They've been silent while the free-speech rights of Canadians are being bartered away.

C-16—if it passes, as seems imminently probable—will add further fuel to the fire in the degenerating dialogue on gender fluidity. In fact, it will be used to end dialogue and replace it with a monotonous monologue praising the spread of (and enthusiasm for) gender confusion. We can assume that churches will be pressed to change their teachings, their protocols and their hiring standards. The reading of the scriptures which reject homosexual practices will no doubt be challenged as "hate speech". The use of single-gender washrooms by those of the opposite biological gender will be proposed, not only in government-owned buildings but in buildings belonging to churches and businesses. The rights of parents to train their children according to their own deeply-held moral beliefs and traditions will be attacked again and again and schoolteachers will be forced to parrot politically-correct dogma to thousands of trusting, wide-eyed children who have come to school seeking to learn practical knowledge and skills.

C-16 is only one item in a growing list of government initiatives which should be causing alarm to every freedom-loving Canadian. It's one that should have had a stronger response from the Conservative Party leadership. By abandoning the principles they once held dear, they've left a vacuum in the House that must be filled if our democracy is to survive. From the trenches in the culture wars, we call on all MPs who value freedom and democracy to rise up and resist the suffocating coils of political correctness. Your honour demands it.

The Christian Heritage Party continues to offer voters a principled choice for life, family and freedom. We will not be silenced by any cowardly restrictions on free speech imposed by a cabal of small-minded politicians drunk with power.

November 14, 2016

Bill C-16, adding "gender identity and gender expression" to Canada's Human Rights Code was tabled by Justice Minister Jody Wilson-Raybould on May 17, 2016 and became law June 19, 2017. This bill replaced C-279 (the so-called "bathroom bill") which had failed under the previous government. Critics continue to be concerned that this legislation poses threats to the safety and security of women and girls as it could be interpreted in such a way as to allow unfettered access by males to washrooms, change rooms and shower facilities heretofore designated exclusively for biological females.

PMO Tells Cabinet How to Vote—(Again!)

Last Wednesday, the House of Commons was the scene of another national tragedy, as the PM's highest-ranking ministers submitted to being ordered about, either directly by the PM or by his "boys in short pants" as the media calls them—the staffers who are charged with ensuring a united front on difficult social issues. One would like to think that ministers of federal departments were selected for their wisdom, their commitment to principles and for the creative thinking that they bring to the table on important issues. How humiliating for them and how embarrassing for the public to learn that the PM does not trust those whom he has selected for these responsible positions to make responsible decisions on behalf of their constituents and citizens across the country.

Bill C-560—the Equal Shared Parenting Bill introduced by MP Maurice Vellacott—would have fundamentally transformed the way courts handle parental involvement with their children in the unfortunate event of divorce. All Canadians recognise the emotional challenges for children when their parents separate. Most Canadians recognise the unfair presumptions made in many divorce settlements where one parent (usually the mother) is granted "custody" while the other parent is relegated to the status of a dependant, needing to coax, persuade and otherwise convince his or her former spouse that he or she deserves some meaningful time with the children they brought into the world together and for whom they have a shared responsibility.

Not everyone will agree (of course) that equal shared parenting is the best model. That's why votes are taken in the House. However, it's a remarkable bit of mathematical happenstance that 33 members of the Harper Cabinet voted against the bill and none voted for it. Six, including Mr Harper himself, did not vote and presumably were absent. Among other Conservatives, including our reliable pro-life friends, most supported the bill. Most of the 80 MPs who supported the bill were Conservatives. The NDP and the Liberals voted against it en masse. Elizabeth May supported the bill. It is obvious that political calculations that go far beyond the merits or shortcomings of this proposed legislation have prompted the leaders of the largest three parties to pressure their members—in this case the Conservative Cabinet—to defeat this legislation.

I certainly have been impressed with the thought and care that Mr. Vellacott put into this bill, with the express purpose of improving the lives of children who are caught in the emotional pressure of divorce and their longing for and need of strong relationships with both parents. The initiative he has taken will no doubt be revisited at some future time when—hopefully—a concern for children will outweigh partisan posturing.

It puzzles me that the Prime Minister or those in his inner circle would feel so threatened by this sincere attempt to improve the outcomes for Canadian children. One can't help feeling that political expediency has once again trumped the principles of "democratic parliamentary institutions" which the Conservative Party says it adheres to. On some other issues the PM has allowed his cabinet to vote according to conscience. Why did he feel that Equal Shared Parenting was an issue on which his hand-picked ministers could not be trusted?

We need a Parliament more devoted to strengthening families and less shackled by partisan expediency.

June 2, 2014

C-560, MP Maurice Vellacott's Private Member's bill (Equal Shared Parenting) was introduced on December 6, 2013. It was defeated at 2ⁿᵈ Reading, May 28, 2014.

The text of the bill may be found here:
https://equalparenting.wordpress.com/2014/03/21/21/

Can Any Good Thing Come Out of Ottawa?

Cynicism did not start in this century nor in this country. Rhetorical sarcasm has been recorded through the ages and political satire extends back through the rise and fall of many empires and dynasties. Even in the religious realm, doubt has been often more evident than faith. When Jesus launched his ministry, Nathanael's first response was, "Can any good thing come out of Nazareth?" The implied answer to his own question was "No". The correct answer, soon proven by the Lord himself was an emphatic "Yes!" Of course, Jesus was actually born in Bethlehem so it might be that Nathanael's question should have been, "Can any good thing come through Nazareth?"

Twenty centuries later, it would be tempting to surmise, based on recent history, that not much that is pure and noble and undefiled comes out of the political machinery that is Ottawa today. Roxanne's Law—designed to protect vulnerable pregnant women from harassment, coercion and intimidation—is defeated and the smug defenders of the abortion industry smile and yawn. Bill C-389, one of several iterations of the "Bathroom Bill" passes and the homosexualist lobby groups go back to the drawing board to dream up their next intrusion on decent society. Where is the fight? Where is the verve? Where is the passion for children and families and vulnerable youth? It lies beaten and bruised somewhere on the campaign trail, beaten and left for dead by the latest media spin, doctored opinion polls, partisan positioning and naked political ambition.

Two private members' bills come to the floor of the house: one brought by government backbencher Rod Bruinooge, and one by soon-retiring homosexual NDP MP, Bill Siksay. The one is to defend innocent life and personal choice, the other to promote transsexual and transgendered acceptance in society, even to the point where "male" and "female", "man" and "woman" cease to have real meaning for the vulnerable generation now being raised in Canada. The response of the Prime Minister to these two bills was revealing.

Essentially, the failure of the Conservative government to rise up and give moral leadership and direction on these bills is a failure to trust the Canadian voters with the choice between good and evil. After all, if voters failed to recognize moral leadership, then all might be lost. The Rt. Hon. Stephen Harper's ongoing bid to form a majority government might collapse. No, it seemed better to him and to half of his trusted cabinet to vote against Rod Bruinooge's bill and make a clear statement that no legislation regarding abortion will ever be considered. Send a message to junior backbenchers that they will receive no support or backing on anything that requires the PM to risk his coveted majority.

As for the opposition MP and his bid to normalize every abnormal sexual appetite and lifestyle? Well these things come to try us. Lay low; don't say too much. Maybe this thing will go away. If we don't make a big fuss over it, perhaps the middle-of-the-road voters out there will give us credit for being open-minded. Those who support the hyper-sexualization of our youth, perhaps they will see that we're not that narrow after all. And in the end, forced to a vote, if Stephen and most of the caucus vote against it, we can at least tell our socially conservative voters and members that "we tried". That seems like the game plan to an outside observer. Bill C-389 received almost no resistance at Second Reading; it flew through committee in 15 minutes with no meaningful discussion. In a motion of concurrence after committee, five Conservatives voted for it, and ten Conservatives did not bother to vote, including the PM. At Third Reading, Mr. Harper was present and dutifully voted against it but still six of his caucus, including high-profile John Baird (hand-picked by

Harper for his tenacity as well as his pugnacity) and Foreign Affairs Minister Lawrence Cannon voted for it. Eleven caucus members did not vote. The bill passed by eight votes.

So can any good thing come out of Ottawa? Massive deficit spending, government sponsored Gardasil vaccinations of young girls, intrusions into the health food and natural supplements industry, more taxpayer-subsidized junk mail, this time from the Senate, partisan bickering and blowhard egotism on steroids . . . the list of complaints goes on. Of course, if we depend on mankind, whether in Ottawa or in the business world to produce good fruit, compassionate and selfless service, etc., we will be waiting a long time. But can any good thing come through Ottawa? Can our elected representatives (and the non-elected ones) be trained, encouraged and challenged to do the right thing and for the right reason? Can God, the one who raises up governments, who gives the throne to whom He will and who holds the nations in the palm of His hand . . . can that same God bring good out of and through our human institutions, even the political establishment in Ottawa? The answer to that is a resounding "Yes!"

The temptation to cynicism is strong but the One who made the universe is stronger. His promise is: "If My people, called by My name will humble themselves and pray and seek my face and turn from their wicked ways, then I will hear from heaven and will forgive their sins and heal their land". II Chron. 7:14

Don't give in to apathy. Get on your knees and fight.

March 25, 2011

Bill C-510, Roxanne's Law, An Act to Prevent Coercion of Pregnant Women to Abort, was introduced by MP Rod Bruinooge

212

on March 14, 2010. This bill was named after Roxanne, a young woman who was killed by her boyfriend because she refused to abort their baby. Every member of Parliament should have supported this bill. Certainly, Prime Minister Harper and the Conservative caucus should have. It was defeated at 2nd Reading on December 15, 2010. Mr. Harper and 47 other "Conservative" MPs voted against it.

Bill C-389, the Bathroom Bill, was—in an unusual move— reinstated from the previous session and passed 3rd Reading in the House on February 9, 2011. It did not make it through the Senate before the Government was dissolved for the Spring Election of 2011. However, a new bill took its place, Bill C-279. It ultimately was replaced by Bill C-16, which was passed into law under the current Liberal Government.

Candidates, Campaigns and Censorship

As I write this article (June 2014), our two by-election candidates are beginning their final week of campaigning before the June 30 vote. David J. Reimer, CHP's Interim Leader, is our candidate in the Macleod riding in Alberta. Linda Gibbons, well-known pro-life activist, is running in Trinity-Spadina.

Once again, a CHP candidate has had unfair treatment by local debate organizers and we need to call them out for violating the spirit of the Canadian electoral process. The only "all-candidates" forum (that we know of) scheduled for Trinity-Spadina was designed—by the organisers—to exclude our candidate. In other words, it was a "some-candidates" forum. Where this kind of shameless manipulation of voters takes place, CHP members (and others) must continue to press the organizers to understand that such bias and discrimination is contrary to the very system of democracy that all-candidate forums, the orderly registration of voters and the privilege of casting a ballot are meant to protect.

There are at least <u>four reasons</u> why organisers of all-candidate forums should NOT be able to include some candidates and exclude others:

1. It is obviously false advertising AND misleading to voters to claim one is hosting an "all-candidates" meeting when some legitimate candidates, registered with Elections Canada are not included.

2. It sets an arbitrary standard of credibility, placing the current better-known parties and candidates on a pedestal (call it an "old boys' club") and giving the impression to voters that the less well-known candidates or parties have nothing to contribute to the public discussion.

3. By presuming beforehand which candidates may be more likely to win or which candidates the audience may be more likely to vote for or which parties should be getting more press, the organisers are ignoring the idea that another candidate may have information or policies to present which the audience has not yet had a chance to consider.

4. Most importantly, creating an opportunity for only a few chosen candidates to communicate directly with voters provides material support to those candidates who are included. Under Elections Canada regulations, organisations (businesses, unions, etc.) are not allowed to contribute to the campaign of any candidate, either cash or gifts in kind. But that is exactly what they are doing by offering this biased coverage. Voters who do not hear from the excluded candidates are more likely to vote for one of the candidates on the stage. This amounts to a campaign contribution in kind and should be made illegal. It is already immoral. It is censorship of the worst kind, a censorship of ideas.

June 23, 2014

The fight for fair and equal treatment for CHP candidates and the candidates of other small parties is ongoing. Parliament has failed to address this issue because MPs who are already elected and the parties they represent are basically happy with the status quo. The well-established parties now represented in the House receive massive amounts of taxpayer funding, free advertisement (regular news coverage), their leaders are invited to participate in nationally-televised debates and in many places, their local candidates are more likely to be given front-page news coverage and a place in local debate forums. The CHP will continue to press for equal treatment for all parties during campaigns.

Dust-up in the House

Tempers flared this week in the House over procedural wrangling on the legitimacy of the Omnibus budget and the majority Government's apparent deafness to any complaints from the Opposition about the process. There were unsuccessful attempts to enter the Chamber by a gathering of First Nations chiefs, indicating their desire to be consulted; there were thinly-veiled threats of lawsuits and court appearances uttered by NDP House Leader, Nathan Cullen. There were uttered but unrecorded angry words (apparently, including "unparliamentary language", otherwise known as "swearing") directed at Cullen by Government House Leader, Peter Van Loan, and a final friendly arm on the shoulder by Defence Minister Peter Mackay, as he cajoled his colleague, the worked-up Mr. Van Loan and led him away to his own corner to cool off.

Although no punches were thrown, the theatrics of this week and the seething testiness of the combatants underscored the deep-seated unease with the current political situation, the non-conciliatory nature of today's partisan politics and indeed the triumph of style over substance. Perhaps it's because Canadians are feeling deprived of their weekly spectator sport and the bloodletting normally associated with nasty outbursts in the NHL. Perhaps it's the constant bombardment of gratuitous violence in the useless TV programming misnamed "entertainment". Perhaps it's the increasing rudeness of participants at all levels of political commentary. Whatever it is, Canadians stop what they're doing and tune in fast when they see grown men about to go at it.

The fact that MPs in the House have different worldviews driving their perceptions of events, the way they describe reality and the solutions they propose for correcting injustice is nothing new. The fact that throughout the centuries, frustrated men have resorted to uncontrolled outbursts and sometimes physical violence is well known to all. Some folks cling to the belief that modern man has progressed in self-discipline to the point where rudeness and rancorous name-calling have given place to thoughtful, respectful discourse but the evidence is lacking. Some people in public life can control themselves some of the time when the rewards for doing so are great enough or the costs of failing to maintain their decorum are high enough. The courts of our land, our prisons, our hockey penalty boxes are full of those for whom the release of emotion seemed—for a small moment—a greater benefit than could be gained by "putting a lid on it".

Losers often fall into the trap of shooting off their mouths in the pain of their losses. All of us who have ever lost a contest or an argument or an opportunity can understand that natural reaction, although most of us have been urged to be "good sports" even in the disappointment of loss. Mr. Van Loan made an error even more tragic. In the moment of victory for his party (based on the passage of the cumbersome Government budget, with all its potentially significant flaws, with its myriad of critics, with the variety of failed procedural tactics designed to stall it) Mr. Van Loan—to all intents the victor—crossed the floor and exposed himself to ridicule and censure by berating his Opposition counterpart, even dropping his verbal gloves and the aura of respectability normally accorded to all MPs.

On the football field, an undisciplined player who can't keep his hands to himself and gets penalized for "holding", "pass interference" or "unnecessary roughness" can lose needed yardage, nullify the great work of a fellow teammate and sometimes cost his team the game. By yielding to his passion Mr. Van Loan has turned over the ball to the Opposition and given them the moral high ground. They don't deserve it but they will milk it. Mr. Van Loan will go back to school where he will learn how to count to ten.

It turns out that the best government is still self-government. An ancient proverb from King Solomon says: "He who is slow to become angry is better than a mighty warrior; he who rules his own spirit is stronger than one who captures a city". Prov. 16:32

Dec 6, 2012

The incident referred to occurred on December 5, 2012. It has since been overshadowed by "Elbowgate", an indiscretion of our current Prime Minister, the Rt. Hon. Justin Trudeau. The beat goes on . . .

Gambling with Other People's Money

Casino Canada is open! As MPs take a break from the drudgery of rancorous partisan debates and otherwise serving their constituents in numerous selfless ways to the much more exciting task of trying to hold onto their seats, their leaders are busy enlarging their carbon footprints and raising the stakes in a media/entertainment docudrama about so-called "democracy".

Jet stops, photo-ops and hip-hops. Spending meaningful time in numerous small towns. Watching the polls. Adjusting the message. Adjusting the tie. Feeling people's pain. Spending people's money.

Every time the big bus pulls up to the one-armed bandit called a fuel pump, there are two major tax wheels spinning—one is the taxes already levied on gasoline and diesel and the other is the steady flow of taxpayers' money into the campaigns of the BIG FIVE. Yes, that's true. Even though the Greens are hopping mad (as they should be) about Elizabeth May being excluded from the biggest media debates, they at least can comfort themselves that they've been given a little gambling money to keep them occupied while Papa Steve and Uncle Iggy spend time watching the Big Wheel spin on the inside. How many times can you pull the lever with $1.8 million burning a hole in your pocket? (that's the amount the Green Party received from taxpayers last year). Between the Bloc, the Conservatives, the Liberals, the NDP and the Greens, there's about $30 million per year of our hard-earned bucks going into the slots. In an election year double that . . . double or nothing!

Every day the stakes go up. A billion here, a few hundred million there. As one American politician once said, "A billion here, a billion there...pretty soon it adds up to some real money!" Yes, the students, the infrastructure, the environment, etc., all targets of the buoyant generosity displayed by the promising leaders as they warm to the task. A round for everyone. Hurrah! This one's on the House! And where does the House get its money? That's a question too deep for voters at a time like this...

Of course, none of these wild and extravagant promises matter much because the parties that lose can't make it happen and the party that wins can only do so by placating the parties that lose. But the real thrill is the gambling itself. At the end of the day, when the big tour buses are parked, when the signs and confetti are cleaned up and the new government presents itself—nearly sober!—to the Canadian voters, all parties can say they've had a great time on the trail. The biggest loser is the Canadian taxpayer who seems to have been rolled in the alley.

Did I mention that the Christian Heritage Party of Canada, the 6th largest party on the ballot, has never received a dime of taxpayers' money? Our party is held up by the prayers and sacrifices of our members. We know the stakes are high—much higher than anything that can be measured in dollars. Nothing less than the future of our nation and the type of society our grandchildren will inherit. For us this race is not a gamble but a sure bet! We know that representing Christian values will always result in blessing— a blessing with no morning-after regrets.

March 31, 2011

After a federal election, current laws provide political parties which receive over 10% of the popular vote a cash payout from the public purse (taxpayers' money) an amount equal to 50% of their expenditures during the past election. After the 2015 election, the Conservative and Liberal parties each received over $20 million into their warchests. On top of this, each candidate *who received at least 10% of the vote receives (back into campaign coffers) 60% of his or her campaign expenditures. This is a huge amount of money and gives the big parties an enormous advantage. It also means that people like me are forced to support—with our taxes—the huge political parties and their policies with which we disagree. It's criminal. One more reason we do what we do.*

Mulcair Attacks Christians as Un-Canadian

From the giddy spires of the NDP Leader's chair, Mr. Thomas Mulcair has again pontificated against the core values of many Canadians, calling them "un-Canadian". His predictable partisan outburst was in response to the revelation that a Christian organization performing humanitarian relief work in Uganda was receiving government funding. Crossroads Communications is busy drilling wells and improving hygiene in Uganda and along with the generous support of many Christian donors, also received $544,813 from CIDA for this work. The newspeg to which Mr. Mulcair's angry accusations were attributed was that this same Crossroads organization had posted on its website its biblically-based position that homosexuality is a "sin" and a "perversion".

Now I am not a big proponent of the taxpayer-funding of charitable organizations, other than through tax breaks to donors. In general, government is a clumsy vehicle for providing relief. The layers of government and the number of bureaucrats required to take the unwilling contributions of taxpayers and transform them into expensive photo-ops for generous handouts administered by those who have been appointed to Cabinet is a little tough to take. As has been famously said: "the problem with socialism is that eventually you run out of other peoples' money" (Margaret Thatcher).

However, we live in a day and age when governments are expected to chip in to every worthwhile cause and many that are not so worthy. The fact that Canada is sinking rapidly into debt may have more to do with lavish MP and other government pensions, with "million-dollar lakes", with corporate bailouts, with tens of millions of dollars given out to the largest political parties and with other luxuries and vote-buying schemes than with the ½-million dollars invested in drilling wells in Uganda. But that's the one Mulcair chose to attack. And why? Because the organization responsible for helping Ugandans actually believes in the values formerly held by the early founders of the Dominion of Canada. And then he has the gall to call Christians "un-Canadian".

Maybe we should look at some other recipients of taxpayers' money. How about Planned Parenthood International which received $6 million of taxpayers' money from the hand of orange juice-sipping Bev Oda? Planned Parenthood doesn't just post comments on their website. They actually kill babies—the largest abortion provider in the world—and they make a lot of money doing it. I didn't hear Mr. Mulcair complaining about that grant, one that actually supported a baby-killing machine. Their religion is the most "intolerant" in the world. They talk about "choice" but brook no opposition. If their "values" had been shared by Canada's founders, many of us might not be here today. If their worldview—promulgated by the likes of Mr. Mulcair—attains dominance in the shifting sands of the Canadian culture wars, we will not recognize our nation in the decades fast approaching.

It's been said before: "Patriotism is the last refuge of a scoundrel". To denigrate people of faith for courageously proclaiming the principles and values of Canada's founders and baselessly accusing them of being "un-Canadian" is a shabby exercise in partisan propaganda and a lazy ruse for those too preoccupied with themselves to try to carry on an intelligent debate. I am a patriot. I love our flag, our land and our people. I love the leadership we can provide in the world if we will base our policies on the unchanging rock-solid truths derived from the Word of God. I refuse to accept the cheap slander of a political opportunist.

February 15, 2013

NDP Theatrics—A "Lost Leader" Waiting to be Found

With the help of the taxpayer-funded CBC, the NDP has been enjoying the luxury of a US-style highly-publicized leadership contest, designed to allure voters into their camp for the distant 2015 federal election. With nothing but some shifting and idolatrous memories of Jack Layton and the Quebec protest vote that launched inexperienced (and in at least one case, patently unengaged) socialist MPs on a path to a platinum-plated pension, the NDP has created—out of the mists—a pageant, a drama, an epic around the rise of "the people" to commandeer Canada's listing ship of state.

The glitz and glamour of a whole series of stage-managed debates, the mock uniqueness claimed by those orange-emblazoned nominees for party chief would have little or no connection to most Canadians were it not for the blatant support and encouragement of the CBC which dutifully foists upon unsuspecting citizens the rhetoric behind the individual claims to strategic or philosophical superiority.

The real question is not: "Which of the seven remaining leadership candidates has the most to offer the NDP?" The real question Canadians should be asking is: "What does the NDP have to offer our children and grandchildren?" The answer to that question hasn't changed for many years: "Nothing of value." Yes, the NDP is committed to the ongoing slaughter of the unborn, something they euphemistically call "choice." The NDP is committed to the further destruction of the traditional family (one man, one woman and usually children). The NDP is committed to socialist principles: the harder you work and the more you save and invest, the more the state will take from you to give to others who do not work but who sometimes (unfortunately) vote. The NDP is committed to creating new and more complex regulations and building larger and more intrusive state-funded institutions to interfere with development and industry. The NDP is committed to introducing ever more regulations and restrictions on what you may say or write and what you may or may not teach your children. The list goes on but it is really a rather boring and depressing platform.

Who would want to lead a crowd so morally confused? I would rather be a follower in a party of principles—a party of moral leadership and fiscal stability—than a leader of a party committed to destructive family policies, discredited economic theories and dictatorial edicts that undermine personal freedom. Those vying for the NDP leadership claim to faithfully represent the values of the party; if they did not, how could they expect the support of their media-manipulated members? That means more of the same: destructive policies that would not only worsen the economic prospects for future generations but would ensure that many members of "future generations" will be killed before birth.

There is only one good reason that anyone should want to run for the NDP: to get to the head of the parade and lead their misguided minions on a 180° march of policy reversals, casting off worn-out and troublesome theories and slogans. However, I doubt that any of the NDP leadership contestants intends to do that. If asked, each would indignantly and categorically deny such a plan. However, the alternative is a pathetic spectacle: seven lost leaders, each committed to leading thousands of lost followers deeper into the quicksands, quixotically claiming that victory is just ahead. The NDP has positioned itself as a party in opposition to God and his principles. What a sad platform!

"The fool has said in his heart, 'there is no God'." Psalm 14:1 God spare us the victory of fools!
March 22, 2012

PM Harper Joins the NDP

In politics, we have learned to expect surprises. We've seen a one-time NDP Premier of Ontario become the leader of the federal Liberals (oops! just before they tanked . . .) We've seen a big-name female Conservative MP recruited by the Liberals (oops again!) to shift the balance of power and we've seen a big-business lumberman elected as a Liberal, only to sit—days after the election—as a Conservative cabinet minister. But when have we seen a sitting Prime Minister in a majority government use the power of his office to attack his own backbench MP, thus strengthening the efforts of the Official Opposition in their frantic attack on logic, science and the most basic of human rights—the right to life?

No, Mr. Harper didn't cross the floor to sit with his NDP colleagues. He didn't have to. He simply announced that a Private Member's Motion put forward by one of his own Conservative caucus was "unfortunately deemed votable by an all-party parliamentary committee," and said that "I will be voting against it." If he had hoped to score any brownie points with Thomas Mulcair's NDP caucus, Mr. Harper was, no doubt, disappointed. The "New Democrats" instead complained that Mr. Harper "could have prevented the motion from being put forward" and that he should have punished his MP for presenting it.

On Thursday, April 26, 2012, MP Stephen Woodworth of Kitchener Centre opened the first hour of parliamentary debate on his Motion 312, a motion calling upon Parliament to establish a parliamentary committee to examine Canada's 400 year-old definition of a "human being", a definition that excludes even a living, breathing infant until it has emerged from the body of its mother.

This latest skirmish within the Conservative caucus and the corresponding attacks from the Opposition mark only the most recent of a dozen or more times when PM Harper has declared his resolve "not to re-open" the issue of abortion. He has stated on more than one occasion that he will resist any attempt to introduce legislation regarding abortion and that if any such legislation does come to the floor of the House "as long as I am Prime Minister, it will be defeated."

Of course, all of those brave and enduringly optimistic souls—who have laboured over the past forty years to shift the culture and to protect the unborn as well as pregnant women from the harm of abortion—know that the debate has never been closed. "Re-opening the debate" is just another bit of linguistic jingoism meant to blame serious protectors of life for upsetting the placid waters of a nation which has accepted the deliberate killing of the helpless. The fact that this gentle motion, calling only for a committee to examine the issues based on current science and medicine, has come under such scathing and relentless attack, simply shows how fearful the pro-abort MPs are of examining the facts. That includes their new comrade, PM Stephen Harper.

For years, going all the way back to the early days of the Reform Party, apologists and strategists of that party claimed that, in order to change the social order in Canada, to have a chance to restore morality, strengthen the family and reduce the number of abortions, prolifers and family advocates would have to accept compromise, "fly under the radar," earn the respect of Canadian voters, work through subtle and incremental channels to achieve results, support loyally the broad-based coalition of social and fiscal conservatives and trust that over time, (a VERY LONG time,) Canadians would democratically choose—through referenda or other grass-roots mechanisms—to protect human life in the womb. Indeed, if Canadians did not choose to protect the unborn, no blame would rest on the politicians representing them in Ottawa. It would simply reflect the triumph of the democratic process and—presto!—the will of the people, supplanting the divine right of kings, would bear any and all moral consequences of social and legal failure to defend the innocent.

In the transition from Reform to Alliance and ultimately to the Conservative Party of Canada, social conservatives were repeatedly warned not to "rock the boat." Protection for the unborn could not be party policy as that would only scare people away and the emerging Conservative Party could never help the prolife movement until they had stealthily achieved power. Once they tasted minority government, their socially-conservative supporters were humoured and cajoled with the obvious explanation that their hero, Mr. Harper could (of course) do nothing for the prolife cause until the CPC had a majority government. Voters could not afford to take any chances on voting for courageous prolife candidates or even a prolife party like the Christian Heritage Party. Mr. Harper needed a majority to tackle the thorny issue of abortion. This, in spite of Mr. Harper's many clear and unequivocal statements that he would resist ANY legislation or discussion of the abortion question.

Well, Mr. Harper has his majority. There are still CPC loyalists pathetically claiming that Mr. Harper will act when he has a majority of prolife MPs. But honest citizens must face the facts: Mr. Harper opposed the Unborn Victims of Violence Bill of his own MP, the Hon. Ken Epp; Mr. Harper opposed Roxanne's Law, the anti-coercion bill of his own MP, the Hon. Rod Bruinooge. Last year Mr. Harper's own Cabinet minister, the Hon. Bev Oda, gave $6 million to Planned Parenthood (with his apparent blessing) and now, with a majority government, Mr. Harper has called the Personhood Motion of his own wonderful MP, the

Hon. Stephen Woodworth "unfortunate" and pledged to vote against it.

When will prolife voters wake up and accept that this prime minister and his party are not prolife? Mr. Harper and those close to him have clearly distanced themselves from the prolife cause. Those brave and courageous individuals within his party who are working so hard to bring the issue of respect for human life to the floor of Parliament are doing so at their own peril. They deserve our strongest support and encouragement for they face the Official Opposition, spiritual opposition, media opposition and opposition from within their own party.

Their cause is just. It is they, and not their detractors, who will receive the plaudits of history. May their courage and determination burn ever brighter. We salute them!

In the meantime, there is only one federal political party committed to the defense of innocent human life from conception to natural death and that is the Christian Heritage Party of Canada. Help us move the debate forward.

April 30, 2012

Political Chameleons—the more things change the more they remain the same

One of the wonders of God's creation is the chameleon. Several species of these lizards share the interesting characteristic of changing from green to brown or other colours, depending on mood, something like the way our faces go red with embarrassment or the way a dog's hackles go up when facing an unwelcome intruder. Some species change colour in response to their environment, displaying green among green leaves and brown when on a brown tree trunk. This ruse allows them to sneak up on their prey undetected and to remain unnoticed by their enemies.

In our variegated political environment, we also have several species of political chameleons—those who display a certain set of values in one crowd and another set when addressing a different audience.

Take family values, for instance. Once upon a time, when the family was esteemed by all Canadians as the most important institution of society, these political chameleons reflected the colours of their surroundings, staunchly protecting the institution of marriage between one man and one woman. But that was long ago, way back in 1999. When the media informed them that the environment had changed, they turned a different colour, confident that they would never be noticed against the new background. But that surprised some of their supporters who thought their first position to have been their true position.

Some of the blue, some of the red and all of the orange chameleons seemed somehow to have taken on a tinge of pink. Still, the blue chameleons flash blue every once in a while, especially when surrounded by their many true-blue friends. They assure them that they have not really turned pink . . . but don't blink! The grant of $400,000 to the Gay Pride Parade sure looked like a change. Some blue chameleons, taking on their bluest hues, said that people had not understood . . . there was only one mutant variety, nothing had changed. Hopping to a different branch, the same speaker said that he had no problem with the grant . . .

Then there were the fiscal policies. At one time, not so very long ago, the blue chameleons glistened in their blueness. As Canadians clamoured for fiscal sanity and government thrift, the blue chameleons stood proudly on their blue branches, displaying thrift and no-nonsense policies as eternal values. But when they felt the branches they were on swaying in the breeze of socialism, they became a little bit red, some even went orange. To some observers, the 2007 federal budget, the highest-spending budget in Canadian history, showed a loss of blue colour and a rise of red ink. A series of expensive elections later and a trip to the candy store—for a stimulus package the red and orange chameleons could only dream of—and for a few moments, it seemed that all the chameleons were the same colour! That caused a different problem. While it may feel cozy to be all the same, it makes it difficult for voters to distinguish the different varieties.

Then there are the Greens. This species does not seem to change colour. It stays on its green platform and does not move. It's a small platform but at least it's green. The red, the blue and the orange chameleons noticed that many were flocking to the Greens and as with one accord, they all began to show a green side. Some went to extravagance in this area, becoming "greener than green". Still, wanting to placate past supporters, they return often to their old haunts where they display their original colours and speak soothing words that have long since lost their meaning.

To the casual observer, it seems that many political chameleons have worn themselves out with their flip-flops and multiple disguises. In a final desperate move, many of them have turned yellow.

There is one political party that does not change its colours but stands out from the crowd in every area. It takes a position and defends it. It is easily recognized by its royal burgundy colour and its unwavering defense of truth. Of course, that's the Christian Heritage Party of Canada.

September 29, 2009

Red Tide, Red Ink, Red Blood

Those who live on the seacoasts of Canada and who enjoy eating clams and mussels know that a "red tide" is a bad thing. It is a discolouration of seawater due to an unusually high concentration of algae. In many cases it is harmful or fatal to various types of wildlife and humans can become seriously ill from eating shellfish contaminated by the algal bloom. Canada has just experienced an electoral Red Tide which has contaminated our national psyche and threatens to harm much of what we hold dear. Our nation has chosen fiscal slavery, moral anarchy and social injustice. It is unbelievable to me and yet it is true: by a combination of misrepresentation in the media and the myopic self-interest of politicians and confused portions of the electorate, effectively hemmed in by narrow narratives, our beloved Canada has come "out of the frying pan and into the fire".

In historical perspective it's fascinating how the heart of a nation could be captured and turned in a few short weeks. The sparring in a couple of debates, a few careless words, a multitude of ever-dimming polls, the threats from Red and Blue to either "defeat Harper at all costs" or "make sure 'just not ready' Justin doesn't ascend to the throne" have once again culminated in a national lemming-plunge of votes for or against the incumbent party. By the way, the campaign slogan, "just not ready", contained within itself an error in judgment. It implied that—given enough time to mature—one day Justin would be ready. It ignored his policy flaws, such as his insistence that no Liberal MP would be allowed to represent the interests of the preborn. It also implied that his youth was the only impediment to his competence, rather than his chosen philosophy. The truth is that unless he adopts another worldview, Justin will never be ready to provide the kind of leadership Canada needs.

It is a sad commentary on public awareness and economic understanding that both Red and Blue could speak about the deficit and balanced budgets, each in his own way, and receive no significant pushback from media or voters. In fact, Justin's promise—to run deficits for several years in order to get things we want NOW—is unprecedented. What thinking people would deliberately choose further servitude to foreign lenders? Yet that is what Canada's people have chosen, with little regard to long-term consequences. Mr. Harper's now-irrelevant claim that Canada has achieved "budget balance" was not seriously challenged by the media as a whole. Most Canadians apparently do not understand the significance of, nor the difference between "annual deficits" and the accumulated national debt. Although his claim did not sway sufficient voters to save his government, it wasn't because voters could see that a one-time $1.8 billion surplus was a poor trade for a $155 billion increase in the national debt which was incurred over the 9 years of Conservative rule. Perhaps they won't notice when our national debt continues to grow over the next four years. After all, consciously or not, they voted for it! That is one promise our new PM will probably keep.

And, of course, our nation has chosen to reject a PM and a party that have been lukewarm at best on the topic of abortion. Our nation has chosen instead a leader and a party committed to the status quo, abortion-on-demand. Worse yet, our new PM is so comfortable with the shedding of innocent human blood that he has said he will not allow any of his MPs to vote for protection for the preborn. I fear for our nation because our people—at least a sizable majority if we include the similarly-inclined but electorally ill-favoured NDP—have chosen death over life and debt over fiscal prudence. I do not claim the Conservatives have been fiscally prudent (did I mention the national debt?) and I don't blame voters for being cynical about the claim but to choose someone who says that "the budget will balance itself"?

Of course, voters in 30 electoral districts across Canada had an opportunity to choose "none of the above" and instead to give their votes to the CHP candidates who so nobly advanced the cause of both fiscal sanity and moral conviction. Some voters did, approximately 15,000 of them, but most took the cautious approach that has—up until now—kept the CHP from gaining national prominence or being seen as a credible threat. Most Canadian voters who had CHP candidates in their ridings chose to bypass them even if they thought highly of their policies and individual characters. They chose to give their votes instead to someone they thought more likely to win.

In this they truly wasted their votes since they neither elected a Conservative government nor sent an electoral message to the big parties and the media. So many thought they had to do something to keep Mr. Harper in office. That is an obviously-failed strategy. As individuals, we do not control the outcome of elections. We have a part to play and a duty to perform. That is to vote for the candidate and the party that best represent our views. The results are up to God. We need to be faithful and let our consciences guide our decisions—not just at the polls but in all we do.

Pray for our new PM and our new MPs. May God guide their thoughts and inspire them to new and courageous policies. The fear of the Lord is the beginning of wisdom. May an awe and reverence for God overtake this Parliament.

I want to heartily thank all our CHP candidates who have given so generously of their time, energy and talents to make a difference in 2015! A big thank you also to their families and their campaign team volunteers and to our many members and supporters across the country who have sacrificed for the cause. My campaign in Ottawa was only possible by the sacrifices of others and I know many of our candidates could say the same.

Thank you all! Together we have declared to our fellow citizens the importance of the biblical principles upon which this nation was founded. For those reading this who are not yet members, we invite you to join us and help bring the CHP's Better Solutions to our needy nation.

October 26, 2015

The PM's Undoing

In any great endeavour—such as running a country—people want to know how much is being accomplished. In Canada today, it behooves us to also find out how much is being "un-accomplished". If a farmer were to plant an acre of potatoes and someone else came behind him, digging them up, "unplanting" them, as it were, that would certainly be his "undoing". The farmer would have nothing to show for all that work and he would be down by the lost value of the seed potatoes.

Right now, our new PM (Justin Trudeau) is making his mark, to some extent, by deliberately undoing the work of the previous PM. Whether these initiatives are his own ideas or those of the cabinet he has appointed, he is uprooting quite a number of the legislative accomplishments of his predecessor. If those accomplishments were bad for the country, undoing them would be good. If, however, some of those laws and amendments were worthwhile achievements, then reversing the efforts of the previous government would be a bad thing. I'm afraid, in most cases, it is the latter.

It's well known that it is easier to destroy something than to build it. Rome wasn't built in a day but it collapsed in upon itself in a short period of time . . . as will our civilization if we continue to abandon moral values and biblical principles. When people talk about "change", they need to be aware that not all change is good. As the saying goes, "Before you remove a fence, find out why it was put there in the first place". So often, even in corporations, a new manager insists on trying things that have been tried before and have failed. The social experiments to which western civilization has been subjected over recent decades should be examined in the light of the results. For instance, more condoms and more explicit sex-ed has resulted in higher incidence of STDs, not lower, more teen pregnancies and more abortions, not fewer.

So what has Mr. Trudeau thrown out that Mr. Harper put in? We'll mention a few items that concern us. Much more information can be found in this article in the National Post: *http://news.nationalpost.com/news/canada/undoing-the-tories-a-guide-to-harperisms-that-the-liberals-have-or-might-kill*

One of the most important pieces of legislation the new Trudeau government has undermined is the First Nations Financial Transparency Act (FNFTA). This legislation was the result of a long campaign by the Canadian Taxpayers Federation, other citizen groups and First Nations people themselves to hold elected leaders and band councils accountable for their spending decisions. Since other levels of government must explain spending to taxpayers it only makes sense that elected chiefs and band administrators also be required to declare revenues, expenses and salaries to the people who pay the bills (taxpayers) and to the people whom they represent (band members).

For the 2014-2015 reporting period all but 38 of Canada's 581 First Nations had complied with the provisions of the FNFTA, a compliance rate of 93.5 per cent. The intent of the law was to compel transparency by withholding funds from bands that fail to comply. The new Liberal government has chosen not to enforce the law, catering to the voices of those who benefit from non-transparency. All indications are that the Liberals plan to repeal the law. This is a clear departure from the "rule of law" referenced in the Charter. The rule of law should establish equality among Canadians. Transparency and public accountability are normal and expected standards for all Canadians but by making exceptions for First Nations bands, the government has declared that all Canadians are not equal. Canadian Taxpayers Federation has much more on this; see the footnote.

On the justice and security front, the Prime Minister has promised to pull Canada's fighter jets out of the battle against ISIS. Although they have not yet fulfilled this campaign promise, the attitude being projected is that Canada no longer stands with our allies against terrorism. The influx of Syrian refugees is a direct result of the cruel deeds of ISIS. By refusing to recognize the cause of the refugee crisis, the Liberals seem to want to put a band-aid on the wound rather than preventing more injuries. If ISIS is allowed to continue to expand, the refugee crisis will only increase.

The PM also plans to repeal the law that would strip Canadian citizenship from convicted immigrant-terrorists. Why? What duty or loyalty do we owe to those who have violated their oaths of citizenship? Protecting our borders and our citizens from danger is the primary role of government. Protecting terrorists from the consequences of their own deeds is no legitimate goal. The appointment of Omar Alghabra as Parliamentary Secretary to the Minister of Foreign Affairs further reveals the direction and thinking of the PM as well. Mr. Alghabra has long been a proponent of Sharia law and does not consider Hamas and Hezbollah to be terrorist groups. Undoing the efforts made by the previous PM to secure our borders and prevent home-grown terrorism is a disastrous course and will no doubt result in injury and loss in the future. Pray that common sense will return on this issue.

The Liberals also plan to reverse cuts to CBC's funding. While most Canadians appreciate our public broadcaster's familiar role in broadcasting news and weather, the left-wing bias of the CBC is hidden only from those who use no other news sources and who fail to think through the issues. CBC's relentless attacks on traditional marriage and family values and their selective coverage of issues and candidates have caused many of us to call for its privatization. Why should my tax dollars be used to promote ideas, philosophies and policies with which I passionately disagree? Funnelling more money to the CBC in a time of declared deficit spending is both an insult to all clear-thinking Canadians and an assault on our freedoms and rights as taxpaying citizens.

Another item of concern (back to transparency issues) is the PM's intent to repeal Bills C-377 and C-525, bills which were designed to force transparency on union officials. Union workers certainly deserve to know how their leaders are spending their money. How can the PM justify helping union leaders and those making over $100,000 per year to keep their financial secrets from their members and from the public?

The list goes on. Hard work is usually admired, but I've always said that if someone is riding a bicycle or paddling a canoe in the wrong direction, the harder they work, the farther they will get from their goal. This PM is going in the wrong direction on many issues . . . and he's pedaling (or paddling) very fast. In his first few months in office, the things he has done and the things he has undone have made our country less safe, less fair and less transparent. Pray for him; he needs wisdom. For a common sense approach to these and other issues, join CHP.

January 25, 2016

Canadian Taxpayers Federation Slams Trudeau Government:
http://www.taxpayer.com/news-releases/ctf-slams-trudeau-government-s-abandonment-of-the-first-nations-financial-transparency-act

Turf Wars on the LEFT—Fighting Over the Moral Low Ground

It has often been said that the first casualty of war is truth. In the latest suicide bombing in the culture wars, Michael Ignatieff has lobbed an old hand grenade into Stephen Harper's nearby forces. It remains to be seen, as the old joke goes, whether Mr. Harper will pull the pin and throw it back.

It began with the Prime Minister's announcement that his government would seek to improve health outcomes for women and children around the world. That's called "Saying it without saying it." He did not specifically mention abortion (or "reproductive services" as the Ministry of Truth likes to call it). His comments had raised red flags for many in the trenches who seek an end to Canada's decades-long war against the unborn, both at home and abroad.

It's true that the announcement deserved some footnotes or qualifiers. But for those on the left, a pause in the conversation is a great reason to start talking, even if they have nothing to say. Mr. Ignatieff waded in on the probability that Mr. Harper— contrary to all past statements and actual history of his behaviour in Parliament—was certainly planning an all-out offensive against abortion and demanded that he specifically include access to abortion and contraception in his promise to aid impoverished women and children. (How the deliberate killing of children can be seen as coming to their defense he left up to the imagination of his audience.) That audience being his Liberal caucus, they did not stumble over this inconsistency but roared back their approval.

The Liberals are running out of room on this one. To their immediate left, the NDP and the Bloc have already staked their claim. That claim is the unequivocal demand that any baby can be killed in any womb for any reason at any time. That claim is that a football player like Tim Tebow should not hug his mother on public television in support of a woman making a life-affirming choice (after all, there could be children watching!)

On their other flank, the Tories have been quietly moving their lines. The uniforms—once clearly distinct on issues such as these—are now a pathetic blend. Camouflage is the colour of choice and choice is the rhetoric of the day. When the party in power refuses to stay politely behind their lines, refuses to defend the unborn, refuses to own up to its supposed agenda, well it's hard to know where to attack. The fact that Stephen Harper, in three separate campaigns, has advanced stealthily on the Liberal position has Mr. Ignatieff crying foul. Mr. Harper's assurances to the non-questioning public in 2008 that he would expect his cabinet ministers to vote AGAINST any legislation restricting abortion seems to have missed the Leader of the Opposition. Or perhaps he lives in wistful remembrance of the days when political leaders could be expected to speak clearly and forcefully about their convictions. If so, he needn't waste his ammo on the Prime Minister. He could end up in a "friendly fire" situation.

If Mr. Ignatieff wants to attack a political party committed to defending the unborn and to supporting   young women as they struggle to make good choices they won't regret, he will have to get over his "Harper hang-up". He'll have to go after CHP Canada, the only morally and fiscally conservative party still on the field, the only party committed to defending innocent human life "from conception to natural death". Mr. Harper may be waiting to see which way the wind blows but we in the CHP understand that it's never wrong to do what's right.

Now Mr. Harper and Mr. Ignatieff should get together and decide: Who will be the leader of their new party? For all the rest of you, you can find our Better Solutions at www. chp.ca

February 23, 2010

The good news on this long-stale debate is that in the Muskoka Initiative, the Harper Conservatives chose not to include abortion in their overseas efforts to improve conditions for pregnant women, mothers and their children. (If only they had done something to slow down the abortion rate in Canada!) At any rate, they took a stand on providing non-abortive foreign aid to assist women and children in other countries with health, hygiene and clean water. It was a nuanced position but at least fell short of promoting abortion—one of the few times Mr. Harper was willing to take any flak in regard to abortion.

The bad news is, of course, that the Trudeau government has changed all that, handing out $650 million to Planned Parenthood International, even assisting them in countries where abortion is illegal and using foreign-aid leverage to push poverty-stricken countries to accept abortion and gender confusion.

When Blue is Yellow and a Pink Rose Turns Orange

The recent electoral upheaval in Alberta certainly turned heads and turned expectations on their collective head. Are collective farms next? Across the country, folks are speculating what this all means and why Albertans, the proverbial rock-jawed conservatives, have suddenly voted in a socialist majority government.

Some say it signals a new day for softer, more sensitive government, a few steps removed from the oil cartels of the mega-rich. Some think it points to real concerns over the environment and caring for the underprivileged. Some think that conservative values have gone the way of the dodo bird and that an economy based so heavily on fossil fuels has come to the end of the road.

While these angles show some understanding of Alberta's rocky descent from economic powerhouse and bastion of personal freedom and independence to a province which has already adopted a cookie-cutter regulatory approach to development (and will no doubt spend the next four years adding new layers to the bureaucracy), there is much more to this story than meets the eye.

Politicians in general are often accused of hypocrisy, of putting on a false front, of speaking out of both sides of their mouths, of failing to keep electoral promises and of waffling on important issues. These accusations are, of course, unfair to many honest politicians who truly do enter politics to serve their constituents and bring positive change to their city, province or nation. In Alberta, however, some of the anger recently expressed at the polls came in response to the repulsive attitudes and actions of a group walking in an entitlement fantasy. That fantasy just evaporated.

The greater surprise to some is that the unhappiness with the PCs didn't translate into broader support for the Wildrose Party. But they (the WR), unfortunately, don't know who they are and the voters of Alberta didn't want to spend the next four years helping them figure it out. In the last provincial election, voters saw a couple of WR candidates expressing themselves strongly on certain issues and their leader at the time, Danielle Smith, distancing herself from them by expressing her support for the abortion status quo and for same-sex marriage. In this election, newly-elected Wildrose leader Brian Jean stayed away from some important topics about which his Parliamentary voting record as an MP was consistent; he even went so far as to disallow one nominated candidate (Russ Kuykendall) because of a very innocuous statement he had previously made regarding his concern over the use of a church basement to promote the homosexual agenda. This fear of being too honest or of representing a view likely to be criticised, brought out the yellow streak in the WR and left voters with tough choices in many ridings.

It didn't help the survivors of the recent WR rupture that their former leader and her coterie of floor-crossers had made a deal with Jim Prentice that apparently lowered both parties in public estimation. To go from attacking the ruling party to becoming its fawning lackeys certainly angered party members and past supporters. It is likely that the misleading polls of 2012 and the stutter-steps that followed also failed to give voters the confidence that the WR could govern—or that they could be relied upon to govern in line with the philosophy that first gave them their momentum.

The WR Party and the PCs, in other words, were both trying to be all things to all people and in this they failed miserably. Both have abandoned the socially-conservative values that many of their supporters were vainly hoping they would champion. In the end, voters cast a crushing protest vote, hoping that the "honest socialists" of the NDP would rise to the occasion and somehow shift the province from its cozy corporate camaraderie to a more caring and sharing society. It is likely that their unrealistic expectations will be disappointed, that bureaucratic bungling will fail—as it always does—to create a stable environment for either businesses or families and that the misguided daydreams of the secular humanists will result in even worse abuses by the state and intrusions on parental sovereignty and individual freedoms.

But the previous housekeepers have been disabused of their notion of eternal security and the abandonment of pro-life, pro-family principles has been exposed as a useless exchange of integrity for power. Without integrity and purity of character, there is no lasting authority. May all who were battered in this debacle dig down and find the foundational principles without which democratic institutions are only a sham. May the citizens of Alberta survive the next four years and—looking beyond collective farms and corporate conglomerates—return to their roots and their worthy heritage . . . a heritage that has been squandered carelessly. Principles matter and voters are looking for representatives who have them.

The Christian Heritage Party has no dog in this fight, no provincial wing in Alberta but our hearts are with solid pro-life, pro-family Alberta citizens who desperately need someone to vote for who will stand unflinchingly on principles. Federally, CHP Canada often stands alone in our refusal to bow to the god of pragmatism . . . to move the goal posts for partisan purposes. If there is no exact standard of right and wrong, no exact standard of what we believe and don't believe then the blue becomes yellow and a pink rose becomes orange. If salt loses its saltiness then it's useless.

This Fall, we face a federal election. We will again hear the many promises that are made to buy our votes. Politicians are often accused of failing to keep their promises. As we recently pointed out, failure to balance budgets and reduce debt load are serious concerns. In today's mass-market politics however, sometimes it's worse when politicians keep their promises—promises they never should have made. Mr. Harper promised never to allow any legislation restricting abortion to pass under his leadership; he has kept that one and 100,000 babies continue to die each year. No doubt, the Liberals and the NDP would keep their promises to institute national daycare and warehouse Canadian children at the expense of families. There is no free lunch. Somebody will pay for extravagant social programs: our children and grandchildren. May we, as a nation of voters, pull back from the precipice on which we teeter and hold politicians accountable for their frivolous, self-serving promises.

It's time to support the Party that WILL stand on principles . . . the principles on which this great country was founded. It's time to say that we will carry our own weight and not live on the backs of future generations. It's time for the Christian Heritage Party of Canada.

If you share our vision of a nation where hard work is rewarded by accomplishment; where children are recognized as a blessing; where government interference in our personal lives is rejected; then join us and help us restore public confidence in the time-tested moral principles which made this country great.

Oh, yes, Canada, it's time!

May 11, 2015

A Better Way to Increase Voter Participation

The Hon. Stephen Fletcher, Minister of State, acting on behalf of the Harper government, has brought forward yet another attempt to re-interest Canadians in the political process.* His solution is to open up two more advance polling days, the two Sundays before Voting Day. He and the Hon. Josee Verner, Minister of Intergovernmental Affairs have speculated that this would "improve Canada's democracy and increase voter participation."

I have a better idea. How about giving voters more REASON to vote rather than more opportunities to do something they obviously have decided not to do? With the advance polls already available, mobile polls, mail-in ballots and guaranteed time off work if required, few voters can cite a legitimate reason why voting is not possible or convenient for them. Many, however, will tell you why they can't be bothered, why voting is a waste of time, why their vote doesn't make any difference and why they don't really care.

Cynicism and apathy have become both chronic and acute. Here are some things politicians could do to improve not just voter turnout but the proper functioning of democracy itself.

Stop wasting taxpayers' money on elections every 18 months to 2 years. Voters have become numb with the constant politicking and bickering, the high-priced and malicious ads and the constant reminder that the opposition can never rest until the government is toppled. In excess of $300 million of direct costs are incurred each time the PM takes the showy pre-election walk to Rideau Hall . . . not to mention the loss of productivity, the endless media cud-chewing and the pricey litter along the highways.

Stop propping up political parties at taxpayer expense. Most of us have to work for a living producing goods or services of value. We accept the responsibility of supporting our representatives in government. But why should taxpayers have to oil the Conservative Party machine (or the Liberals or the NDP or the Bloc or the Greens)? Thanks to over $30 million worth of taxpayer funding, we subject ourselves to advertising ad nauseum and the smaller parties with something to say have to fight the traffic with only the sacrificial donations of their members.

Stop wasting taxpayers' money on gold-plated pensions. Most hard-working Canadians are honest enough to admit that they don't think politicians should be paid MORE than they're worth or that they should have a luxurious retirement income while the rest of us working stiffs have to scrimp to get by.

Keep your promises. Do what you say you'll do. Don't do what you promised not to do. Don't make promises you can't keep. Stop buying votes today with money borrowed from tomorrow.

Deal with the "democratic deficit" of our "first-past-the-post" system. Proportional Representation, in combination with a Preferential Ballot would eliminate the tired myth of the "wasted vote" and would restore some sense of values proportionality.

Keep Voting Day a day of national community interest. By the time a large segment of the populace has already voted in one of the multiple advance options, there just isn't the same nationwide sense of being joined together as a community seeking the greatest good for our society. If further options become available, such as the 2 Sundays proposed, employers may resist the requests of their employees to exercise their democratic rights on Voting Day. Not to mention that the pressure to campaign and vote on Sunday is a direct insult to millions of Canadians who really appreciate having one day of the week set aside from political friction and frenzied activity.

Ensure all voters are well-informed about all their options. The big parties and their telephone-polling accomplices like to make voters think they have only 3 or 4 options and they want them to vote quickly—before they find out about the other parties and the important issues the big parties have been avoiding. Surely the 5-week period of an average campaign is not too long to allow all citizens to hear from all candidates. Voting early does not change the governing party any sooner. Patience is a virtue and voters are ill-served by attempts to force their hand.

Return government to its proper role—defending its citizens and keeping just weights and balances. The social engineering of recent years and the attempt to be Santa Claus to every isolated bloc of voters has done little to earn respect and much to provoke hostility among the citizenry who just want a fair chance to feed their families, safe streets to walk on and freedom from repressive bureaucracy.

Don't just make it EASIER to vote. Make it more IMPORTANT to vote. Train voters to "use it or lose it". Instead of pandering to apathy, help voters recognize the responsibility that rests upon their shoulders. Suggested protocol: Voters who fail to vote in 2 consecutive elections lose voting privileges and would be required to re-register to regain them.

To accommodate voters who will be away on Voting Day, one advance polling day, one week before Voting Day should be allowed as well as mail-in ballots.

What are the downsides of the 2 additional advance polls as proposed by the government?

250

Having polls open on Sunday turns that day into another frenzied politically-oriented day like any other. Canadians have resisted this in the past.

- The two additional days will cost taxpayers more, especially if one of those days is a full-on voting day.
- It would force Elections Canada workers to give up their Sunday rest and family day.
- It would reduce the significance of Voting Day and would likely be a step toward eventually forcing all voters to vote on Sunday.

It's time to be honest about the state of the nation. Some of our citizens have lost the passion for the democratic process because they have not seen the benefits. Democracy's image is tarnished and those who have been entrusted with positions of responsibility need to work at restoring it.

April 28, 2010

for reference: press release from the Minister of State (Democratic Reform) - April 26, 2010: Harper government Introduces the Increasing Voter Participation Act. (Ottawa)- The Hon. Steven Fletcher, Minister of State (Democratic Reform), today with the Hon. Josée Verner, Minister of Intergovernmental Affairs, President of the Queen's Privy Council for Canada and Minister for La Francophonie, moved ahead with the Government of Canada's 2010 Throne Speech commitment to increase voter participation by giving Canadians more chances to vote during federal elections.

"Increasing the number of advance polling days means giving Canadians more opportunities to vote and will help to increase voter participation," said Minister Fletcher. "That is why our

Government is improving Canada's democracy by adding two additional voting days for voters."

The Increasing Voter Participation Act, introduced today, adds two new advance polling days to the campaign period. The first additional day would be on the Sunday eight days before election day and the second would be on the Sunday immediately before election day. More importantly, all 65,000 regular polls will be open on the Sunday before election day. This will maximize the opportunity for Canadians to vote at advance polls in their own neighbourhood and will be particularly helpful for Canadians living in rural areas who often must travel long distances to vote.

"Voter participation in the political process is the cornerstone of our democracy," added Minister Verner. "Our Government believes it is important to encourage citizens to participate in the democratic process."

Bullets, Ballots and the Politics of Frustration

We live in frustrating times, in confusing times, in desperate times. From municipal politics to provincial to federal and certainly in the minefield of international politics, there is a growing angst as well as a disappointment in the process of choosing leaders and policies that are hoped will improve and not diminish the human condition.

Human history is littered and stained with collapsed empires, slaughtered peoples, slavery and dominance, opulence and poverty and the steady undertone of downtrodden people "yearning to breathe free." The human heart longs for justice and the human mind and spirit strive to achieve it. Periods of disconsolate acquiescence to seemingly permanent injustice are interspersed with flashes of brilliant and engaging upheaval as classes or races or clans or guilds or nations stir themselves in rare displays of unity to reverse decisions, to replace assumptions and to renew that ageless quest for recognition, respect and reward.

We see our neighbours to the south now agonizing over who shall hold the reins for the next four years. By most accounts, those years may resemble an economic train wreck. Payments are coming due and the unfortunate heir to the highest office in the most powerful nation on earth will, without a doubt, have to disappoint many, fool some and accept compromise on many fronts in order to accomplish anything worthwhile.

On this side of the border, in a land far from home, the citizens of Quebec have just elected (by a small margin, with a small percentage of the eligible voters) an alternative to the Liberals who have governed Quebec these past 11 years. The Parti Quebecois, under new leader, Pauline Marois, were elected on Tuesday night and are forming a minority government. While separatism is part of their platform, many feel that voters were not choosing separatism but rejecting former Liberal leader Jean Charest. It's happened before. In the "orange crush" of 2011, Quebeckers surprised the nation by electing a number of inexperienced NDP MPs in a move that showed not so much their loyalty to Jack Layton but rather their unhappiness with the ruling Conservatives. In the Spring of this year, Canada watched the misguided mayhem of the student revolt in Quebec; the "solidarity" movement that it sparked was a key in solidifying the public opposition to the fading Liberal government.

And now, in the aftermath of Tuesday's return to power of the PQ, Canadians must deal with the tragic events of that night. When the ballots were counted and the PQ was seen to be in the ascendancy, one man gave vent to his frustration by shooting to death a fellow Canadian, a sombre reminder of the high stakes in play when clashing worldviews produce levels of disappointment verging on despair. In spite of the frustrations and disappointments with politicians and the political process, Canadians must resolve to maintain our confidence in the "supremacy of God and the rule of law."

We extend our condolences to the family and friends of Denis Blanchette. We extend our congratulations to Pauline Marois and her new government. Like all governments in human history, they have been granted an opportunity by God—the one who raises up governments and can bring them down—to enact just laws, to represent their constituents well and especially the weakest and most vulnerable, the children of Quebec, born and preborn. What they spoke of during the campaign is not as important as what they do with their mandate. May they not squander it.

September 7, 2012

Don't Talk While I'm Interrupting!

Democracy is a good deal better than dictatorship. At least our ancestors thought so and many died so that we could enjoy the privileges of citizenship in a democratic nation where most decisions are a group effort and national direction is guided in large part at the ballot box. The possibility, however, of maintaining a civilized society depends also on the moral character of those who make the rules and that of those who vote them in. Democracy can be defined by regulation but enacting laws is only the beginning. Without personal integrity in leaders, the best of constitutional law can be made irrelevant.

In last night's "leaders debate"—which some reporters are at least recognizing as limited to the "main" party leaders, we saw a breakdown in civil discourse (nothing new in Canadian politics) which—if allowed to continue—will accelerate the erosion of public morality in Canada. Young Mr. Trudeau distinguished himself by trying to extinguish real debate. He repeatedly overwhelmed Mr. Harper by interrupting him as he was trying to speak. The moderator, predictably, did nothing to restore the "rule of law" which Mr. Trudeau brought out as a convenient phrase to try to shame the elder Conservative leader on the topic of revoking the dual citizenship of convicted terrorists. While shouting over and drowning out the Prime Minister's remarks, the cocky leader of the Liberal Party abandoned decorum and respectful dialogue, not to mention the "rule of law" governing debates.

Are we really a country that rallies to the person who shouts the loudest, interrupts the oftenest and denies his opponent the opportunity to be heard? Freedom of speech is a great thing but unless one's message can be heard, that freedom is irrelevant. Yet, based on some post-debate analysis, many Canadians say that

Trudeau won the debate. Not in my eyes. People who want to censor the ideas and opinions of others are either afraid of those ideas, recognizing their value and strength or they are so arrogant as to presume that no ideas are worth considering other than their own. As I mentioned at the beginning, democracy is better than dictatorship but a sham democracy begins to resemble a dictatorship.

In a dictatorship, only the ideas of the leader or the elite are allowed to be published or broadcast. In a dictatorship, citizens are compelled to demonstrate their loyalty to a person, a party or an ideology. In a dictatorship, those who think for themselves are shamed, excluded and denied access to jobs, housing and influence.

The current campaign environment brings out some of those exclusionary tendencies. We in the Christian Heritage Party feel this pressure in a unique way during elections. While Mr. Harper was shouted down, insulted and hindered in his ability to present his opinions, the leader of the CHP was not even allowed on the stage. Nor, by the way, were the leaders of the Green Party, the Bloc and a number of other smaller parties. Across the country, CHP candidates have faced varying levels of exclusion, based solely on the size of our party and our past electoral results (which, in turn were partly influenced by exclusionary practices). Where is the forward-looking openness of which we hear so much?

The CHP has had local candidates refused a place in local debates. Does this make sense? Why can Chambers of Commerce, TV and radio stations and newspaper chains pick losers and winners? Because Parliament has established rules which ignore fairness and favour those parties already in power. National media have generally failed to recognize, mention or in any way report on the

256

campaigns of CHP candidates. Yet our candidates, our party and our leader have to meet all the same registration requirements as the Big Three. We're under the same reporting requirements and spending limitations. (Don't worry; the CHP will not be spending $50 million on this campaign like some other parties may. They can do it with the help of taxpayer subsidies; we subsist on the generous donations of our members and don't spend money we don't have.)

So enough whining and back to last night's debate. In many ways the CHP supports the foreign policies of the beleaguered Mr. Harper. We stand with him on the war against ISIS. We stand with him on the importance of properly screening refugees and with reaching out especially to refugees fleeing religious persecution (those in the most dire need would be Christians and Jews who are being killed for their faith). We stand with him on the revoking of citizenship for convicted terrorists. We question the wisdom or necessity of C-51—which some claim will sacrifice freedoms without meaningfully improving our security—but we agree that security is a high priority.

One other statement of Mr. Trudeau deserves to be challenged and the major media will not do it. He spoke of the importance of protecting Canada's "most vulnerable" and immediately promised to make abortion even more available than it is today. Who is more vulnerable than the preborn child? Why is no major media outlet pointing out this hypocrisy? Why does Mr. Harper not point it out? As we all know, Mr. Harper has chosen not to defend the preborn "refugees" already within our borders who are not only rejected but also killed. We continue to defend their right to life.

With that I ask that all who are reading this (all of whom, by definition have been granted the tremendous privilege of being born) exercise the right of citizenship and help guide our nation with your vote. If you have a CHP candidate in your riding, please give him or her your vote and your support. If not, please ask the Conservative candidate where he or she stands on the issues of life, marriage, justice and freedom. Ask him or her what he or she will do—if elected—to defend life and restore traditional marriage? Vote accordingly. If you have no pro-life candidate in 2015, determine in your heart that you will not let that happen again.

The "main" opposition leaders—those on the stage last night— attacked the PM recklessly, rudely and personally. Rudeness does not particularly qualify an individual for public office. If you want policies that consistently defend innocent human life and a commitment to righteous governance and a return to civility within our democracy, join CHP and help us turn the tide.

September 29, 2015

Reviewing this article in the Spring of 2018, I was struck by the manner in which Justin Trudeau, who went on to win a majority and to become the Prime Minister, has indeed become a dictator, demanding allegiance to his ideology and censoring any opinion different from his. Limiting access to the Canada Summer Jobs program is his latest outrage. By demanding that every applicant submit to Liberal policies regarding abortion and gender confusion and denying funding to those who refuse, he has become a tyrant.

Along party lines, he has pushed through bills and motions (Like C-16 and M-103) intended to limit public commentary contrary to his edicts. May the people of Canada wake up, rise up and vote for a return to civility, morality and democratic principles!

258

Harper Settles for Tripoli Senate

If you can't get what you want, change what you want. That seems to be one way of redefining success. For years in the early days of the Reform Party and "The West Wants In!" campaign, Stephen Harper and his fellow reformers talked about smaller government and other reforms to make Canadian government more responsive and democratic. One of those goals shouted from the unrepresented hinterlands and spoken boldly from the Opposition benches is now more of a wish-list thing . . . that is, a reformed Senate for Canada.

The language used in the old days was Triple-E: Elected, Equal and Effective. Everyone knows that Mr. Harper has now taken control of the Senate by appointing a whole slew of unelected (and some perhaps unelectable) Tory Senators to help him pass legislation with a minimum of foot-dragging. Real Senate reform and the real election of those Senators may still come . . . someday. Now that Mr. Harper has a majority in both the House and the Senate, he may be able to restructure government significantly. How he proceeds in that regard is still to be seen. Most Canadians realize he has already succeeded in concentrating power around the PMO and in his expanded cabinet.

However slowly democracy may be advancing on the home front, we now have other ways to measure our influence, including our recent involvement in Libya's civil war, a war which seems to have reached its logical conclusion, with the overtaking of Tripoli and Muammar Gaddafi's stronghold. Without NATO's air strikes and what began as enforcing a "no-fly zone", it is doubtful that the beleaguered rebels could have toppled the strongman / dictator. What is far from clear is what kind of regime will be established when the oppressed become the dominant players.

This writer believes the cure could be worse than the disease. Let's all pray that I am wrong.

This year has been a year of tumultuous and chaotic change, beginning with the Arab Spring. No doubt the pent-up frustrations of the citizens of Yemen, Tunisia, Egypt and Libya provided fertile ground for foment. There is also no doubt that the Muslim Brotherhood and other manifestations of Islamic jihad have poured fuel on the fire in the not-unrealistic expectation that these nations will become a cohesive springboard for increased terror and pressure on Israel and for the spread of Sharia throughout the world.

The amazing thing is that Canada and its NATO partners jumped into the fracas in Libya with so little discussion or debate. There is no shortage of dictators in the world against whom Canada could wage war at any time if that were deemed useful and expedient. The civil war which has raged in Sudan for twenty years and cost over two million lives is just one example of innocent citizens being brutally killed by those in power. In fact, in our own country, 100,000 innocent Canadians are killed each year by our government. We call it abortion. Stephen Harper doesn't want to discuss it. Why is Libya chosen for an area in which Canadian troops and supplies should be deployed because a madman is abusing his power?

Canada should look closely at its alliances. While we wish to be a good neighbour to the US, jumping into every war in which they entangle themselves should not be a pattern we can't break. With Barack Obama at the helm, we need to really question whether our complicity may lend support and legitimacy to regimes which will become a threat to real democracy in the future. I suggest Mr. Harper get back to making a Triple-E Senate work at home before claiming victory in a Tripoli Senate in Libya.

260

Of course, now that Libya has been thrown open to the winds of change, Canada should use any political capital it has earned with the rebels to stress the importance of religious freedom, freedom of speech and equality for women in its government-in-transition. My expectations are not high but we should not be afraid to promote the kind of democracy we believe in—even if we have not achieved it yet ourselves.

August 25, 2011

Two months after this article was written, on October 20, 2011, the dictator Muammar Gaddafi (numerous spellings for his name) was killed by NATO-supported rebels, and three days later his Libyan government fell. As anticipated in this article, the nation descended into chaos. Various Islamic factions fought over the oil-rich state.

On September 11, 2012, The US diplomatic compound in Benghazi, Libya was attacked and burned and the US Ambassador, Chris Stevens was killed, along with three other Americans.

In 2014, ISIL jihadis became numerous and effective in Libya. In 2015, Sharia law, including lashings and public executions became prominent. Some ISIL forces were driven back by Western-backed forces but Libya continues to be a bloody battleground, and a place of extreme violence and persecution.

Western governments which believe in freedom should be very careful about upsetting delicate balances of power in countries that do not operate according to the rule of law. Be careful what you ask for.

Writ Large: the 2015 General Election from Month to Month to Month

Since the major national media forgot to call the leader of the Christian Heritage Party to ask my opinion about what will be one of the longest election campaigns in Canadian history, I am offering this public response to the unnecessarily premature launch of Election 2015. Now that the campaign has begun, our candidates will be getting out on the streets and up to the doorsteps across this nation to tell voters about Canada's only federal pro-life, pro-family, common-sense, small-government, freedom-loving party. The CHP is in the running and we are determined that our message will be heard!

Never would I have guessed that the Prime Minister would have used his advantage of incumbency to subject Canadians to an 11-week election campaign. Sure, he faced mounting pressures to do so: the third party lobbies were spending a lot of money to sway public opinion against the Conservatives and yes, the Conservatives had a big wad burning a hole in their pocket . . . so why wait? The timing appeared advantageous to the ruling party and some speculate that they felt confident that they could outspend their opponents and simply overwhelm the public with "positive spin".

However, things are often not what they appear. Right out of the gate, the PM faced questions about the timing and the length of the campaign. Here's where he stumbled, only minutes after asking the Governor General to dissolve Parliament. He was asked about the cost of the campaign to taxpayers. I fully expected him to answer these questions in a straightforward manner. He did not.

Instead of acknowledging that taxpayers will share the cost of a campaign over twice the length of average, he claimed that he called the election early so that taxpayers would not have to pay for the campaign. "It's important that these campaigns be funded by the parties themselves rather than taxpayers," he said. He could have talked about the unfairness of unions using the dues of their members to attack the government. He could have owned up to the additional cost to taxpayers and simply said, "There's too much at stake to leave this in the hands of third parties". But, by blatantly denying the facts and repeating his assertion that taxpayers will not be paying for the 78-day campaign, he gave the impression of a desperate man willing to ignore the truth in order to retain power. I wish he had told the truth.

The truth is that the extended campaign period will cost taxpayers over one hundred million dollars more than a normal 5-week campaign. The direct cost alone of Elections Canada offices and personnel will likely increase from an average historical cost of $375 million to about $500 million, according to estimates from the Canadian Taxpayers Federation. Then there are the rebates to political parties and candidates. Taxpayers will rebate them for their expenditures up to 50% and 60% respectively for each party or candidate who achieves 10% or more of the popular vote. Parties, which were allowed to spend $25 million in previous campaigns, will now be allowed to spend over $50 million. The rebate cost to taxpayers in 2011 was approximately $60 million. Expect that to more than double.

How does an economist like Mr. Harper not seem to understand the implications to taxpayers? Mr. Harper is not stupid. I have to conclude that he knows very well that taxpayers will be bearing the financial costs as well as the disruptive social costs of this election marathon. Perhaps, he just hopes Canadians will forget how the campaign started and focus on other issues. What might those be?

Certainly not abortion, not if the PM has his way. The fact that we are terminating the equivalent of 4,000 classrooms of children each year is something he does NOT want to talk about. But we do. We think how you treat the vulnerable and defenceless is at least as important as balancing the budget. In fact, protecting life might help us to balance the budget. Approximately 900,000 babies have been killed by abortion since the Conservatives have been in power. Had they been born, they would have added to the nation's economic growth, first as consumers and later as producers. Children need food, toys and clothes. They need teachers. As young adults, they buy houses and cars and build businesses. Children have value, not only for their intrinsic worth as human beings but also for their creative potential.

What does Mr. Harper want to talk about? Several times, he has mentioned balanced budgets. The PM claims he wants to run on his economic record. Does he have a record to crow about? He spoke as if the Conservatives have been consistently running balanced budgets. On the contrary, the past 7 years have been 7 years of budget deficits, not surpluses. During the 2008 election campaign, he stated emphatically that the Conservatives would NOT be running a deficit; then they ran the highest deficit in Canadian history. During the 2011 election, he promised that the budget would be balanced by 2014-2015. It wasn't. Now he claims that the budget will be balanced by next Spring. But, economic trends indicate otherwise. The Conservatives have added about $144 billion to the national debt. Debt service charges cost Canadian taxpayers about $71 million every single day! The fact that the Liberals or the NDP would likely do worse does not mean that chronic deficits are acceptable. Those who have had the opportunity to govern must stand on their record. The promises of politicians are often viewed with suspicion. Buying votes with taxpayers' money is always a strong temptation. At the end of the day, money spent has to be repaid and the only source of revenue is taxes. The Christian Heritage Party has consistently promoted mandatory balanced budgets and a plan to pay off the national debt like a household mortgage.

Even now, on the eve of this campaign, the PM and his cabinet ministers have been flying across the country doling out money to a variety of their favourite causes and constituencies. To deny that this has been a "softening-up" campaign to gain public favour using taxpayers' money is a transparent attempt to fool voters. Does the PM really think that Canadians will believe his story that "since he wants the parties to play by the rules, he's called a 78-day election campaign to keep things fair".

No, this was a move of desperation and calculated, or prepared for, long in advance. It was changes in electoral finance under Bill C-23, which was passed last year, that increased the spending limits and gave us this prospect of 11 weeks of partisan posturing.

The Christian Heritage Party comes off the blocks with the wind at our backs, our principles intact, our candidates committed, and our hearts hopeful that 2015 may be the year when voters choose to send some of our candidates to the House of Commons! God helping us, we intend to bring common sense, decency and a respect for justice back to Canada.

August 4, 2015

A Canadian is a Canadian is a Canadian . . . Really?

During the long and rocky federal election of 2015, Justin Trudeau, at the Munk Leaders Debate, objected loudly to the provisions of Bill C-24 which allowed for the stripping of Canadian citizenship from dual-citizenship convicted terrorists, famously stating that "a Canadian is a Canadian is a Canadian".

In February of 2016, as Prime Minister, his government acted on his simplistic slogan by introducing legislation reversing parts of C-24 and effectively ensuring that people like Zakaria Amara, (a Jordanian-Canadian member of the Toronto 18 terrorist group who pleaded guilty to plotting to set off a bomb in downtown Toronto) could not lose his Canadian citizenship. The Liberals' Bill 6 became law in June of 2017. Immigration Minister John McCallum, told reporters, "We believe very strongly that there should be only one class of Canadians, that all Canadians are equal, that a Canadian is a Canadian is a Canadian from coast to coast to coast".

Ensuring that foreign-born terrorists are treated equally with law-abiding Canadians was deeply offensive to many concerned citizens. Was it a "matter of principle" as the PM claimed or was it just another ploy to garner support from an angry class of disenchanted ideologues?

If the PM really wanted all Canadian citizens treated equally, why has he given such prominence to promoters of Islamic causes? People like MP Omar Alghabra, Parliamentary Secretary to the Minister of Foreign Affairs, a man who has repeatedly sought to introduce Sharia Law into Canada. People like MP Iqra Khalid with her ties to the Muslim Brotherhood and the sponsor of M-103.

If the PM really wanted all Canadian citizens treated equally, why has he arrogantly and openly denied pro-life and pro-family organizations access to the Canada Summer Jobs Program?

If the PM really wanted all Canadians treated equally, why has he waived fiscal transparency for First Nations chiefs and band councils while (rightly) expecting it of other levels of government?

Why is the PM denying free speech to Christian organizations in regard to abortion, homosexuality and the dangers of Sharia Law while allowing thousands to violate every measure of human decency in the Gay Pride Parades in which he participates enthusiastically?

There's a simple reason for all of the above discrepancies: The PM and his strategist-handlers are identifying and isolating voter-blocs which they assume can be counted on to give Mr. Trudeau another majority in 2019—by giving them special rights:
- By opening the border to unvetted refugees and illegal migrants, he hopes to secure the immigrant vote and build that base for the future.
- By legalizing recreational pot, he hopes to get the votes of an increasingly confused bloc of first-time voters who may see him as "cool".
- By parading shamelessly with lewd sex-activists, he hopes he can secure the votes of the gender-confused.
- By allowing First Nations band offices to operate under their own rules, he hopes to be seen as a reliable arbiter of indigenous rights.

On Valentines Day of this year, the Prime Minister announced that his government will recognize and ensure—in a new way—special rights for indigenous peoples in Canada. With flowery

267

speech, he promised that his government will enact legislation and follow through with action designed to enshrine and enforce a new understanding between indigenous and non-indigenous Canadians. Again, this sounded hopeful to those who have seen or lived through the tragic days of the residential schools and the dysfunctional poverty of life on many of Canada's reserves.

On one level, the PM was right: the inequities of the past do need to be addressed; a new partnership must be forged if all Canadians are to achieve the quality of life and dignity to which we all aspire.

But is the PM's promise of special treatment, special status and special privilege truly the way forward? And if "a Canadian is a Canadian is a Canadian", how can we accept a completely different reality, a completely different set of circumstances, a completely different set of rules for this demographic subset of the Canadian population?

The PM claims—of course—that his promised new approach is based on existing Constitutional rights and existing agreements. It's true that the British North America Act (1867), the Charter of Rights and Freedoms (1982) and the Indian Act (1876) all contain special provisions for aboriginal people, today represented by 614 First Nation peoples. Past acts of the Canadian Government towards indigenous peoples (such as land confiscation, residential schools and denial of voting rights) are rightly regarded as unjust. But much has changed.

Today, Canada wants to be known as a nation of inclusivity, of equality of opportunity and of justice. How can we achieve this when special privileges, unequal access to resources and unequal standing before the law are proposed as inviolable "rights"?

268

Canada has changed dramatically since 1867. Indigenous people, since 1960, are recognized as full citizens, able to vote for their federal, provincial and municipal representatives. Much remains to be done but Canadians must face these challenges together. We cannot undo the past but we must take responsibility for the future.

For the good of future generations of Canadians, we must end the era of special rights. If "a Canadian is a Canadian is a Canadian" then the government should act like it.

The Christian Heritage Party of Canada endorses the Charter Preamble, not only for its support of the "supremacy of God" but also because of the "rule of law". One law for all Canadians under God's direction: that is the recipe for national prosperity, security and social peace.

If you believe in the equality of all Canadians, join CHP Canada today.

February 20, 2018

Changes to Citizenship with Bill C-6:
https://www.canada.ca/en/immigration-refugees-citizenship/news/2017/10/changes_to_the_citizenshipactasaresult ofbillc-6.html

Our Christian Heritage

"Canada is founded on principles that recognize the supremacy of God and the rule of law."
Canada's Charter of Rights and Freedoms

And So It Begins...

Since becoming a Christian in 1976, I have understoo
persecution of Christians would one day come to Canada. The
Bible warns believers that "...all who will live godly lives shall
suffer persecution". 2 Tim. 3:12 Jesus told his disciples, "If they
have persecuted me, they will persecute you". John 15:20 The
Book of Revelation refers to those who will be and have been
beheaded for their faith in Jesus. Through the centuries, followers
of Christ have sometimes enjoyed periods of calm and have also
endured periods of turmoil. Those who name the name of Jesus
have had seasons of public acceptance where their beliefs have
been the common shared beliefs of their fellow citizens. They
have also had seasons of distress, where they have been maligned,
imprisoned and put to death. As believers, we are taught to boldly
declare our faith and to trust in the Lord's care for us, no matter
what the circumstances, because unlike those who adhere to the
religion of atheism, we do have the hope of eternal life.

What does this have to do with politics in 2015? After all, the
CHP is a political party, not an evangelistic association. It has to
do with how we face the turmoil around us and how we respond
to those who would like to silence our voice. We live in troubled
times. Across the waters, our brothers and sisters are facing
persecution of the worst kind. Men and women are being tortured
and beheaded, little children are being brutally killed, women are
being raped. This senseless violence is forcing thousands, probably
millions, to leave their homes and seek refuge from the storm.
This is not a new phenomenon. Over the millennia of human
"civilization", ravaging armies have swept through the
countryside and across borders, killing, enslaving, raping and
pillaging. In the last century alone, Communism, with its atheistic
worldview, conquered much of the world, subjugating and killing
millions by starvation, violence and demands that the peoples

under their power submit to their ideology. Cadres of chanting party members became pitiless killers subject to the whims of their party leaders.

In Germany, during the 1930s, Hitler rose to power and the people of Germany were forced to submit to his godless philosophy. Rather than rejecting this madness, a segment of the population became his deadly enforcers and brought the World into its Second World War. Why did the good citizens in Germany not stand up against the dictator, a pitiful, self-absorbed and formerly insignificant troublemaker? Because of fear. They allowed themselves to be silenced and their families and their nation paid the price. Once he gained control of the press and the government, his unyielding military machine carried the nation inexorably to a horrific destruction.

Here in this nation, many still hope that religious persecution is far off. They pretend that the things that happened in Germany, Russia and China cannot happen here. Persecution begins in small ways yet carries big consequences. Like the fires now raging through California (which began with a small spark, a candle, a cigarette), the attacks on our freedoms—the freedoms to speak, to worship and to raise our children according to our beliefs—have begun to stifle the voices of conscience in Canada and the US, formerly bastions of democracy and personal liberty.

Some Christians feel that it's not our responsibility to challenge the forces of evil which now threaten our nation. They say—from the security of their heretofore peaceful homes and their heretofore peaceful churches—that the role of God's people is not to confront evil but only to preach the gospel. What they don't realize is that their freedom to preach the gospel is already being taken away. Oh sure, if you keep your head down and keep your speech politically correct, you may believe you have freedom. But if you speak up on the issues of the day, you'll find the doors are being shut, the blinds are being drawn and the freedoms you thought you had are being attacked.

In the US, we saw recently County Clerk Kim Davis jailed for refusing to violate her conscience and refusing to participate in pandering to the gender agenda. Even I was shocked that she was jailed; that event reveals a measure of the hostility felt by those who reject a Christian point of view. In Canada, just last week, we saw Jesse Rau, a Calgary City bus driver, being fired for publicly expressing his unwillingness to drive the rainbow-painted "Pride" bus. The media has twisted this story and the timeline of what happened needs to be straightened out. The reason he was fired was not for refusing to drive the bus (that never happened) but for publicly declaring that God is opposed to homosexual behaviour. More and more companies and government departments (not the least of which is the public school system) are being made complicit in the promotion of gender confusion. Those who stand in the way are ridiculed, maligned and—if they won't submit to the New Order—punished.

There is more to the story of the "Pride" bus. Jesse is not the only person whose sense of morality is being violated. Every Calgarian waiting for a scheduled bus may find him or herself forced to decide: Am I willing to ride on this symbol of defilement? What if I have an appointment and that bus is my only choice?

The world has forgotten but we who know better must not forget what happened to Sodom and Gomorrah. The world considers that a fairy tale; we know that it is historical truth. But let me tell you: Sodom and Gomorrah did not become such wicked cities overnight. They got there little by little. A court decision here. A media broadcast there. A little compromise, a little complacence.

By the time judgment fell, God could not find ten righteous men in the whole community.

Those in the pro-family, pro-life, pro-marriage, pro-freedom movement know and understand that the goalposts have shifted. The boundaries of acceptable behaviour have been distorted. Men now call evil good and good evil. We who know better must speak up in defence of God's standards. One thing you can do today is to encourage those who are on the frontlines, people like Jesse Rau, a young husband and father who is now out of work. He took his stand for all of us and our children. You can also write the City of Calgary and ask them to reinstate Jesse and repaint the bus. Calgarians should not be forced to support the homosexual agenda.

The CHP stands in support of traditional marriage between one man and one woman and we stand opposed to the destructive tide of perversion sweeping our land and confusing our children. We will not sit idly by while our nation is destroyed.

September 16, 2015

Common Sense and Compromise

When seeking to understand the thoughts, words and actions of those with whom we disagree, every one of us tries to analyze those thoughts, etc. through our own lens. How could we do otherwise? That is how the world makes sense to us—even if it leads us to conclusions we sometimes find difficult to accept.

When we see others doing and saying things which conflict with our concept of ethics, we're puzzled because we assume that they share our understanding and our ethical standards. That's when "common sense" appears so glaringly uncommon.

Most of us apply a definition to the word "common" as meaning "frequently occurring" or "usual". It would help if we used the word in the context of something that is shared, something that we have "in common". The old "village common" was a grassy area where everybody's cow, horse or goose could wander and graze; the villagers had equal access to it. They had it "in common". Most of us in any city share a "common" water supply.

There was a time when most villagers and most citizens of a country shared common values, common interests and a common understanding of the world. That made it much easier to find common-sense solutions to problems. In Canada today, and in much of the world, those with conflicting worldviews are seeking to find common ground in problem-solving but are frustrated by deep division. In city halls, provincial legislatures and in Canada's Parliament, there is much talk of "focusing on the things upon which we all agree" but often those agreements are shallow; attempts to reach real unity are often hampered by fundamental differences. Those of us whose worldview is not shared by all are often accused of being divisive. The reality is that those divisions already exist; we merely point them out.

Many atheists and secularists want Christians—for instance—to jump on the bandwagon and cooperate with them in the promotion of abortion, gender confusion and euthanasia in legislation and public school curricula. They think we should "celebrate diversity" with them, ignore the moral imperatives protecting innocent human life, welcome false teachings regarding creation and sexuality and passively submit when they tell us to keep our beliefs to ourselves. We could do this . . . if we shared their worldview. We could compromise—as so many already have—if we really did not believe the things we profess. If God were a figment of our imagination, if He had not created "male and female", if He had not created this world in which we live, if he had not told us to "go into all the world and preach the gospel", then we could compromise with the world. But to do so knowing what we know and believing what we believe would mean to abandon the Truth and to accept a different narrative. It would mean we would share their values and hold them "in common".

In the movie, "*Chariots of Fire*", Eric Liddell's father says, "Compromise is the language of the devil". Of course, there are times when negotiating small points to achieve larger goals acceptable to all can be useful, even necessary. If compromise meant only the sacrifice of personal goals for the greater good, we would all be willing to compromise, to "give and take" so that society could move forward. In our day though, compromise has come to mean that deeply-held convictions must be sacrificed on the altar of pragmatism. Because our society does not share common values, pro-lifers are expected to "compromise" and allow others to kill babies. Because we hold convictions not shared by those in power regarding sexuality, we are told we must "compromise" and allow others to proselytize gender confusion to young children. The list goes on.

The sad facts are that many of those who do share our worldview have accepted the bullying of the secularists and have not used their voices to defend freedom of speech. They've not used their votes to elect politicians who will not compromise on life, marriage, religious freedom, freedom of speech and fiscal sanity. It's easier to float downstream.

We cannot accept that reasoning and we must not accept cowardly pragmatism. We live in challenging times but we have the Truth that sets men free. We have Better Solutions for the problems that plague mankind. We have hope for a generation which has been robbed of purpose. We must work to make a biblical worldview common again. Only when men and women, boys and girls are imbued with the knowledge—that they are made in the image of God and that He has rightful dominion in their lives—will we find a return to common sense, common interests and common values. If we hope to ever restore righteousness in Canada, we will have to root out cowardly pragmatism.

March 3, 2017

Does God Have Rights?

The Supreme Court of Canada has now ruled unanimously against public prayer in municipal chambers across this land. From their places on the bench where they are assumed to be interpreting Canada's Constitution and Charter, they now have set themselves up as arbiters of Canada's shared beliefs and designers of Canada's social constructs. They have put inordinate emphasis on the word "supreme" as it relates to the body and office they represent and have completely ignored the foundational "supremacy of God" in the Preamble to Canada's Charter of Rights and Freedoms.

When the Preamble states that "Canada is founded on principles that recognise the supremacy of God and the rule of law", it implies that God (the God of the Bible) has authority, not only over the stars and planets which He created and all the complexities of matter and energy pulsing and interacting in a cohesive and harmonious symphony, but also over the mundane affairs of state. If He created us, by His hand and in His image, He also has authority to direct us in accordance with His plans. His commandments—written first in human hearts and then written for all mankind on tablets of stone—are kind, clear and effective. In Western societies, with shared value systems, we all accept the rightness of precepts like: "You shall not commit murder", "You shall not commit adultery", "You shall not lie" and "You shall not steal". Yet today there are some—including apparently nine unelected Supreme Court justices—who presume to separate a people from their God and to place themselves as higher than the Most High. They presume to interpret laws while ignoring the supreme Lawgiver. This is tragedy and does not bode well for our civilization.

We ought to learn from history. Pharaoh tried to prevent the Hebrews from worshipping God and lost his firstborn along with

3 million slaves. The elite and powerful men in the court of Darius tried to prevent Daniel from praying publicly to God. They made a law against it but Daniel continued to pray. They tried to punish him but God upheld Daniel's position and punished his accusers (read Daniel 6). The rulers in Jerusalem tried to prevent the apostles from speaking in the name of Jesus but God intervened on their behalf. They said, "We ought to obey God rather than [mere] men". That's what the Supreme Court justices are. They are mere men and women, some of them acting out their unbelief and seeking to impose it on Canadians in spite of our Christian heritage and foundation. They will fail but in making this decree they are telling God that we don't need His blessing, His provision or His protection. We need all of the above if Canada is to maintain her stature among the nations and to continue to be a rock of refuge and a source of blessing in the earth.

Banning God from public places only makes sense if there is no God. If He exists—and is all-knowing, ever-present and all-powerful (as we believe He is)—excluding Him from the public square is the most foolish thing a nation could do. "The fool has said in his heart, 'There is no God'." Psalm 14:1 Let us not become fools; let us become wise. Respecting Almighty God is the place to start: "The fear of the Lord is the beginning of wisdom". Prov. 9:10

April 17, 2015

This article was first published in the Vancouver Sun in response to the Supreme Court decision on April 15, 2017 ruling against public prayer at municipal council meetings. See CBC article below.
http://www.cbc.ca/news/canada/montreal/supreme-court-rules-against-prayer-at-city-council-meetings-1.3033595

Haters of Wisdom, Lovers of Death

There is much talk about hate in these days and as the death toll rises in cities and malls around the world, in our schools and in our streets, it is evident that hatred—deep, burning, cruel and bloodthirsty hatred—has gripped the hearts of many.

Despite the commentary on national television and the hand-wringing of the talking heads, community leaders and heads of state, the descent into moral and spiritual chaos seems to be accelerating rather than abating. All the finger-pointing and sombre reflections seem to have no power to impede the carnage of self-infatuated individuals who are willing to perish in a hail of bullets for the satisfaction of causing others anguish and making mothers cry.

We naturally ask ourselves: What is at the root of this violence and destructive behaviour? Is there any way to put an end to the mayhem?

In the book of Proverbs, chapter 8, God gives wisdom a persona and allows her to speak to "the sons of men", to humankind. The whole passage is a beautiful entreaty, laying out the benefits of seeking wisdom. The last verse gives a warning for those who choose to reject wisdom. It says "He who sins against me wrongs his own soul; all those who hate me love death". Prov. 8:36

Who would love death? Death is something most of us try to avoid. Yet God makes it clear that there are some who are attracted by death or at least who—by their actions—invite death. What does it mean to "hate wisdom"? It means to reject wise counsel, to choose to ignore sage advice, to do one's own thing in spite of warnings.

Human nature does not naturally want correction. Human nature does not rejoice in limitations. We generally don't like speed limits, stop signs, restrictions, rules and regulations or any other limitations that might hinder or prevent us in any way from doing exactly what we want, when we want and how we want. In addition, we don't want any negative consequences for the things we choose to do.

God, the maker of heaven and earth, the author of life, has given each of us a free will so that we can choose our behaviours. For our good and the good of society, He has also ruled that there are consequences to bad choices. He wants us to make good choices and—to protect us—He has placed barriers and warnings along the path. His instructions are designed to give us a good understanding of the choices which will lead to long-term happiness. Not all members of the human family appreciate these warnings. Some will drink and drive. Some will smoke in spite of warnings on cigarette packages. Some will ignore warnings about drug use, casual sex, workplace hazards, illegal business practices, etc.

The bloodshed we are witnessing around the world is the natural result of people hating and rejecting wisdom. Some have rejected God's claim to the protection of innocent preborn human life. Even the tired battle-cry of "choice" reflects the desire of people to engage in uncommitted sexual activity without having to deal with the natural consequences . . . in this case, pregnancy. That "choice" has led to the death of over 3.5 million tiny Canadians over the past 40 years. Those who hate wisdom love death.

Others want to ignore God's clearly-articulated plan for the lifelong commitment of marriage between one man and one woman. They want to redefine marriage to include members of the same sex and some want multiple partners. Research proves that same-sex activity and multiple-partner sexual activity lead to higher rates of disease and higher rates of suicide. These consequences serve as warnings which reinforce God's prohibition against sexual aberration. Staunch promoters of sexual experimentation don't want God's advice. They want to do what they want, when they want, how they want and without consequences. So our society continues to stumble down that road. We continue to allow our children to be indoctrinated in our schools. We continue to see our young people falling into lifestyles which will prematurely end some of their lives. Those who hate wisdom love death.

Our collective awareness today is focused on the mass shootings, bombings and stabbings which have affected people in so many places around the world and which may at any time erupt on our shores. What does this have to do with "hating wisdom"? There are several connections: First, in our political correctness, we and our neighbours in the US have rejected God's wisdom. We've taken His Word out of our schools. We've forbidden His name in many public settings. His wisdom instructs us to seek Him with all our hearts and not to trust in our own limited human understanding. But we—our nation, our politicians, our courts—have rejected His wisdom. We've chosen to go our own way. We've substituted polling numbers for His guidance and we've deprived our young people of His instruction. Whether it's "lone-wolf" unhinged shooters or wannabe ISIS devotees, those who have rejected the sovereignty of Almighty God have chosen delusion and "God has given them over to a reprobate mind to do things which are not convenient". Rom. 1:28 Mass shootings are very inconvenient. Explosions at airports and in busy malls are senseless because they've been done by people who have rejected God's wisdom. Those who hate wisdom love death.

What can we do? Is there any hope? Yes, of course. God calls us to greater obedience. He calls us to be salt and light in our communities and in our nation. The path ahead is not easy. The path ahead will require sacrifice. We must boldly proclaim the truth. We must call the nation back to God, back to His wisdom. He has answers. Those who love life will choose to love His wisdom. The Christian Heritage Party is not a church; however, we know that our nation needs to return to the wisdom and guidance of our Creator. Knowing that, we boldly proclaim—in the sphere of politics—the good news for which the world is waiting.

July 25, 2016

Red Square, a Time Machine and Mindless Masses

Over 100 days have passed since (some) Quebec university students took to the streets to demand that their tuition fees (the lowest in Canada) be kept at their unsustainable levels. Quebec's efforts to raise rates by $350 per year to achieve—after 5 years— what would still be the lowest rates in the country (?) have been viciously attacked by a collage of students, professors, strident unionists and would-be Marxists reliving the unfinished escapades of a deprived youth they never experienced.

Nearly 100 years have passed since Russians (who really were deprived, mistreated and hungry) rose up and deposed the Czar (subsequently executed, with his family). The tragic and brutal history of the Russian people under the czars, the wars in which they were entangled and the details of their short, mean lives certainly were a fertile breeding ground for rebellion and savagery, much like Paris in the years of the arrogant and pompous extravagance and injustice that preceded her Revolution. There are more similarities: the monstrous beheading machine, La Guillotine, was the tool of vengeance gone wild in Paris and the shameful slaughter of the innocents in her heyday was a foreshadowing of the hard and cruel tortures and deaths of millions in the aftermath of the Russian Revolution. It is said that Stalin may have killed—directly—30 to 50 million of his own citizens, many with bullets, many with starvation, all of them tormented with fear and terror. The torture and murder of innocent people who are somehow blamed for the sufferings of others or callously executed on the basis of false accusations of treason seems somehow to have followed the orchestrated overthrow as surely as night follows day.

Today, the "risen masses" in Quebec seem grasping for a cause to call their own. Their hunger and thirst is not for bread and water—of which the participants in this revolution have plenty. It is not because of the callous execution of their fellow-citizens; although if they keep pressing their unreasonable demands, breaking the law, destroying property and threatening or injuring innocent bystanders, they may eventually coax or bait La Belle Province into actions that would create a few "martyrs" and thus retroactively justify their extreme and lawless behaviour.

No, this revolution is simply a rebellion looking for a cause. The "access" to education they say they want is now squandered. The cost of protecting the public from their unruly rampages has been very high, both for the students and the state. 100 days is a long time to do nothing but cause trouble. No job, no income. No classes, no diploma. And now the Red Squares have drawn in their union comrades to raise the stakes in this contest. They wished for an "Arab Spring" for Quebec and for Canada. The results of last year's Arab Spring in the troubled Middle East are coming in; the chickens are coming home to roost. What was touted as a quest for democracy in Egypt and Libya has been exposed as a Muslim takeover and the Brotherhood has stepped forward to take its prize and impose its Sharia-based tyrannical oligarchy on the very citizens who bravely faced down the tanks a year ago.

In Canada, we believe in the supremacy of God and the rule of law. Without God in the picture, the rule of law can become arbitrary, harsh and unfair. The rule of law is supposed—under the guidance of a just God—to treat all citizens equally, to assume innocence and not guilt, to hold all equally accountable for their behaviour. As Canadians, we must use our personal influence, as well as the authority vested in the state, to entreat these young people—our fellow-citizens—to take an honest look at their grievances and the inconveniences they have imposed on their fellow citizens. Rebellions that end in bloodshed have happened before. Justice has suffered, the people have suffered and civilization has suffered. May it not happen in Canada, not on our watch.

May 25, 2012

Separation of Mosque and State

As I write this, Canada—under the direction of our new Prime Minister—is hurriedly preparing to welcome Syrian refugees by the tens of thousands and Canadian military bases are being turned into domestic refugee camps. Muslim prayer mats and Korans are being purchased by Canadian taxpayers for use on the bases and plans are being made to build Islamic "worship centres", known in the real world as mosques.

The pomp and circumstance of all this panicked generosity is to present Canada as a "caring nation" and to show the depths of compassion and concern we have for the struggling and destitute. How long can such a fantasy be sustained? While military personnel—heretofore given their due respect as defenders of our nation—are being turned out of their lodgings to accommodate this wave of "instant immigrants", our men and women in uniform abroad are being called off of their mission in Syria where they have been trying to defend the homes and cities from which these refugees are fleeing. Rather than defending the right of these people to exist and to remain in their own country, Canada now offers the "consolation prize" of a new life in Canada, even if we must throw caution to the wind and suspend our own military preparedness to do so.

Of course it must be pointed out that our PM does nothing to protect the most vulnerable and defenceless among us. On our shores, far from the front lines in Syria, approximately 100,000 Canadian babies are killed each year, a practice he strongly supports. If they were allowed to be born, each of them would already have a home. They would not require translators or ESL classes. They would not need taxpayer-funded Korans. They would not displace our military. About 274 are killed every day and our PM shows no concern.

In the blur of the "Syrian refugee crisis" the starving masses of South Sudan—many of them Christians—have not been mentioned. The UN estimates that over a million are on the verge of starvation and at least 40,000 will die imminently unless they receive aid. Persecuted Christians are being killed by the thousands and driven from their homes in North Korea, Eritrea, Afghanistan, Pakistan, Somalia and Libya, to name but a few countries and mostly in the name of Islam. There are literally millions of refugees in the world. We know we cannot help them all but why are Syrian refugees singled out as the "poster child" recipients of Canadian compassion?

The shocking travesty of Canadians being forced to fund a foreign religion can hardly be comprehended. Our own Christian heritage is mocked or ignored and the name of our God, whose values have been the foundation and guide of our great civilization, is often excluded from the public sphere. Yet Canadians are expected to sacrifice not only to provide food and shelter for the refugees but even to promote and encourage the practice of Islam on our military bases. Since when did Canada become responsible for the promotion of any religion?

The withdrawal of our fighter jets from the frontlines in Syria can only be seen as a defeat. To pretend that sending a few specialized units to train beleaguered nationals is "another way" of defeating ISIS is folly. We are either committed participants in the desperate struggle to defeat the many-headed horror of terrorism or we are casual observers. History will not be so kind as the liberal media in assessing this unnecessary retreat and the self-absorbed distraction of our ill-conceived refugee response. The CHP calls on the government to renew the battle against ISIS with vigour, to defend Syrian villagers in their own homeland and to stop the madness of mass, ill-vetted refugee importation.

February 10, 2016

The above was written in response to this story on The Rebel by Ezra Levant on February 8, 2016
https://youtu.be/ZRMNyE0CZWc

White LIES Matter!

According to public opinion, politicians are generally classed as liars, tossed in with the stereotypical used-car salesman (my apologies to all the honest and hard-working used-car salesmen reading this column . . . and all the honest politicians out there who have gotten a bad rap). This moniker is not entirely unearned (by some), only misapplied. Just because some politicians seem incapable of telling the truth, that doesn't mean that all politicians should be painted with the same brush. In fact, all politicians should be held to a very high standard when it comes to truth-telling. Their promises—to voters and taxpayers—should mean something.

Truth is important. For the survival of a civilized society, access to the truth is essential. Every criminal trial is an attempt to determine the facts, that which is completely true. The well-known courtroom promise to "tell the truth, the whole truth and nothing but the truth" is intended to create a society, a culture and an environment where a person's word is reliable. Decisions will be based on the statements of eyewitnesses. People's lives and property hang in the balance. That's also true of politicians, educators and media. Voters make decisions based on their words. When those words are not "the whole truth", voters will make bad decisions based on false information.

Sometimes people refer to "little white lies". That phrase refers to untrue statements employed to accomplish a good purpose. Some people think it's ok to lie if it prevents some negative consequence. "The dog ate my homework" comes to mind.

Where does such thinking lead? Politicians may campaign on "balanced budgets" as the Conservatives did in 2015 after racking up over $144 billion in new debt during their ten years in office.

Politicians may promise "no new taxes" as Ontario Liberals did under Dalton McGuinty, who earned a Pinocchio from Canadian Taxpayers for winning the election on that promise and subsequently raising taxes in spite of it. In some other cultures, "white lies" are taken for granted. Promoters of radical Islam have made lying an honourable thing if it is done to further the expansion of Islam. Lying to unbelievers to promote Islam is called "taqiyya". Such a concept is entirely foreign to Christian culture. Jesus even called Himself "the Truth", an indication of the value of truth in our society.

In the U.S., presidential candidate Hillary Clinton claimed—regarding her private email server—that:
• Nothing marked "classified" was sent or received.
• No classified material was emailed through her private server.
• She only used one device for sending and receiving.
• All her work-related emails were returned to the State Department.
• Her lawyers had read her emails individually and in detail.

Testifying before U.S Congressional House Committee, FBI Director James Comey answered that ALL FIVE of those statements were false. They were lies. Were they "white lies"? Is there such a thing? Is a liar fit for high office?

Back to Dalton McGuinty: In the 2003 Ontario provincial election, then Liberal leader Dalton McGuinty promised that—if they formed government—the Ontario Liberals would "balance the budget, not run deficits and not raise taxes without the explicit consent of Ontario taxpayers . . ." Of course, Ontario Liberals broke all three promises, along with many others. The tragedy is that Ontario voters did not learn from their mistakes but elected them again and have been paying the price ever since.

What we need to realize is that if a man will lie to you about simple things like taxes and debt, he cannot be trusted with things more important and more complex—things like educating your children according to your values or protecting innocent human life at both ends of life's journey.

As taxpayers and as voters, we have a responsibility to elect men and women who can be trusted to tell the truth—all the time. We need discernment of character. On top of outright lies we also must face the more confusing barrage of deceptions. Words like "choice" and "autonomy" are meant to sell us on ideas which we would otherwise reject. The social engineers on the left never use phrases like "baby-killing" or "killing old people to save money". Yet those goals are hidden within their policies. "Free Trade" sounds good but apparently it only applies to some. "Saving the planet from climate change"—who could be against that? It may mean just another tax grab which does nothing to save the planet. All of us are against "bullying". That distraction has been used for more than a decade to cover for the introduction of sexual confusion in our public schools.

We in the Christian Heritage Party believe that moral integrity includes a solemn reverence for the truth. Unless we, and all those who love life, liberty and family are willing to put truthfulness and character above political expediency, we will have nothing to offer Canadians. Let's offer Canadians the truth that can set them free. Truth has nothing to hide. Truth is its own reward.

August 8, 2016

Wrong Conclusions; Wrong Solutions: How the West Fails to Fix its Problems

Every math student knows that problems can only be solved when there is enough information given to which one can apply a formula. Sudoku enthusiasts use the process of elimination to fill in missing information without which the rest of the puzzle cannot be completed. So it is with the very real puzzles of our times—social unrest, environmental degradation, international conflict and relational dysfunction, among others.

Beginning any investigation with the wrong clues could lead a careless detective down back alleys, wild goose chases and dead ends. When reliable evidence is discarded or ignored, the likelihood of a successful solution is decreased . . . or at least postponed. When lives hang in the balance, delay is critical and methods matter. Firemen want to know where the fire is, where the nearest fire hydrant is, are there any people in the building, etc.

In recent decades, social planners and law enforcement agencies, courts and legislators, schools, media and a vast array of advocacy groups have sought to understand and respond to the destructive events and trends of our day; they inevitably assess situations through the lens of their own training and perspectives. Lawmakers and high-level bureaucrats can't avoid the issues of the day: the soaring national debt, toxic air and water, purposeless and unmotivated youth, suicide, disease epidemics, broken homes, senseless mass murders, falling literacy and functional incompetence, alcohol and drug abuse, teen pregnancies, homelessness and poverty, terrorist violence, partisan rancour, corporate corruption and more.

As our society has moved away from a Christian worldview, away from a shared commitment to biblical morality, so we have consciously or unconsciously begun to interpret circumstances differently and to apply solutions more suited to a socialistic, "new age" paradigm . . . even if they don't work! Fishing in a bucket is way easier than fishing in the ocean but the likelihood of catching a fish for dinner is considerably smaller.

Here are a few examples of current issues, misguided responses and some Better Solutions from the CHP:

Childcare: Since many families are struggling to pay their bills, often both parents feel the need to work outside the home. Therefore, some claim that the government must use taxpayer dollars to pay for institutionalized childcare.
Better Solution: Provide a "family care allowance" to make it possible for one parent to stay at home nurturing the children, creating stronger family bonds and reducing the tax burden. Job openings created will reduce unemployment for youth entering the workforce.

Brutal violence and murder: The tendency in vogue is to blame weapons, not people. We saw this in the recent terrorist attack in San Bernardino. Radical Islamists used guns but in 9/11 they used utility knives and airplanes. It's the ideology and the hatred that lead to murder.
CHP's Better Solution: Hold people accountable for their violation of God's laws against murder. Restrict gratuitous violence on TV. Teach the sanctity of human life by protecting human life at all stages.

Sexual disease and teen pregnancies: Our educators have told them to use condoms for "safe sex". We see the results all around us. Moral restraint has been cast off. STDs are epidemic.

Better Solution: Teach young people that their bodies are a sacred trust from God and meant to be kept pure for a lifelong marriage to one individual; endorse abstinence before marriage and fidelity within marriage.

Government spending: Governments tend to raise taxes or run deficits, passing along our unfunded expenditures to future generations.
Better Solution: Cut spending. Focus on real needs. Stop buying votes with boutique handouts to certain demographics. Government MUST live within its means.

Youth anger, gang activity, graffiti and bullying: The tendency is to say, "Kids have nothing to do. Build them a pool or a pool hall." However, crime doesn't occur because of lack of entertainment but because of a lack of an eternal perspective.
Better Solution: We know that much anger, resentment and insecurity results from divorce and broken families. Work harder to prevent divorce. Eliminate the concept of no-fault divorce. Restore tax incentives for those who keep their marriage commitments and remove economic incentives for divorce and common-law relationships. The Darwinian view of life taught in most schools robs children of a sense of purpose and destiny. We should teach schoolchildren that they are made in the image of God and that He has a plan and purpose for their lives. They are not meaningless blobs of tissue; they are moral beings with potential and responsibilities. Teach them that actions have consequences, either good or bad.

Unhealthy sexual behaviours: Since some citizens struggle with gender identity and some choose homosexuality, many believe that children should be taught that homosexuality is "normal". In schools, young children are instructed in all aspects of sexual behaviours and are encouraged to make their own choices.

Better Solution: Recognize that the biblical narrative is correct, that God made "male and female" and warned mankind against violating these natural boundaries. Teach children to respect others but encourage them to choose biblical marriage—a lifelong commitment between "one man and one woman to the exclusion of all others".

Youth unemployment: Some think the government should "create jobs" through tax-funded make-work projects.
Better Solution: Reduce tax burdens for businesses and institute an affordable "beginner's wage". Help companies to invest training time in inexperienced youth who then can "earn" their place in the workforce.

Drug abuse: Since enforcement is difficult, the government now plans to legalize and regulate marijuana.
Better Solution: Enforce drug laws; impose fines on traffickers. Eliminate the "revolving door" of judges undermining the work of policemen.

Refugees: Some feel that Canada needs to open its doors to all in need. Worldwide, it is estimated that there are 19 million refugees, due to war, famine and disease. We can't take them all.
Better Solution: Find out what's driving refugees from their homes and try to help them where they are. When accepting refugees, use every means to screen out potential terrorists. All new refugees and immigrants MUST be held to a high standard of loyalty and socially acceptable behaviour.

Summary: So often the "easy way" to solve social problems seems to be to hire more people, send more money and create new departments. Except that it rarely solves the problem. If we really want to change our nation and reduce poverty, debt and violence, we will have to properly identify the problems and then look for answers that are reliable. Our problems are not new and neither are the answers. In Jeremiah 6:16, the Lord implores His people to "look for the old paths, the good way; walk in it and you will find rest for your souls". As of today, Canada has not done so. Our society is addicted to "change for the sake of change". If we want real solutions to our real problems we will have to return to the Lord.

December 7, 2015

Political Climate Change

When US President Donald Trump announced that the US would withdraw from the Paris agreement on climate change, he signaled a change in the political climate of the world. Against the dire warnings and angry invective of left-wing leaders and media commentators, President Trump declared that the Paris agreement was a bad deal for the US and for the world. For that reason, the US is withdrawing. Canada should do the same. It's time we changed the climate of lock-step submission to political correctness and challenge the assumptions behind the Paris Accord.

Pressure for ideological uniformity on this issue has caused many nations—including Canada—to implement economic policies which can only end in disaster. The decisions made in Paris in 2015 committed world governments to unachievable, unaffordable, unrealistic and unnecessary targets. The costs are high. The predicted results are insufficient to warrant the expense.

First of all, focusing on CO2 as the main culprit in climate change is presumptuous. There is no hard evidence that CO2 is even the cause of climate change. There are certainly many benefits to improving engine efficiencies, reducing the wasteful use of non-renewable resources and reducing the dispersion of man-made chemicals into our air, soil and water. However, to focus on CO2, a natural, beneficial gas, needful for plant growth, is not only illogical but also economically foolish.

The Paris Accord, glibly supported by our Prime Minister and our Minister of the Environment, would cost world governments trillions (yes, that's right, thousands of billions of dollars) over the next 100 years. Proponents claim that after the first hundred years, the sacrificial and costly measures proposed in the Accord will reduce global temperature rise by .2 C. That's 2/10ths of one degree Celsius! That's if all the calculations are correct and all the signatories follow all the protocols. Hardly a worthwhile achievement for a program guaranteed to cost trillions of dollars.

The US is also concerned, and rightly so, that China and India—two of the world's major polluters and two of the economic giants threatening US jobs and fiscal balance—are being handled with kid gloves while the US, and other successful western democracies, are being asked to bear the brunt of the economic impact. Canada should have the same concerns. We have been on a debt-spiral for years, even under the Harper government and now, under Trudeau's Liberals, the floodgates have been opened and the red tide of government spending and waste has seriously threatened our ability to return to fiscal balance. Pursuing a phony war on carbon will hinder both our efforts to achieve economic growth and any plan to balance the budget and pay down the debt.

Another reason to be suspicious of the motives of the global elite who keep calling so insistently for government initiatives like the Paris Accord is that their spokespersons are not walking the talk. Big names like Al Gore, Suzuki, Obama and even our own PM, Mr. Trudeau, fly about in their jets and attend endless international conferences (including the Paris conference) with their entourages and never seem to lose any sleep over their own carbon footprints. Under Prime Minister Trudeau, Canada sent 383 delegates to Paris in 2015. That's more than twice as many as the US delegation and having them there cost Canadian taxpayers about $1 million. Extravagances like these not only cost money but use a lot of carbon (1). How about PM Trudeau's private jet flying him to Medicine Hat last year to boost the Liberal brand during the by-election? Isn't that a lot of carbon for one man's travel? How about his helicopter flight to the Agha Khan's luxury Bermuda hideout? Not saying the man doesn't deserve a vacation but what if every Canadian spent their holidays burning all that helicopter fuel? Of course, most of us couldn't afford it (2).

Whether or not taxpayers are picking up the tab for the lifestyle choices of big-name environmentalists is an important point, but not the only one. More importantly, how can we believe their exaggerated and urgent claims when they continue to live as if their own personal choices are not on the table? They ask for sacrifices from their fellow-citizens but seem unwilling to give up their lifestyles and carbon-consuming possessions. I'm not sure how many properties Al Gore owns but he purchased a pretty exotic mansion in California for nearly $9 million. (3) Obama has just bought a mansion for $8.1 million. (4) Suzuki has multiple pricey properties but his main residence in Vancouver sits on land valued at over $8 million. (5) All these properties require carbon outputs to heat, cool and maintain. Sure, Al Gore may purchase carbon credits to salve his conscience but the reality is that the carbon is being consumed and CO_2 is being produced. I'm not up in arms about their CO_2 footprint; only about their hypocrisy in dictating low carbon use for others but burning it themselves as if it didn't matter.

Yes, the climate is changing. As it did during the Great Ice Age. As it did during the Medieval Warming Period. Mankind has a responsibility to look after the earth and there's much we should be doing but for politicians to pretend—as they did at the Paris Summit—that we can control the earth's temperature merely by setting targets and spending boatloads of money is foolishness.

Thanks to Donald Trump, the value and costs of the Paris Accord are now being questioned. Canada should also re-examine our global commitments regarding carbon and make sure our lofty sentiments are based on science, not hypocritical hype.

People who are worried about rising sea levels should re-read the biblical account of the Great Flood. Genesis 6-8 (6) The extreme weather events of Noah's day had nothing to do with carbon but everything to do with mankind's rejection of God's rule. We in Canada should make sure that we are conducting our national affairs according to His precepts. The One who formed the sun, the moon, the stars and our planet is able to control the weather and the climate. If we ignore His principles, no Paris Accord can help us.

June 5, 2017

1)http://news.nationalpost.com/news/canada/canadian-politics/smyth-canada-sent-383-people-to-the-u-n-climate-conference-more-than-australia-the-u-k-and-u-s-together
2)http://www.cbc.ca/news/politics/trudeau-agakhan-bahamas-ethics-1.4034413
3)http://www.newsbusters.org/blogs/nb/noel-sheppard/2010/05/03/stunning-pictures-al-gores-new-9-million-mansion-media-totally
4)https://uk.news.yahoo.com/obama-residence-harry-potter-castle-102852573.html
5)http://www.torontosun.com/2013/10/11/the-two-suzukis-theres-saint-suzuki-the-one-you-see-on-cbc-and-secret-suzuki-the-capitalist-millionaire
6) https://www.bible.com/bible/1/GEN.6.kjv

Hot Rock Soup with Ice Topping

I remember that Grandpa used to like to have warm milk in a cold glass. To retain the best qualities of that comforting drink, you actually have to consume it right away. Grandpa also liked to have his water boiling BEFORE going to the garden and picking the ripe ears of corn for corn-on-the-cob. That way, they were nice and fresh. Not like some of the tasteless produce that gets picked green so that it can withstand the grueling days of transport to the cities where it will be consumed. Those were different days, when hot things stayed hot and cold things stayed cold and fresh ideas and fresh corn were not canned and regulated as they are today.

While it might be hard to imagine keeping a glass cool for even a minute after filling it with warm milk, this planet we're walking on is even harder to understand. Having just come from Lloydminster, Saskatchewan where the -38 degree weather made my old Chevy pickup reluctant to start, I'm trying to grasp how those raw winds and icy roads can exist as a thin layer over a spinning ball of molten rock hurtling through the universe. It's even harder to fathom how we fragile human beings can survive between the harsh extremes of temperature that routinely dominate our living area.

We know that we require water in liquid form and—somewhere between the heat of the desert (and the hot lava beneath our feet) and the icy poles at the strangely magnetized axis-ends of the earth—we find enough water to quench our own thirst and water our camels. Without that liquid water we would die. Those of us who acknowledge God think about the distance of the earth from the sun, the angle of the earth's axis, the speed of the earth's rotation and the composition of the earth's atmosphere that traps the sun's rays. All these factors and more play into the animated

3-D puzzle, the complex interactions of matter and energy that allow us to drink from a bubbling brook or drill into subterranean pockets of cold, clear water. Drill a little deeper and you might hit oil, deeper still you might find hidden lakes of superheated water. A little deeper and you touch the liquid rock that every so often bursts it bounds and boils to the surface.

We have—within our tactile reach—such extremes of heat and cold as seem almost impossible to coexist; yet there they are. Our own existence can seem impossibly fragile were we not aware of the nature and character of our impossibly all-powerful, all-knowing, all-loving God. He is the One who designed the solar systems, who created fire and gases, indeed all matter and energy. He has created us and our world in the vastness of space and mystery. He has placed our world in its orbit and set the bounds of every star and planet. The laws of physics which govern our rotation and trajectory, centrifugal force and gravity are all His. In short, we are here by His permission and design and for His glory. He covers the molten rock with fertile fields, bounteous seas and even icy glaciers and gives us a place here with our fellow-creatures because of His own plans and purposes.

In our social-political-philosophical world we also have extremes which seem so contradictory as to come from or belong to different planets. And we have people who carry such opposing views within their own thoughts, unable to grasp even the contradictions so evident to others. The same people can blithely cast a ballot supporting the murder of 100,000 innocent babies each year while erupting in condemnation over the shooting of 100 dogs. The same folks will cringe and complain at the exhaust of an idle car but say nothing about the hot air and induced exhaustion of an idle man. The pollution of the minds of children with perverse images and teachings is justified while the introduction of sense and reality on issues of sexuality is

304

condemned. The existence of absolute truth is denied but those who disagree with this assessment are considered to be wrong. How can one be wrong when there is no standard to measure by?

And so, against the grain of faulty logic and deliberate deception, we must continue to present the Truth to all those who may be able to receive it. Since we don't know beforehand whom these may be, we simply speak the Truth to all and pray that the Maker of stars and Designer of planets will also open the hearts and minds of men. Without His guidance and revelation, our thoughts are foolish but when He pulls back the curtain on the intricacies of the universe (as He has done for so many inventors and scientists), the non-contradictory patterns of His ordered beauty and power are seen. Then men and women are drawn to the Source of all truth, the Giver of all life and the One who can bring all creation into harmony with His plan and purpose. What a privilege to be alive in these days of discovery and revelation!

August 5, 2014

Changing the Climate: Who Sets the Dial?

In all areas of social interaction, the reporting of news and its interpretation can always be looked at and handled in two ways: the newsman can either be reading the thermometer or setting the thermostat. In the case of Canada's own CBC and many of its contemporaries in the Mainstream Media, we've long seen the forcing of social change through biased reporting, selective coverage and thinly-veiled leveraging of information. Abortion, same-sex marriage, guesstimates of the earth's age and opinions about the origin of life clothed in the respectability of "science"— all these have been paraded, parsed and punctuated for years. As each successive campaign winds down, these thermostat-adjusters can always be heard attempting to close the debate by issuing a series of stories with the general tone of: "scientists agree" or "conclusive evidence convinces skeptics."

Speaking of climate, weather, temperature and thermostats, the CBC has apparently concluded that the time is right to end the "climate change / global warming" debate. In a recent article online, *Droughts show global warming is 'scientific fact' (1)*, CBC quotes a "new study" they claim proves beyond reasonable doubt that the planet is, in fact, warming and at an alarming rate. They reference recent droughts to prove their point. (I can imagine new debates erupting between the "droughters" and the "doubters.")

There are several problems with the way this information is presented as well as what important info is left out altogether:

- First, there is an assumption that if a global warming trend can be demonstrated, it naturally follows that it is man-caused and, more specifically, the result of our "carbon footprint."

306

- The presence of data showing a warming trend based on the relatively stable period of the '50s and '60s is like considering a bump in the road as a long-wave trend. The few years since data has been systematically measured and documented are really a very short timeline in the bigger scheme of things. We know that there were significant droughts in biblical times—spanning multiple years—as well as evidence of warmer climates 1,000 years ago when Greenland had more agriculture than it does today.

The dial-setters in the MSM seem quite comfortable with conjecture presented as "scientific fact" when it supports their worldview and agenda. Even the study quoted here hypothesizes global warming because of the "unlikely" number of droughts occurring in recent years. They say it is unreasonable to believe that doesn't statistically indicate global warming. How much proof does it take to convince them of a fact they try to ignore? All the evidence in the world—from the existence of one humming atom to the wingbeats of a hummingbird to our own ability to reason and debate—shout that there is an omniscient, omnipresent, omnipotent God, a sentient being capable of controlling the paths of the planets and the climates of millennia. The special creation of man, with mind, will and emotion is demonstrated in countless ways so that "deniers" are "without excuse." Yet still, these MSM wizards keep looking for "the God particle" or presume to speak of "discovering the origins of man."

In another recent CBC article, *Artificial cooling of Earth could reverse global warming (2)*, the author speculates that mankind (the apparent culprit for all our climatic and anti-climactic ills) could take steps to reverse the process by painting roofs white, spraying the clouds with sea water or spraying sulphur into the air. The article states, "Notions of manipulating the climate to impede global warming have been on the fringe of scientific discussion for some time, but is moving increasingly toward the mainstream." Remember when someone thought it was a good idea to bring rabbits to Australia?

Policy statements pushing for man to experiment with manipulating the earth's climate are both frightening and naïve. Frightening, because although nobody really knows for sure what, if any portion of "climate change" is due to the activities of mankind, there are so-called "scientists" arrogant enough to think they could do a better job than God of regulating sun, wind and rain. Naïve, because military and commercial civilian "manipulators" have been at this for decades already, seeking to regulate the weather. It is reported (and denied) that airplanes routinely disperse nanoparticles of barium, potassium, calcium and aluminium, all in an effort to "control the weather". People may disagree about the effectiveness of such methods but the fact remains that government agencies, farmers and utility companies hire weather modification companies to perform cloud seeding for hail suppression or to increase or decrease rainfall in a particular area.

This phenomenon is not discussed in polite company but it should be. If Canadians are being told not to idle their cars due to concerns about supposed effects on climate, why is it okay for companies to deliberately pump chemicals into the atmosphere for the express purpose of changing the weather (and on a larger scale "the climate"). There needs to be a national discussion about the right of citizens to not have someone tampering with their weather. Check out the influence of Harvard professor David Keith who is promoting "climate geoengineering" around the world. It is unclear at this point how far his ideas have gone but government representatives are meeting with him and that gives cause for concern.

CBC, of course, could not resist throwing this nugget into their article, ". . . curb greenhouse gas emissions, mainly from burning fossil fuels, responsible for climate change . . ." There you have it! Rock solid proof. CBC says that fossil fuels are "responsible for climate change." I know the climate changes in my truck when I'm burning fossil fuels and I turn the A/C unit on. But that's my personal climate. I don't want CBC and their "scientist" friends adjusting the thermostat for the whole planet. A much better step would be to acknowledge the One who made the heavens and the earth, repent of the many ways in which mankind has offended Him, call on Him for His mercy and ask Him to send the "early and the latter rain."

"Elias was a man subject to like passions as we are, and he prayed earnestly that it might not rain: and it rained not on the earth by the space of three years and six months. And he prayed again, and the heaven gave rain, and the earth brought forth her fruit..." James 5: 17,18 As Bob Mumford said many years ago, "Aren't you glad not everyone can make the sun stand still?"

August 6, 2012

1. *http://www.cbc.ca/news/world/story/2012/08/04/climate-change-real-scientist.html*
2. *http://www.cbc.ca/news/technology/story/2011/12/02/technology-solar-radiation-management.html*

Going Ballistic in Korea

Temper tantrums have long been a way of life for the dictator-family now represented by Kim Jong-un of North Korea. Histrionics and hyper-venting are so much easier than diplomacy. Today, those denunciations and threats reached a new peak as the hawkish ruler of the Communist North (speaking through the National Defence Commission) declared that the DPRK would be launching more tests in retaliation for UN sanctions. These tests would be of long-range missiles, capable of reaching targets in the United States, as well as "higher-level" nuclear tests, thought to involve enriched uranium.

The significance of these statements can be measured—in part— by the fact that they were issued somewhat in defiance of Communist China, North Korea's only ally in the region and by the stark revelation of Kim Jong-un's plans to eventually send nuclear warheads to US cities. The announcement claimed that the US lives by the "law of the jungle" and that only force, not words, can induce US policy toward the DPRK to change. China, notably, had voted with the UN recently in condemning further nuclear tests by the North, a departure from its staunch support for the Communist regime in the past.

An interesting aspect of this thrust is the apparent lack of any attempt to conceal the militaristic plans and purposes of the DPRK. It's like the shock value of these naked threats has some satisfaction all its own for Kim Jong-un. While he boasts, threatens and attempts to throw a long shadow, his equally unsavoury counterpart in the Middle East, Mahmoud Ahmadinejad, the President of Iran, takes a far different approach. Ahmadinejad seeks to convince the world that his purposes are entirely peaceful. "Nothing to see here; move along…"

Iran also is under international sanctions for its suspected but unproven nuclear weapons development program. Oil revenues are down and income taxes are up as the stakes in this nuclear game of cat-and-mouse continue to rise. In the Middle East, of course, Iran has allies in its war with the US. The many various manifestations of Islamic regimes both new and old, the Muslim Brotherhood which spans international boundaries and the flaring cells of Al-Quaeda sprinkled throughout the region—all united in their hatred for Israel and resentment against the US—preclude any easy or straightforward response to Iran's cloaked weapons plans.

Unholy alliances have developed before between countries far apart geographically and culturally; the common cause of hatred can make sworn enemies into uncomfortable allies or even "blood brothers" for a season. Let us pray that the leaders of the world's democracies find the wisdom to defuse every ticking bomb. They have a ticklish challenge: appeasement gives the madmen opportunity to build their weapons and publish their pernicious lies while confrontation gives the madmen excuse for their mad designs.

The UN towers—omnipresent but impotent— over so many of these disputes and challenges. Statesmen and poet-philosophers outside its imposing orb must seek to encapsulate for their own peoples the narrow paths by which massive destruction may be averted, if indeed such a thing is possible. Threats and accusations raise the stakes and technology—real or imagined—fuels the fire. Impossible situations like this have been corrected before. When Saul and his army trembled in perplexity, David showed up with his five smooth stones. Pay attention to the greengrocer and the cab driver; one such may have been entrusted with the key to unlock these riddles.

January 26, 2013

The problems in North Korea and Iran far predate the advent of the Trump era. A series of mismanaged foreign relations have led to the very dangerous situation we face in both countries in 2018.

Since this writing, dramatic events have taken place with the summits and negotiations between President Donald Trump and Kim Jong-un. We're still holding our breath to see how that unfolds.

Inviting Judgment

Foolishness and pride are a deadly combination. When they become the hallmarks of the persona of the President of the United States, they are harbingers of catastrophic world events because—while he is just a man—the circles of influence within which he operates affect all nations and all peoples. Inviting judgment on oneself is foolish; committing the resources of the United States of America to opposing the will of God or supporting those who do is like painting a target on the US and arrogantly declaring the US immune from God's wrath.

During his tenure, President Barack Obama has launched a series of attacks on the person and sovereignty of Almighty God:

- He's pushed the most aggressive poor-choice policies of any US administration yet, even exceeding the Bill Clinton years. Clinton was arrogant enough to defend partial-birth abortion. Obama, as an Illinois State Senator, opposed the Born-Alive Infant Protection Act, preferring to let the surviving victims of abortion die in cold dark rooms than to respond as any decent citizen would to protect a living, breathing child. As the POTUS, he has appointed only the most committed abortion advocates to positions of power and influence.
- He's arrogantly pushed back and pushed down any attempt to resurrect and protect the traditional family and traditional marriage, introducing heightened gay activism to the military and every possible realm of American life, including his "Fathers' Day" message.
- He's reveled in the adoration of unthinking masses of people both at home and abroad, shamelessly basking in their mindless worship in a personality cult of which he is the central figure. When Herod received the worship of the masses without redirecting it to God, he perished on

the spot but this man is so comfortable in his role as "President of the World" that his smooth and demeaning speeches are hard to listen to without cringing in embarrassment.

- He's flaunted the laws of finance and seems no more concerned than if he'd dropped a penny on his way to the slot machine. While adding to America's devastating debt load by the trillions, he stands before audiences of distinguished educators, generals, heads of state and pontificates to them in measured tones of self-acknowledged brilliance.

Not yet out of the wars for which he freely criticised his predecessor, he's waded cheerfully into new conflicts and encouraged his friends and allies to do the same. Never thinking for a moment about the 1.5 million Sudanese who have perished in the past couple of decades (or the many other victims of repression and injustice), he applauds the sacking of cities and throws US weight into a Libyan battle whose end may yet produce a harsher regime than the one it purports to oppose.

And now, on the eve of an historic visit by Prime Minister Netanyahu, he takes upon himself the role of game-changer, demanding that tiny Israel submit herself to his redrawing of borders in order to promote "peace and justice for the Palestinians". Prime Minister Netanyahu's wise response to Obama's arrogant and foolish theatrical performance is worth reading (1).

My point is this:
God is not mocked. A man who has had the great honour of being elected to represent the people of any great nation owes a duty of allegiance and humility both to his God and to his people. God holds all people accountable for their transgressions and for their

314

pride. Those who have had the confidence (or the audacity) to stand between God and man, between nations, and claim to represent the people and claim to have the wisdom to lead the country ought at least to have the wisdom and humility to submit those globe-impacting decisions to the one who made the earth and everything in it. "The fear of the Lord is the beginning of wisdom." Prov. 9:10

While there are great and legitimate differences of opinion among Western thinkers—even among Christian thinkers—about the role of the nation of Israel in these last days, few are so shallow and narrow (outside of the Muslim world) as to believe that Israel does not have a right to exist. Mr. Obama's recipe for the creation of a Palestinian state and a lasting peace in the Middle East is a recipe for disaster and the destruction of Israel. While he parades around Europe in pomp and pageantry, world leaders and statesmen must deliver themselves and their nations from his madness. They must summon the courage to tell him to his face that this time he has gone too far. They must warn him and promise him that they will not support his vision of a weakened Israel. Are there any leaders left in Europe "man enough" to point out the folly of following this narcissist to destruction? If not, we all will pay the price. In Canada, Prime Minister Harper has an opportunity to set the pace and lead the world in its approach to the Middle East. The President of the USA has failed.

May 26, 2011

Benjamin Netanyahu's speech to a joint session of the US Congress, May 24, 2011:
https://www.theglobeandmail.com/news/world/transcript-of-prime-minister-netanyahus-address-to-us-congress/article635191/

Canada's Angry Foreign Affairs Minister Promotes Gay Agenda Around the Globe

Long known as the PM's bulldog in Parliament, Foreign Affairs Minister John Baird is not shy nor slow of speech. Quick to react and quick to respond, his value to Canada is not determined by his ability but by what drives him. Just days ago, he earned the respect of many around the world for explaining why, in the interest of safety and to send a clear message to Iran, Canada was shuttering its Iranian embassy. While this move displeased the left-leaning MSM, it showed support for Israel and it showed a Canadian strength and discipline that is sorely needed on the world stage. He and the Prime Minister are to be commended for facing down the nuclear-seeking mullahs. The importance and significance of that act was made crystal clear when—a few days later—the mighty USA was humiliated by having several of its middle-east embassies overrun and its ambassador to Libya assassinated in Benghazi and paraded through the streets.

Thank you, Mr. Baird, for your forceful and competent resolve re. Iran. But now our Foreign Affairs crusader has taken it upon himself to loudly and emphatically put homosexuality as a major target category of international human rights violations—one that requires Canada's intervention—lumping it together with women's rights, the mistreatment of racial minorities and the abuse of people whose religious convictions differ from those of the dictators under which they live.

I object. First of all, sovereignty should mean something. The right of sovereign nations to enact laws reflecting their cultural traditions is a long-standing principle. Of course, we reject the killing of innocent citizens of any country whether on racial terms, religious groupings or even personal lifestyle choices. But as we all know by now, the "gay agenda" being foisted upon the bewildered citizens of Canada and other Western countries has nothing to do with the isolated instances of "gay-bashing" and the execution of known homosexuals in foreign lands. It is simply a thinly-veiled attempt to ensure that the homosexual lifestyle is promoted in our streets and schools as "the new normal" and that anyone who speaks out against the imposition of homosexually-explicit, culture-eroding "education" is deemed to be hateful, narrow . . . and increasingly silent.

Note to Mr. Baird and Mr. Harper: Please review your mandate and your responsibilities. Christians are being murdered throughout the middle-east and their churches are being burned. This is not a Pride Parade moment. Canada still has some respect in the world. Use that respect to confront these actual horrifying abuses of good people trying to live good lives. In China, where an abusive government forces abortion on unwilling women and where political prisoners are routinely tortured and executed, Canada could and should have something to say. Last I heard, however, Canada is extending its right hand for more business dealings with China. Of course, Canada's new moralizing on the virtues of homosexual practice may come in handy when China's disproportionate male population comes of age. All those years of the "one-child policy" have created a sex-selection-abortion nightmare. A generation of lonely males may make John Baird their "poster boy". Move over, Svend Robinson; the "Conservatives" are in power.

September 23, 2012

Remembering the Sacrifices Made for our Freedoms

This week we will be pausing to reflect on the courage, heroism and selfless sacrifices of our men and women in uniform who gave "the last full measure of devotion" for our country and for our freedom. It always strikes me—when attending a sacred service for those who have so nobly died—how far we are from the bullets and the privations of war. We may stomp our feet and shake off a few snowflakes. They lay in frozen muddy trenches under the relentless blast of shot and shell with no refuge and no shelter from the elements nor from the brutal instruments of death.

How did they do it? How did they find the courage to rise up out of their trenches and advance across open fields in the face of enemy fire? How did they keep hope alive when the daily toll on their friends and comrades was so numbingly tragic? Perhaps until we find ourselves in their boots, in their trenches and in their desperate frame of mind, we'll never know. But the human spirit is capable of rising to great heights when called upon and the tales of individual bravery in war are inspiring on a level we can hardly comprehend.

Why they did it is easier to see. They knew that the future of the human race was at stake. They knew that their children's happiness, freedom and very lives hung in the balance. Although they faced the daily temptation to yield to fear, to surrender to brute force and to compromise with dictators, they chose instead to lay it all on the line and to put the lives and freedoms of others ahead of their own. They chose to sacrifice their comfort and security for the uncertain hope that they might preserve a nation where human decency and Christian values might prevail.

They took the risks. Some said they could do no other. Some realized that there would be no safety in retreat, no security in compromise. They realized that unless they stepped forward and put their bodies in harm's way that all mankind would be subject to the brutality and destruction being unleashed across the waters.

And so they stormed the beaches and surged into the strongholds. Many fell and did not live to see the victory. They knew it would be so and still they went bravely forward. We cannot thank them enough. We can only bow our heads in reverence and gratitude.

Today, our challenges are of a different sort. Those seeking to destroy our way of life often do so without bullets, shells or declarations of war. They work quietly from within, undermining our society's foundations, subverting truth, misleading our children and imposing quietly on us regulations, restrictions, taxation and social pressures just as deadly and harmful as those imposed by martial means on the battlefields of war. Our family structures, our peaceful neighbourhoods, our shared spiritual values and our close-knit communities are being taken captive. The faith our fathers once knew is being mocked in front of our children. The sanctity of our parents' marriages is being defiled. Patriotism and national pride are derided and the strange lusts of the world are given honour in our institutions of higher learning.

Our fathers, those who gave their lives on the battlefield, would never have accepted this takeover of our society. They would not have quietly allowed their children to be taken captive. They showed us how earnestly we must contend for our nation and for our children's future. They faced bullets and torture. We face only mocking and political correctness. For now. They understood that there is a time to stand firm before all that is holy is swept away. We must follow their example or one day wear our chains in shame. Let's honour the fallen and let us pledge to do our part to maintain that for which they so nobly gave their lives. Lest we forget.

November 9, 2015

The Conclusion of the Matter

Let us hear the conclusion of the matter: Fear God and keep His commandments; for this is the whole duty of man.   Eccles. 12:13

The Conclusion of the Matter

I would be sorely remiss if I didn't offer some sort of bridge between this varied selection of articles representing circumstances and events spanning more than a decade and the current conditions we face today.

Many of these articles were written when the Conservatives were in power, including four years with a strong majority. If you've read this far, you'll know that we often disagreed with the decisions of that government, especially in regard to its failure to protect innocent human life. We also criticized their failure (as we saw it) to courageously rein in spending, allowing the national debt to increase by nearly $150 billion during their nine years in office.

We believe the Conservatives could have taken stronger steps to restore traditional marriage and to resist the "gender agenda" which has now hit the public education system with full force in most provinces and is being fought in courtrooms and human rights tribunals in many different aspects and on many different levels.

In spite of articulate attempts by some of the best Conservative MPs (thank God for those brave souls) to introduce sensible and measured pro-life legislation, Mr. Harper made it clear that he would oppose any efforts to protect the preborn with legislation and he did. He also refused to exercise the Notwithstanding Clause (Section 33 of the Charter) to prevent the imminent implementation of Assisted Suicide. The current CPC Leader, Andrew Scheer, has indicated that he will follow the same course. Even if the Conservatives elect a majority and even if they allow individual backbenchers to present private members' bills and motions, without the support of the CPC leader, those bills will be doomed to failure.

It is sad that the previous government under PM Harper felt that avoiding difficult and divisive topics would prevent their loss of the House in 2015. Failure to represent biblical morality did not win the election; it did, however signal that the party leadership would continue to compromise on moral issues.

We have always believed in thanking our elected representatives when they do the right thing. We appreciated Mr. Harper's bold stance in support of Israel and his efforts to resist Sharia and terrorism at home and abroad. We appreciated the verbal commitment to balanced budgets even though their 9-year record was mostly a string of deficits. We appreciated his efforts to improve financial transparency.

However, we believe that as long as a government tolerates the shedding of innocent human blood, the trampling of freedom of speech and the imposition of sexual anarchy and pornographic lewdness in the streets of our cities, it cannot expect the blessings of God on its crops, its finances, its security or its respected place among the nations of the world.

That being said, I must state clearly that our current federal government under PM Justin Trudeau is far worse, has done far more damage and endangers future generations of Canadians in ways that were unimaginable even 20 years ago.

The fear of the Lord is the beginning of wisdom. Therefore, where there is no fear of the Lord, no respect for the Almighty Creator, there is no wisdom. Zero.

Moreover, when people reject God and His moral principles, He gives them over to delusion, confusion and to "do things which are not convenient". Rom. 1:8 Our current PM and his pathetically-loyal MPs and Senate appointees are doing many things which are not only "not convenient" but are morally and fiscally destructive. Canada's economy, our security and the opportunity for our children to live happy, peaceful and fulfilling lives are severely at risk.

To date, the Liberal PM has:
- increased funding for abortion at home and abroad, even where it is currently illegal
- implemented assisted suicide with thousands of lives already taken from us
- imposed an unhealthy sexual agenda throughout the bureaucracy and extending into provincial education systems, robbing young children of innocence and privacy
- imposed his personal viewpoints on Canadian charities, demanding verbal commitments to Liberal talking points in open defiance of Charter protections
- created an atmosphere antithetical to the exercise of freedom of speech, freedom of religion and freedom of association
- opened Canada's borders to masses of unvetted migrants while rejecting calls to help at-risk Christian minorities
- given special status and protection to radical Islamist ideology and protected known terrorists from the consequences of their actions
- racked up huge additional debts which create a burden on the next generations
- unleashed on Canada the destructive effects of legalized mind-altering marijuana, known to result in increased traffic fatalities and other damaging consequences

The list could go on and on but of course, we hope it doesn't. Many Canadians who may have naively voted for Mr. Trudeau in 2015 because of his youth and fresh new face are taking a sober second look at his record and asking themselves if they really want four more years of his arrogant disregard for the traditional values which made Canada great.

We in the CHP will continue to offer voters the opportunity to choose biblical morality, an unapologetic defence of Truth, a commitment to Life, Family, Freedom and Justice. The future of Canada rests largely in the hands of the voters. It is God who raises up rulers and brings them down again Daniel 2:21 but He also allows people, in a democracy, to choose their leaders. Choose well.

Choose you this day whom you will serve . . . as for me and my house, we will serve the Lord. Joshua 24:25

Blessed is the nation whose God is the Lord. Psalm 33:12

Thank you for allowing me to share my thoughts with you. May God guide us all as we seek to restore righteousness and morality to the political sphere in our beloved Canada.

For more information on the Christian Heritage Party of Canada, visit:

chp.ca

For more from the author and a list of live links to the urls footnoted throughout the book, visit:

rodtaylor.ca

Made in the USA
Lexington, KY
16 November 2019

57149904R00202